Exhibitions in Museums

Leicester Museum Studies Series
General Editor: Dr Susan Pearce

PUBLISHED:
Susan M. Pearce, *Archaeological Curatorship*
Gaynor Kavanagh, *History Curatorship*
Eilean Hooper-Greenhill, *Museum Education: Theory and Practice*

Exhibitions in Museums

Michael Belcher

Leicester University Press
Leicester and London

Smithsonian Institution Press
Washington, D.C.

© Michael Belcher, 1991

First published in Great Britain in 1991 by Leicester University Press
(a division of Pinter Publishers Ltd)

Editorial offices
Fielding Johnson Building, University of Leicester,
University Road, Leicester, LE1 7RH

Trade and other enquiries
25 Floral Street, London, WC2E 9DS

British Library Cataloguing in Publication Data
A CIP cataloguing record for this book is available
from the British Library
ISBN 0-7185-1299-5

Published in the United States by the Smithsonian Institution Press.

Library of Congress Cataloging-in-Publication Data available
ISBN 0 87474 913 1

Typeset by Witwell Limited, Southport
Printed and bound in Great Britain by Biddles Ltd, Guildford and King's Lynn.

Contents

List of tables

List of figures

Acknowledgements

A number of individuals and museums have given me assistance in assembling material for this book, and I should like to acknowledge their help and express my gratitude. Those museums which have assisted in providing photographs or other illustrative material include: Bradford Art Galleries and Museums, the Trustees of the British Museum, the Burrell Collection, Glasgow Museums and Art Galleries, Catalyst, the Museum of the Chemical Industry, Edinburgh City Museums and Art Galleries, the Imperial War Museum, London Transport Museum, the Manchester Museum, the Museum of London, the Natural History Museum, Northampton Museums, the Norfolk Museums Service, the Royal Academy of Arts, St. Albans Museums, the Victoria and Albert Museum, York Archaeological Trust. I am also personally indebted to Sue Pearce, who as General Editor has given patient encouragement and editorial advice; however, I must myself accept responsibility for any errors or omissions. Also to be thanked is Rosemary Davison for her patience and able typing of the manuscript. Finally, I must thank my family, Marie, Irene, Justine and Charlotte, who have lived with it for the last two years.

General preface to series

Museums are an international growth area. The number of museums in the world is now very large, embracing some 13,500 in Europe, of which 2,300 are in the United Kingdom; some 7,000 in North America; 2,800 in Australasia and Asia; and perhaps 2,000 in the rest of the world. The range of museum orientation is correspondingly varied, and covers all aspects of the natural and the human heritage. Paralleling the growth in numbers comes a major development in the opportunities open to museums to play an important part in shaping cultural perceptions within their communities, as people everywhere become more aware of themselves and their surroundings.

Accordingly, museums are now reviewing and rethinking their role as the storehouses of knowledge and as the presenters to people of their relationship to their own environment and past, and to those of others. Traditional concepts of what a museum is, and how it should operate, are confronted by contemporary intellectual, social and political concerns which deal with questions like the validity of value judgments, bias in collecting and display, the demystifying of specialized knowledge, the protection of the environment, and the nature of our place in history.

These are all large and important areas, and the debate is an international one. The series *Leicester Museum Studies* is designed to make a significant contribution to the development of new theory and practice across the broad range of the museum operation. Individual volumes in the series will consider in depth particular museum areas, defined either by disciplinary field or by function. Many strands of opinion will be represented, but the series as a whole will present a body of discussion and ideas which should help to redress both the present poverty of theory and the absence of a reference collection of substantial published material, which curators everywhere currently see as a fundamental lack. The community, quite rightly, is now asking more of its museums. More must be given, and to achieve this, new directions and new perspectives must be generated. In this project, *Leicester Museum Studies* is designed to play its part.

SUSAN M. PEARCE
Department of Museum Studies
University of Leicester

Introduction

Few people who have recently visited a cross-section of museums in Britain could deny that they now contain a wide range of exhibitions which are meaningful, stimulating and, above all, relevant to today's visitors. It is also true to say that the post-war years have seen unprecedented developments in museum exhibition presentation. Stimulated by such events as the Festival of Britain, museum exhibitions began to take on a new look which received a considerable impetus in the late 1960s as a result of the nation's increased awareness of design. At this time, there were probably no more than half a dozen qualified designers working in museums and very little use was being made of design consultants. Indeed, the design profession itself was still relatively new, and certainly museums were only just beginning to recognize the fact that the designers had a role to play in the museum team (Belcher 1982). Over the years, greater realization and utilization of the skills of the designer have undoubtedly brought about a high standard of excellence and achievement in the field of exhibitions. This has been matched on the part of the curator with high standards of scholarship and an innovative approach to exhibition themes and the interpretation of objects.

This book has been written for all who are concerned with the preparation of exhibitions in museums. It is not a design grammar, nor a survey of design solutions to exhibitions. These approaches have been undertaken with considerable success by Margaret Hall and Michael Brawne. What this book attempts is to provide an introduction to the various factors which relate to exhibitions and to bring together, for the benefit of all concerned with their provision and preparation, those aspects which might be considered as 'essential knowledge'. It is a book intended for the student, but one which hopefully will also serve as a useful source of reference for the more experienced.

Part one. *The interface between museum and public*

1. Museum policy

All but the most private of institutions, created for personal gratification or for the exclusive use of a closed group of people, need to be aware of the *interface* which exists between an institution and its public. The interface may be defined as the points of contact. Most will be under the control of the museum concerned. They will range from the physical contact of visitors entering and progressing through a museum building mainly to visit the exhibitions and possibly meet staff to the more tenuous contacts, made, perhaps, when reading a museum poster or publication. Many others, which may be described as the indirect contacts, occur through a third party, such as the media. These are less easily controlled. In an organisation which exists to serve the public, and is market-conscious the importance of the interface cannot be under-estimated.

The museum, as a provider of a service to the public, needs to be aware of its role. So too do the public whom it serves, since they have a right to know what it is they are paying for, possibly by a contribution through taxation, or by direct payment at the door. The public also may wish to be assured that the tasks entrusted to museums in terms of safeguarding what might loosely be described as a 'nation's heritage' are incorporated in its role and are being adequately pursued.

Unfortunately, statements of policy emanating from museums on anything other than collecting have been all too rare. Ask any group of junior curatorial staff (let alone the public!) if they know what their museum's policies are, and, in all probability, only one or two of any group of twenty will be able to respond. This does not, of course, necessarily mean that only perhaps 10 per cent of museums have policies—but it does suggest that, whether museums have policies or not, only about 10 per cent of junior staff seem to know about them. No doubt this reluctance to commit an institution to set objectives is, at least in part, based on a fear that it might in some way create restrictions which will prevent the museum from being flexible and being able to respond to new opportunities. This of course, need not be so, and the fear of committing objectives to paper will deny the creation of a rational sense of purpose which is so necessary to the well being of any organization. Indeed, consideration of a museum's exhibition activities cannot sensibly be done unless it *is* related to the museum's objectives and overall policy.

Theodore Low (1942), commenting on American museums, wrote:

Unfortunately, the vast majority of our museums have failed to accept the responsibility entrusted to them by the founders and have blithely tossed the original ideas out of the window. Nor did they substitute anything in their

place. Indeed, of all institutions, both public and private, which have flour-
ished in this country, few, if any, have wandered so aimlessly toward undefined
goals as have the museums. To be sure, some worthwhile efforts have been
made to fling wide the golden gates and let the public in, and no one would
deny that some false barriers to public learning have been rudely shaken. And
yet, when one reviews the scene today, it is very apparent that museums still
lack a definite goal, still are elaborating on past procedures rather than looking
to the future, and still are content with minor sallies into the field of public
education.

Low's comments, admittedly made several years ago, and in America,
nevertheless prompt the question to be asked of a museum: 'Is it an
institution wandering aimlessly towards undefined goals?'

The Times on 19 March 1990 carried an article by Simon Tait entitled
'Another fine old mess?'. In it he made the point that, today, it is not so
much that the goals of museums are undefined as that there is confusion
as what the true role of a museum in the current economic and political
climate might be. He quotes the directors of some of the country's
national museums, among them, Sir David Wilson, Director of the
British Museum, who says; 'I have never seen the museums in such
disarray. Those in the provinces are slipping backwards and the natio-
nals, for the first time, are split. They simply don't see eye to eye.'

It is on issues such as how they should rectify the shortfall in their
funding and to what extent they should compromise scholarship with a
more popularist approach that their opinions differ most. Fortunately,
those concerned for the future of scholarship, the importance of museum
objects and free access to this unique resource by members of the public
have a champion in Sir David Wilson. He is quoted as believing that:

the question of where museums are going is not just a matter of money, its
philosophy. There is an all-singing, all-dancing element which is impossible
in the really big national museums. I am more and more convinced that people
want to see objects properly displayed and described and they don't want
television in the gallery or music in the background.

Another national museum takes a rather different view. 'The Fate of the
Natural History Museum' is the subject of a paper submitted for debate at
the Annual Meeting of Individual Members of the Museums Association
at its Annual Conference in July 1990. This has been put forward
following controversy surrounding the museum's corporate plan for
1990-95, which some feel would effectively disembowel the museum
overnight. (A similar controversy erupted over plans to restructure the
Victoria and Albert Museum in 1989.) Penny Wheatcroft, the author of
the paper, states that in the plan 100 posts were to be lost which would
cut major areas of research. She says:

The policy stems from the false premise that a national museum can be made to
run as a business, rather than a public service. Museums can never compete on
equal terms with theme parks and other organisations purely devoted to

entertainment, because we have the added responsibility of caring for the national collections, carrying out research and providing access to the public.

With such important policy decisions at issue, there is a need to have them clearly defined in order that they may be fully known and considered.

So each and every museum should define its role, and, this done, consider how it might go about attaining its aims and objectives. Additionally, a museum should stipulate its primary services (including its communications function) and consider both secondary and support-ing services which may be deemed necessary or desirable in the context of providing a service to the public. A further consideration will be the economic viability of such proposals.

The manner in which a museum determines and controls the interface with the public will result in the creation of the museums's *image*. And this should not be a haphazard occurance, but should emanate from the purposeful implementation of the museum's *communications policy*, via its *communications strategy* through the *communications plans*.

Of paramount importance, from both functional, visual and psycho-logical criteria, is *design*. For the design of the total museum—that is, every tangible aspect of the museum system and particularly those elements which are part of the crucial public interface—will form a major aspect of the museum's visual image and therefore its communi-cations policy. In this context the nature of design, in terms of its quality in the solution of problems, must be seen as essential to the success of the museum.

The various decision statements—that is, the overall policy, specific area policies and strategies—can be brought together in what may be described as a museum's *grand conceptual plan*. This should, as far as is possible within the museum's context, be suitably imaginative and comprehensive. It need not, in this form, be compromised by fears, either real or imagined, of diminishing budgets, for the purpose of a conceptual plan is that it should set out what it is desirable to achieve if resources and opportunities permit. The logistics of implementing either part or all of the plan should be contained in what may be described as the museum's *corporate* or *business* plan.

The corporate plan should be ambitious yet realistic. It should set out what can reasonably be achieved and worked for over a given period of perhaps three to five years. As such it becomes a most useful document in establishing a baseline against which the effectiveness of an organization can be measured through clearly defined targets. For it should set achievement levels or productivity figures in all areas of the institution's activities and relate them to a time scale and resource plan. Thus, at the highest level, it will commit an institution to specific courses of action which should not easily be changed. Nevertheless, like all other policy and planning documents produced by an institution, the corporate plan will need to be kept under constant review, and changed as circumstances may dictate.

Museum policy

A prerequisite to formulating a statement of museum policy is an acceptance of a definition of what a museum is. The most widely applied definition (and therefore to some extent the most flexible) it that provided by ICOM and adopted by the Eleventh General Assembly in 1974:

> A museum is a non-profitmaking, permanent institution in the service of society and of its development, and open to the public, which acquires, conserves, researches, communicates, and exhibits, for purposes of study, education and enjoyment, material evidence of man and his environment.

A more specific definition was that formulated by the Museums Association and approved at its Annual General Meeting in 1984. It read:

> A museum is an institution which collects, documents, preserves, exhibits and interprets material evidence and associated information for the public benefit.

An explanation of the definition is given in the Museums Association's *Museums Yearbook* (1990). While the explanation of words like 'collects' as embracing 'all means of acquisition', 'documents' as emphasizing 'the need to maintain records' and 'preserves' as including 'all aspects of conservation and security' is relatively obvious, other definitions are less so. For example, 'evidence' is used to guarantee the authenticity of material as 'the real thing' and 'associated information' represents the knowledge which prevents a museum object being merely a curio, and also includes all records relating to its past history, acquisition and subsequent usage. 'Exhibits' is meant to confirm 'the expectation of visitors that they will be able to see at least a representative selection of objects in the collections', and 'interprets' is taken 'to cover such diverse fields as display, education, research and publication'. Contained in the phrase 'for the public benefit' is the notion that museums are the 'servants of society'. Clearly, the explanations of the definition provide a useful basis for a statement of intent and indicate those areas which each museum will need to consider for further clarification and indeed rank in order of priority in relation to its own situation and aspirations.

Probably the definitive model for statements of intent was that incorporated in the Act of Parliament to facilitate the creation of the British Museum and passed in 1753 (see Lewis, 1984). It stated:

> Whereas all arts and sciences have a connexion with each other, and discoveries in natural philosophy and other branches of speculative knowledge, for the advancement and improvement whereof the said Museum or collection was intended, do and may, in many instances, give help and success to the most useful experiments and inventions; . . . [and that] the said Museum or collection may be preserved and maintained, not only for the inspection and entertainment of the learned and the curious, but for the general use and benefit of the public.

More recently a useful model has been produced by the Royal Ontario Museum (1976). This sets out the museum's basic objectives towards achieving its goal, which it defines as:

furtherance of man's understanding of himself, his society and the natural world of which he is a part.

It relates the objectives of collecting, employment of scholars, participation in man's search for knowledge and the interpretation of that knowledge to the social context in which it operates, and goes on to specify ways in which the objectives will be achieved. These relate to a broad exhibition theme, to museum growth, to decentralization and province-wide responsibilities, and to internal organization and physical facilities.

The need for a clear definition of the *raison d'être* of each individual museum in Britain has never been greater. In a rapidly changing economic climate, with the political emphasis on enterprise, profitability and competitiveness, the demands on museums to participate in this style of economy are considerable. The omission of the word 'non-profit-making', which appeared in the 1974 ICOM definition of a museum and in subsequent definitions such as that of the Museums Association (1990), is evidence of this new trend. Both political and economic pressures are being applied to museums to encourage them to undertake more profitable activities and diversify into areas which once were only peripheral. Indeed, there is also pressure on certain institutions to capitalize on their assets—even to disposing of collections and, at time of writing, the government is seriously considering an enabling Bill so that national museums may more easily dispose of items in the national collections. Not surprisingly, this has provoked considerable opposition from the museum movement and its supporters.

David Mawson (Chairman, British Association of Friends of Museums) in a letter to the *The Times* (2 December, 1988) on the subject of the then proposed Mappa Mundi sale by Hereford Cathedral[1] wrote:

It is because of such sales that many of our groups are very concerned about the Government's proposed 'powers of disposal' for the trustees of the Tate Gallery, the National Gallery and the National Portrait Gallery. If similar, well publicised, sales were made by these galleries there would be enormous damage done to the fund-raising efforts of supporting groups and future benefactors would be discouraged.

Some of our members consider that no such powers of sale should be granted, even with safeguards, as it will open the door for future Governments to reduce the grants to national galleries and will force them to sell works to provide for running costs and repairs!

However, although most museum professionals oppose museums disposing of their unique collections, others do see the need for museums to be more commercially active. Dr. Neil Cossons, Director of the Science

Museum, London, stated in an article in *The Sunday Times* (1 May 1988):

> they [museums] should have freedom to raise money by whatever means are available. They should be given borrowing powers.
>
> several museums have opportunities to develop their property and enter into partnerships with others so that their collections could become assets for urban regeneration.

Already one can see ample evidence of this move towards the 'commercial museum enterprise' going beyond the familiar museum shop activities which gained momentum in the late 1960s and early 1970s. The Science Museum, as mentioned above, and another of London's most popular museums, the Natural History Museum, have both introduced charges for admission and are actively assessing the market potential of many of their other services. Also in London, the Victoria and Albert Museum is entering into commercial partnerships to market 'exclusive' ranges of products (e.g. wallpapers, fabrics, etc.) based on items in the museum's collections. It will market these through leading high street retailers. This capitalizes in an intelligent manner on one of the museum's greatest assets—the collections—but in a way which preserves the originals and yet brings them to a wider audience.

The principle of public museums becoming autonomous trading companies is an important one. For too long local authority museums have had little or no incentive to generate income, since they could not easily benefit directly from their enterprises, with the monies earned going to the authority in general rather than to the museum specifically. Similarly, certain national museums have also lacked this facility until recently when tight rulings have gradually been relaxed or circumvented.

Clearly there is enormous potential for museums to diversify and use property and skill resources in a more entrepreneurial way. And, if this trend continues, it is not difficult to see a time when many museums will be running companies in property or trading *as their main activity* in order to finance, on a small scale, a museum operation in the traditional sense. Whereas once the problem for museums was to strike a balance between, as Flower (1893) put it: 'the two distinct objects . . . research and instruction', today, with all museum functions competing for a share of the available funds, a balance perhaps needs to be struck between entrepreneurial and academic pursuits.

The need to aportion resources to the competing and often insatiable demands of the various areas of the museum system is what makes a policy essential to rational and purposeful decision-making. For example, purchases could so easily absorb all available monies and so limit other activities; similarly basic costs of accommodation and staff, once met, might leave insufficient funds to support anything but minimal activities across a broad front or a significant advance in one particular area.

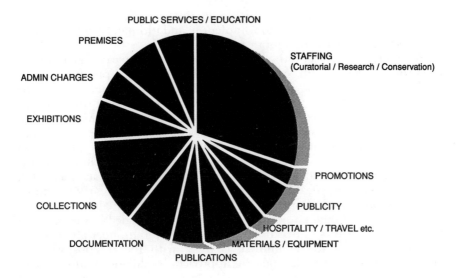

Figure 1.1   An approach to apportioning resources in order to meet competing demands

However, writing a policy statement is, in itself, of limited value. It must be seen as part of a larger process. The emphasis should be on the *implementation* of the policy which will produce the tangible results. For, with good management practice, Low's 'aimless wandering' can be counteracted by a policy statement which results in an organization that deploys its resources effectively (and therefore economically) to achieve its declared goals.

Preparing a policy

The preparation of a policy statement should take into account any existing statement, possibly dating from the inception of the museum, and any changes that there may have been to the museum's original purpose. Also important is an awareness of any constraints, and legal or political factors which might affect the viability of a policy statement. It would also be prudent to anticipate how other interested parties (e.g. museums, educational institutions, donors and lenders of items in the collections, etc.) might react to the statement.

The preparation of the policy, whether it be a new document or the modification of an existing one, will need to be co-ordinated at the highest level, although inputs in the form of contributions and comments may be encouraged at various levels throughout an institution. It could be, for example, that a group of senior staff get together and produce a draft document. This could then be circulated within the museum for comment prior to completion, and ultimately submission to the controlling body for adoption.

An alternative model is the formation of a working party (maybe by the controlling body) with specific terms of reference to produce a draft policy statement. The group may include representatives from the controlling body plus the museum directorate, senior staff from various disciplines and selected specialized interests. 'Friends of the Museum' and maybe informed 'outsiders' or consultants, all of whom have a particular interest in and knowledge of the museum's functions, albeit from different viewpoints, may be usefully included. Clearly not everyone eligible should, or indeed would want to, be included in such a group, even if it were practicable. It may be prudent to invite written contributions from staff, but only those who indicate a definite interest and an ability to contribute in a positive way might be included in the working party, which, if it is to function efficiently, should number about ten.

Whatever form the committee charged with the responsibility of formulating the policy may take, its approach should not be introspective and, in normal circumstances, it would need to consult widely. Those to be consulted in Britain might include government departments, Her Majesty's Inspectorate, regional and local authorities, local education advisers and other museums. Educational establishments at all levels should be included, and so should local societies, regional arts associations and similar organizations, area museum services, development boards, tourist, leisure and similar organizations. Funding bodies and local chambers of commerce should not be left out, and indeed all the various organizations and individuals who have an interest in the context in which the museum operates should be given a chance to make their contribution.

Assuming preparation of the policy document has been undertaken within the museum, it should normally be approved by the chief officer before being submitted for approval and ratification by the controlling body. In other circumstances, where policy emanates from the controlling body itself, depending on the nature of the organization, it would be passed to the chief officer to implement.

The policy statement

The exact form and content a museum chooses for its policy statement will be determined by its circumstances and aspirations. As has been indicated, it will need to contain sufficient information to be useful, but will need to be flexible in order to meet a variety of circumstances. It

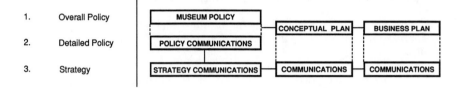

Figure 1.2   Relationships of planning and policy papers

should not be seen, however, as irrevocable and should be the subject of periodic review.

Included in the policy statement should be:

1. A general statement of intent—the *raison d'être* of the enterprise.
2. A list of general aims and objectives which define, in broad terms, the role of the organization.
3. More specific statements of policy in relation to the main aspects of the museum's work, which would normally include: acquisition and disposal of collections; nature of collections; research; documentation; preservation and conservation; fieldwork; communications; education; design; professional standards; organization and methodology; funding and sponsorship; commercial enterprises; public services; special needs; ethics; race, sex, religion, and health and safety.

Writing a policy statement which addresses and clarifies the museum's position on both fundamental and contentious issues will clearly have considerable benefits, the most important of which are:

1. The useful process of getting a group of professionals to stop and consider what they are doing and think what they should be doing—with the resultant benefit of gaining direction.

2. Clarification of the museum's purpose as a point of reference for those working within it, i.e.:

(*a*) Museum committee members, trustees or governors, in order that they should have sufficient knowledge of the institution which they serve to enable them to contribute effectively.
(*b*) The chief officer, who, perhaps more than anyone, needs a clear and accurate perception of the direction in which to lead the organization.
(*c*) Individual members of staff, who should benefit from having an understanding of the organization's role, and therefore acquire a greater sense of purpose, which should improve job satisfaction and performance.

3. The provision of a definition of the museum's role for use by outside organizations and individuals who have an interest in the museum. These may include:

(*a*) Government departments, local authorities and other agencies concerned with the provision of a museum service.
(*b*) Funding bodies who would reasonably expect this information when considering the provision of support.
(*c*) Professional and academic bodies, who may also need to know the museum's stance on issues of mutual interest.
(*d*) Other museums, which, in order to avoid duplication or conflict of interest, might need the information.
(*e*) The press, for whom having the definitive version of museum's policy might avoid mistakes and misunderstandings.
(*f*) Politicians, who, for many of the reasons listed above, may also benefit from being accurately and adequately informed if they are to make informed political decisions on museum issues.
(*g*) Concerned individuals who contribute to the museum by direct or indirect taxation, by donation or by payment of a fee and may either wish to know or whom the museum may wish to inform of its policy.
(*h*) Any groups or individuals that need to know the museum's policy in relation to their particular endeavours or aspirations—and the service they can expect.

Note

1 Proposals for the sale were abandoned when a substantial donation was made to facilitate the necessary repairs and obviate the need for the sale.

2. Museum communications policy

Communications policy

We have already seen in the section 'Preparing a policy' that among the subjects to be addressed in the museum's policy document should be 'communications'. The statements made may then be amplified in a more comprehensive communications policy document, which will, no doubt, be one of a series of such papers which develop policy themes in more detail. These need to be read in conjunction with the policy document and with other detailed theme papers, for, clearly, within the various topics there are considerable areas of overlap, and 'communications' in particular embraces many other museum activities. Especially relevant in this context are the subjects 'education' and 'design' and should they not be afforded separate detailed policies, they would need to be incorporated within the communications policy.

The issues any museum might wish to address will be peculiar to that institution and its aims and objectives, but they may well include the following:

1. The nature of the museum's approach to communicating.
2. The type and content of material to be communicated.
3. Identification of the people with whom the museum wishes to communicate.
4. The levels at which communication is to be effected.
5. The modes of communication and the languages selected.
6. The image which the museum wishes to project, and the importance of design.
7. Priorities and resources.

All these areas will be explored in what follows.

The nature of the museum's approach to communicating

A museum will need to consider its rationale in respect of its approach to communicating. The main issue to be addressed will be the extent to which the museum should be involved in educating, informing and entertaining, and for what purpose. Thus a set of clearly defined aims and objectives should be devised. These may then be amplified and a set of approaches identified with which the museum particularly wishes to be concerned. The medium of exhibition would be expected to feature prominently in these as the main vehicle for communicating information about the collections. A statement might therefore be made on the ratio of permanent to temporary exhibitions and to what extent travelling exhibitions might be produced and circulated to other centres. Accessibility to the museum's collections is fundamental to a museum's communications policy and therefore such controversial issues as charges for admission and other charges in respect of the communications function (e.g. pricing policy for museum publications) will need to be considered in conjunction with the appropriate section of the museum's overall policy.

The museum's involvement with such activities as distance learning material and publishing as means of communication also needs to be addressed.

The type and content of material to be communicated

The central issue here is how the museum should use its collections, and appropriate aims and objectives will need to be developed. The relationship between primary and secondary collections might need to be discussed if this approach is favoured. Also, if space limitations are a factor, the issue of permanent, temporary and travelling exhibitions may again need to be addressed.

Particularly important when discussing type and content of material will be the main themes and topics which the museum wishes to communicate. Since collections can be arranged in countless different ways, the selection of appropriate themes is a fundamental issue which needs to be resolved. The main alternatives are either a systematic approach based, for example, on chronology, taxonomy or material type, or a more journalistic approach. This may be no less methodical in the way it groups material, but will use it selectively in order to tell a particular story—a three-dimensional essay. If a museum wishes its exhibitions to convey powerful messages, or to take a particular stand on political, commercial or other controversial issues, then these need to be considered.

Identification of the people with whom the museum wishes to communicate

To develop 'an exhibition programme which will make the collections both accessible to a wider public and stimulate international interest . . .' wrote a national museum in relation to its exhibition policy. Even this brief and simple statement provides an indication as to how those responsible might set about formulating a programme in order to achieve the desired results. Drawing up a list of those people with whom the museum specifically wants to communicate is a useful first step, to be followed by considering how best their needs might be catered for. A rationale for this approach is that the museum wants to serve a community. It recognizes that it comprises many sections and groups. It also feels that within its collections it has something of interest to communicate to most groups. It seeks to identify what might usefully be communicated to whom, and to relate this to its policy. This approach is very close to the marketing strategy which might seek to identify markets and satisfy them with suitable products.

Groups of people for whom the museum might wish to formulate a specific policy could include the young, those at various educational stages and in particular those taking GCSE and comparable examinations, specialist groups and local societies. It is likely to consider local residents, visitors to the area, special-needs groups and ethnic minorities. It may also wish to make special provision to communicate with the poor and the unemployed, or conversely with the very affluent for whom paying an admission charge of several pounds and purchasing a catalogue at several times that amount would present no hardship. In order to categorize people, reference may also be made to the standard market research social categories A, B, C, etc. Thus, in developing this theme, general aims and objectives will need to be established and, as necessary, amplified.

The levels at which communication is to take place

The levels of communication must obviously relate to the selected groups of people with whom communication is to be effected. Whereas the functional details may well be discussed in the communications plan, clarification may be warranted at policy level. Some museums, for example, first set a specific communication level to all exhibitions, pitching it in relation to the intellect and knowledge of someone approaching O levels or GCSE. Others relate it to a notional reading age, which for some people has been set as low as twelve, the level of some of the more popular tabloid daily newspapers. But not only reading ages need to be considered in this context. All aspects of communications and educational technology will need to be considered, and this will include specific approaches. For example, museums may consider the use of the highly interactive, participative approach. Like that in the London Science Museum's 'Launch Pad' gallery, or the application of computerized question-and-answer facilities, which are now a feature of many museums.

The image the museum wishes to project and the importance of design

Emanating from the various facets of the museum's policy, and in particular the section concerned with communication, is the *image* the museum wishes to project. Purposeful and deliberate consideration of how the museum wishes to appear is probably one of the most important, yet frequently the most neglected, of tasks. For there is a tendency to think that an institution has no control over an image: that it is something which simply occurs over a period of time, and that, once acquired, it is set for all time.

The truth is that a good image has to be worked for and actively maintained. Here, too, it is necessary to establish clearly defined aims and objectives, for the museum has the opportunity to adopt any of a wide range of images. For example, if it wishes to appear professional, authoratitive, friendly and approachable, it will need to take very positive steps in order to achieve this. Likewise, if it wishes to be thought of as being involved with topical issues, be they controversial or political, then this image will need to be evident from its approach to its communications policy and plan. A museum can also be a 'high profile', visibly active organization or it can adopt a 'low' profile, and appear passive. Similarly, a museum can decide to adopt an approach which places it in the centre of a community or one which distances itself from it.

Increasingly, museums are coming to realize that design is a matter of such importance that it warrants a specific commitment by the institution in a formal statement of policy, with aims and objectives laid out. Although design may be considered in relation to image, and is very important in relation to a communications policy, it should be involved in every facet of the museum system and therefore warrants being included as a topic in the overall policy statement. In relation to communications the museum will doubtless wish to develop and strengthen a concept of corporate identity and ensure that it is adhered to throughout the organization. It may also wish to associate itself with the highest standards of design and actively help to promote the recognition of particular forms or exponents of design.

Priorities and resources

A museum, in preparing a policy statement, will rightly seek to identify those aspects of its function, and of its aims and objectives, which it regards as important. However, in a large and complex system such as a museum which undertakes several different functions, most of which compete with each other for resources, problems can occur if some indication of specific priorities is not given. A museum can no longer be all things to all men, and at times when its fundamental duty to safeguard and advance knowledge may be questioned, it is useful to determine overriding principles if not specific priorities. Additionally, the apportioning of resources in terms of finance, accommodation and manpower will need to be undertaken in support of the aims and objectives. Useful as general statements on priorities and resources will be within the policy document, it is within the museum's corporate or business plan that they will be expanded upon and related to a specific work programme.

Museum communications strategy

If the museum's communications policy sets out the general principles and rationale of its work in this area, the *strategy* should be concerned with the organizational aspects of implementing the policy. As such it determines the system, setting out how the work is to be done and by whom. Because this clearly relates to the decision-making process of the museum and to its management structure, the organizational elements of the strategy would need to be undertaken by or approved by the senior staff and probably the Chief Officer personally.

There are various models which could apply, depending very much on the type and size of the museum. Ideally a named senior officer—rather than an anonymous committee—should be charged with the responsibility of implementing the communications policy and, to do this effectively, should be given executive powers. This could be at Deputy or Assistant Chief Officer level or at Head of Department level if more appropriate.

In a museum committed to a corporate management philosophy, the senior officer would normally be a member of the management team with a brief to report on communications matters. This would ensure that all senior staff have the opportunity to discuss and formulate management decisions on communications in the context of the total remit of the museum.

Alternatively, a steering group might be formed of senior staff and chaired by the Chief Officer. This group might have as its remit the co-ordination of communications activities within the museum as a whole. In a small museum, however, or in one organized along more autocratic lines, committees might be dispensed with, and individuals made accountable in a line management model for their areas of responsibility. Clearly the approach of the officer charged with the responsibility for communications will depend to a great extent on the personnel resources he has at his disposal. Should he have responsibility for a large department covering many related fields of expertise such as graphic and three-dimensional design, educational technology, and so on, he may draw selectively on this expertise and form a working party. This group would need to combine with a similar curatorial working party which could advise on those aspects which relate specifically to the collections and their interpretation and care. Together, the two working parties would form a communications group.

The Royal Ontario Museum, which embarked on the task of formulating and implementing its communications strategy in the early 1970s (ROM 1976), decided to form a committee, which it called the 'Communications Design Team'. This it placed under the supervision of the Assistant Director of Education and Communication. In this instance the committee consisted of a small group of people with a knowledge of such relevant areas as learning processes and communications theory; human factors design; display design; curatorial functions; audio-visual techniques; graphic design; object technology; preparation, conservation and security; evaluation, management and technical services. The terms of reference for the team embraced responsibility for the development and detailed design of all exhibits and visitor guidance, including written and audio-visual aids. Included specifically in the team was the Curatorial Department, which 'will retain absolute control over the integrity of the information content of the exhibit'.

However, the way in which any individual museum approaches the tasks of first formulating the strategy and then preparing the communications plans will depend on the expertise it has available and how it is organized. The same may be said of how the plans will be implemented. In many museums the expertise will be grouped within a design or exhibitions department and the head of unit will liaise direct with his curatorial counterpart. Both will bring into the project members of their staff as the needs dictate. But should a museum lack sufficient communications expertise on its staff, it may decide to bring in outside contractors. Some museums do this anyway, as a matter of policy. In such cases the museum will need to be satisfied that it is able to (1) prepare a suitable project brief, (2) ensure adequate liaison and accountability, and (3) monitor progress and evaluate the work (as well as pay for it!). Even if a museum does not decide to employ consultants to undertake specific projects, it will almost certainly wish to consult many of those groups and individuals who advised on policy—together with selected specialists on aspects of the communications strategy and, in particular, involve them in the planning process.

The plan, therefore, is something which needs to be adopted at the highest level, and implemented via the Chief Officer and his management team. It should, at least in part, circulate within an institution and be something with which all senior staff are familiar. It may also be usefully circulated outside the museum to those organizations and individuals who would be interested in knowing the museum's intentions. Indeed, some local authorities now insist that all organizations within their purview produce such plans, and use them not only as statements of an organization's intentions but also as baselines against which their effectiveness can be measured.

Communications conceptual plan

Like the other major areas which make up the museum's activities and are included in the museum's policy document, 'communications', as a topic, should be represented in the museum's 'grand conceptual plan'. Those responsible for preparing the plan would be identified within the communications strategy. A likely group would include senior and interested members of staff who had the necessary expertise together with various outside specialists who, it was thought, had a specific contribution to make. The group would be led by the senior member of staff with responsibility for communications.

Its task would be that of taking the museum's policy on communications and stating how it might ideally be achieved. As has been stated, the plan should not be over-concerned with the administrative and economic problems of implementation, but should set out what is desirable if resources and opportunities permit. As such, it should recognize actual (as opposed to imagined or even convenient) constraints, and set out what the museum realistically wishes to achieve, consistent with its policy. It must therefore be practical and well thought out.

Essentially it will need to address the two interrelated issues of concept and physical opportunities. For the first, it must consider the museum's approach to communication with the public, and in particular expand the subject areas which the policy identified as being those with which the museum wishes to be involved. For the purpose of exhibitions, this might include a schematic system of organization of the major topics. Once this has been established, and links between topics identified, it should be related to the physical accommodation—both actual and planned—of the museum, because the physical opportunities afforded by both existing and planned new buildings must be considered. The conceptual master plan will be about creating a blueprint which sets out what the museum regards as the ideal solution to its communications problem, and so it should aim for completeness. The plan will be what the museum deploys its energies and resources to achieve. It is the ultimate goal which may not be attained for many years—indeed, possibly never. Inevitably it will need to be reviewed periodically.

Communications action plan

Like the conceptual plan, the communications action plan also forms a part of a more comprehensive document which covers all aspects of the museum's work, namely the museum's corporate or business plan. And whereas the conceptual plan identifies the long-term goals, the communications action plan incorporated in the business plan should be regarded as an attainable, if optimistic, target, to be achieved within a specified period of perhaps three or five years. As such, it should be compiled with a good knowledge of what undertaking such projects entails, and be founded upon experience, feasibility studies and accurate costings. Thus the plan should identify the specific projects, such as new gallery developments which the museum intends to undertake in a given period, and incorporate them into a programme.

The main purposes of such an undertaking are to clarify thoughts on planning and put forward a clearly defined programme of work which the museum must carry out. It therefore determines immediate priorities and facilitiates management objectives. In this way it becomes the target which all museum staff can work towards achieving. Whilst the communications section of the business plan will list those things which the museum hopes to accomplish in exhibitions, publications and similar media, other sections will deal with related areas such as acquisitions, target building programmes and income levels. This then

combines to form an objective, integrated plan of the museum's activities
for the ensuing period.

3. Museum image, marketing and design

Museum Image

Mention has already been made of the importance of a museum's image, and its significance in relation to the interface between museum and public and to the communications policy and plan. Bearing in mind its importance, it is unfortunate but true that, for many people, the image associated with museums is not a complimentary one. Indeed, the word 'museum piece' has passed into daily usage, as the dictionary tells us, as a derogatory term, meaning 'fit for a museum' i.e. old-fashioned, quaint, or worse! It is also well known that, in the not so distant past (and, regrettably, even at the present time), some museums have been (and are) exceedingly dull, lifeless places with unchanging, uninspiring displays gathering the proverbial dust. Additionally, many of the staff were, and are, non-communicative and certainly not welcoming to the public. It used to be said that someone interested in archaeology, natural history or whatever, and wanting to do research, would choose to work in a museum, where they could be left in peace, rather than enter academic life in a university or polytechnic where they would be disturbed by students wanting information!

This poor presentation and public face have meant that for many people, who perhaps have not visited a museum recently, and are in their middle years or older, their last experience of a museum has possibly left them with the lasting impression of dullness. Therefore, whenever the topic of museums is raised, they are likely to relate their unfortunate experiences, so planting in the minds of their circle of friends or their children similar expections of museums and thereby perpetuating a particular (if largely out-of-date) image.

Someone with no preconditioning should obviously approach a museum with a relatively open mind. However, some degree of pre-conditioning is inevitable, since, in order to find out about a museum in the first place, some knowledge of it is necessary. The manner in which this is obtained—perhaps by word of mouth (through listening to a speaking voice which is enthusiastic or discouraging, irrespective of what is actually said) or through an advertisement, leaflet or press report—will mean that certain expectations will inevitably be aroused.

A helpful way to consider the formation of an image is as a balance, poised on a central pivot with equal pressure either side maintaining an equilibrium. This then responds to both increases and decreases in the

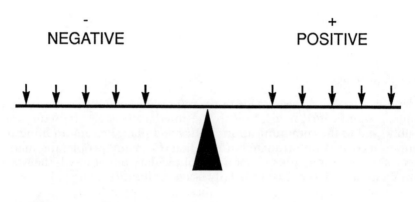

Influence on Image

Figure 3.1 Negative and positive influence on museum image

pressures applied, moving it from the neutral to indicate either negative
or positive attributes.

It is a truism that people who are happy, satisfied and content will
think nice, positive thoughts, whereas unhappy, frustrated, disappointed
and tired people who are then subjected to a long, cold wait for a bus (or
cannot find a parking place or lavatory) will not. And even if none of
these things is directly attributable to the museum (like the weather),
nevertheless, experiences encountered on a visit to a museum will be
associated with that museum—for better or for worse! Thus a museum
should seek to identify those elements which might exert negative
influences on its public with a view to eliminating them where possible,
and, at the same time, identify and develop positive characteristics.

Fundamental to the image issue is the museum's own identity. This
unique set of characteristics can then be 'packaged' for marketing within
the overall image which the museum wishes to project. Identity is
essentially related to the type of museum and the material it exhibits.
National, university, regional, local and private museums each have an
identity relevant to status and also in relation to collections, for these, be
they tanks, scientific instruments, modern paintings, children's toys,
antiquities or whatever, provide the museum with its particular character. Other influences are the type of building in which the museum is

housed, be it period or modern, and its location, in a major city, town or country village.

The various ways in which people come into contact with the museum, i.e. the museum interface, are those which are most important in terms of museum image. These are the factors which particularly affect the way in which people think about museums, and most have been identified and explored in the many opinion surveys which museums have undertaken to find out what their visitors think. The major areas for consideration include design; publicity; services and facilities; dealings with museum staff and the environment, and these are briefly discussed below.

Design

In this context design essentially is intended to mean visual appearance, and as such it is an aspect which permeates most aspects of a museum's activities. It may also be enhanced by a specific house style or corporate identity. This enhancement would normally embrace a 'logo' or 'trade mark' which, even when standing alone (without illustrations or supporting text) would identify the institution but, when used in conjunction with other material, serves as a unifying element to all the diverse communications channels which the museum might employ.

This enables the public to identify quickly museum material and, through frequent exposure, maintain the identity of the museum as an active organization in the public's mind. Stationery, including letter heads, is important in this respect, as are all printed material, advertisements, and so on. Thus the form of the device which a museum adopts as its 'logo' will do much to promote this image.

The type of design a museum selects as right for it is, in effect, its house style, and this should extend into all areas of the museum and include such aspects as interior design. It should also be apparent in the exhibition galleries—but not be so rigid as to prevent individual exhibitions from having their own identities and, more important, reflecting the character of the material displayed.

Publicity

A museum's generated publicity should be its conscious attempt to utilize the most effective of media in order to promote its chosen image. Thus the type of material it devises (or which is devised on its behalf by an advertising agency) will, to a very large extent, determine how a large number of people regard the museum—without necessarily having visited it. In this, it is the use of its corporate identity scheme, together with the visual images and words which it selects, that form the message it wishes to communicate, and, once committed to paper or film and published, the 'style' is set. So if the publicity is sophisticated or austere, jocular or common, this is how the museum will be identified and where it will find its mark among the various groups of people who will see the material and take note of it.

A problem for a museum, like any other institution or individual, is that not all publicity is self-generated—some is thrust upon it. It is said by some that any publicity is good publicity, since it raises the profile of the museum in terms of public awareness. This may be so; however, adverse publicity will do little to enhance the intended image of a museum and this may have serious consequences in both political and economic terms.

Services and facilities

A museum's image will also be reflected in the range and type of services it offers, and fundamental to this are the exhibitions which feature the museum's collections. Indeed, in many people's minds this is the reason why museums exist. As has already been said, the type of material on display will play a large part in determining the character of the museum, and how it is displayed will also contribute in a significant way to the image projected. Thus the style of presentation and communication—the choice of prose, the use of audio-visual and interactive devices, and so on—all contribute to the overall image.

In addition to exhibitions, other public services such as catering facilities, lavatories and shops also occupy significant roles in the museum/public interface. It hardly needs to be said that a museum which provides expensive 'nouvelle cuisine' food in its restaurant has a rather different image and is appealing to a rather different type of client from one which provides a take-away burger-and-chips booth. It is clear that the extent to which a museum caters for, and makes a conscious, positive effort to anticipate and provide services for its visitors is a prime indication of its attitude and therefore of its image.

Environment

The importance of design has already been discussed, and obviously the appearance of the museum will do much to create the mood which, in turn, has an effect on the image projected and obtained. How the museum environment appears—not just in design terms, but also in terms of atmosphere and whether it is a comfortable and welcoming or minimal or aggressive—is another significant factor in contributing to the museum image. An aspect of this is the museum's approach to maintenance and cleanliness. Litter-strewn, graffiti-clad exteriors or uncared-for lavatories do little to endear a museum to its visitors, and evidence of a disregard towards the environment might suggest a similar attitude towards care of the collections and concern for visitors.

Dealings with museum staff

All museum employees, irrespective of their status and role are representatives of, and represent to the public, the institutions for which they
work. Thus whenever a member of the public comes into contact with a
member of the museum staff, the impression given is significant in
determining, for that individual, the image of the museum. Obviously,
certain staff have particularly important roles to play in terms of public
relations, but an institution benefits from staff at all levels who are at ease
when dealing with people and who communicate effectively and
courteously. Among those with important roles are clearly those
members of staff who communicate with the media and who make public
statements on behalf of the museum. But also important, particularly as
far as individual members of the public are concerned, are the first
members of the museum staff with whom they have contact. Thus anyone
positioned near the entrance or on duty at an information desk needs to
be friendly, welcoming and polite if that is how the museum wishes to
appear. Moreover, all officials at all levels need to be courteous and
professional in their dealings with the public, whether it be in person, by
phone or by letter.

Particularly unfortunate first impressions of an organization are
sometimes given when telephone switchboards are overworked and
understaffed. If the public (and professional colleagues, too) experience
long delays in making contact with people, or curt rather than courteous
treatment, they will obviously gain an adverse impression of the
museum. Protracted delay in answering letters also has a similar effect.

A museum, then, needs to be very much aware of the particular aspects
which play such an important part in determining its image. But it
would be a mistake indeed to think image applied only to a museum's
dealings with the public. It has a professional image to maintain too, and
its standing with other museums and academic institutions will be
determined by the manner in which it conducts its business.

In conclusion, a museum might usefully ask itself such questions as:
'How does the museum think it appears to its clients?' 'How *does* the
museum appear to its clients?' 'How does the museum *want* to appear to
its clients?' A periodic reassessment of a museum's image through
providing detailed answers to these questions, can undoubtedly be a
useful exercise, for, as has been indicated, images can, through hard
work, be improved.

Museum marketing

For many museums, marketing is not altogether a new phenomenon.
Indeed, some museums, from fairly early in their development, have been
aware of the benefits of publicity and have actively engaged in it. And
today many museum staff regard their publicity and promotional work as
their marketing—mistakenly thinking that they are the same thing. They

are wrong, for publicity, important as it is, is but one aspect of marketing. The concern which museums have been showing for their visitors comes closer to what marketing is about. This gathered momentum in America in the mid-1960s and soon spread to Britain, where it manifested itself in a whole host of visitor surveys. Museums wanted to know who their visitors were, where they came from, what they did in the museum and what their interests were. Many impressive sets of data were published and museums did indeed achieve their objective of finding out about their visitors. However, there are few recorded instances of how the information obtained in surveys has been used as a basis upon which changes to the service provided by museums have been implemented.

As so often in the past, museums are again operating in a climate of change. This time the changes which have a particular relevance to museums are the economic pressures which are being put upon them, the need to find a way to help alleviate this problem for themselves, and the growing competition for the attention of the public which is coming from all branches of the leisure industry, and indeed, from other museums. Because of the prevailing interest in economic viability and commercialism, it is particularly important that each museum looks seriously at the concept of marketing and its relevance to the museum's function, aims and objectives. In what is becoming a highly competitive activity, museums will need to take account of the concept of marketing if they are to operate successfully in these changing circumstances.

The nature of marketing

Marketing is a concept of business which puts the customer at the centre of the activity. It is embodied in a cyclic approach based on market research, service/product development, selling and promotion, quality control and after-sales service. Put simply, it is about identifying, anticipating and meeting the needs of the community or groups within it (that is, the customers) for a service which is compatible with the aims and objectives of the provider. The very nature of the concept pre-supposes that any organization adopting such an approach will be dynamic, flexible and, above all, responsive in providing a service which takes account of the findings of market research.

Marketing, therefore, is very different from the popular concept which equates it with advertising, that is, persuading people to buy things they don't want. Indeed, it may be seen to be almost the opposite, that is, the making available of things people do want and will buy.

Developing a marketing strategy

For some, marketing is not dissimilar from the chicken-and-egg syndrome of deciding what should come first—developing a product or service and then finding a niche in the market place for it—or first finding the niche and then developing the product or service in response to the need. For museums the *raison d'être* should have been clarified by the application of the definition of either ICOM or the Museums Association, and further expanded in the policy document with clearly defined aims and objectives. Within this paper there should also be statements of policy relating to the museum's approach to marketing.

Once the need for a marketing strategy has been accepted, the first stage in establishing one is to undertake a resource audit in order to assess the services or products which the museum might provide from existing resources (and thereby also permit identification at a later stage of any weaknesses or omissions which may need to be rectified). The resource may be categorized under three headings:

1. *Staff*, i.e. the skills, scholarship, knowledge and technical competence, assessed and quantified where possible.
2. *Services*, i.e. the range of service activities currently being pursued, which will probably include exhibition provision; lectures and other public events; educational services and publications.
3. *Facilities*, i.e. museum accommodation, including galleries; lecture theatres; restaurants; transport; equipment, etc.

Following the resource audit, the second stage is to clarify how the resources might be used. This may initially result in a reaffirmation of the museum's aims and objectives, and even justification of the *status quo*. However, if approached slightly differently by asking the question 'How might the museum *maximize* the use of these resources?', then new ideas and initiatives might result, particularly if the exercise is conducted in a manner which encourages creative thinking, such as 'brainstorming' sessions. The implications of new ideas, if they are accepted, may require a reconsideration and revision of the museum's aims and objectives, or some adjustment to the deployment of the museum's resources. Following the generation of new ideas and their consideration in relation to the museum's aims and objectives, the next stage is to undertake some form of feasibility study and test whether the proposals are valid in terms of demand.

Alternatively, if more general information on the demand for museum services is required prior to generating any new ideas, then some form of market analysis is required. This is where market research is essential and where comprehensive research programmes need to be undertaken to produce a position audit, using, for example, the 'SWOT' (strengths, weaknesses, opportunities, threats) approach to discover:

1. General attitudes towards the museum and its services.
2. Why people *don't* come to the museum (whether they know it even exists) and what would attract them to it.
3. Why people do visit the museum—an evaluation of existing strengths.
4. An evaluation of the image currently projected by the museum (both negative and positive factors).

5. A critical appraisal of existing visitor services—identifying any weaknesses or omissions.

6. An evaluation of existing professional services together with an appraisal of demand.

7. What the various groups which make up the potential consumer market might want from a dynamic museum service and the price (if applicable) they might be prepared to pay for it.

8. The nature of the competition (both actual and potential) from other organizations operating in related areas, such as: museums, heritage centres and educational institutions; the leisure industry; the entertainment industry; commerce (which might include such things as craft and antiques fairs, etc.); restaurants and the service industries.

9. An evaluation of the factors (i.e. economic, social, political and geographical) which might influence future trends—and thereby have an effect on the museum service of the future. These might include increased leisure time; population trends; accessibility and transport; educational systems; levels of disposable income; European links, etc.

As the data become available and are given meaning by placing them in suitable contexts, so a picture emerges of possible avenues to evaluate further and consider in the light of resources the implications and the uses to which the resources might be put. From this will evolve a marketing strategy which, subject to its being compatible with the museum's aims and objectives, may be modified or implemented.

Minda Borun (1977) in her study of museum effectiveness which was undertaken in the Franklin Institute, Philadelphia, believed that a museum should aim to become 'a flexible, self-evaluating, self-correcting institution in touch with the needs and desires of its public'. Her investigation dealt with the educational role of the museum, whereas the above statement has wider application. Nevertheless, her thinking was clearly in line with the notion of marketing, and probably few museum specialists who are concerned with the effectiveness of the service they provide would take issue with this aim, provided, of course, that what the public want is broadly in line with what the museum wants to provide. Major difficulties occur, however, when either the museum wishes to provide services for which there is no demand (like exhibitions to which nobody comes) or when a need is identified which is outside the accepted museum policy (like everyone wants entertainment). This then demonstrates just how flexible and responsive the museum is prepared to be, for museums should not necessarily submit to the pressures of popularization and the fads of fashion. Some will, admittedly, in consequence relate only to a very small market niche—but they may well do so very successfully.

The nature of museum design

Museum design is concerned with the function and the appearance of every facet of the museum system, because it embraces all tangible evidence of the museum's activities. It also involves many different design disciplines and may be regarded as the application of those disciplines to the museum situation.

As a system devised to undertake certain clearly defined tasks, the museum can benefit in many ways from the expertise of the professional designer. On the large scale, there is a need to provide a physical environment in which the museum can operate, and this will include the building or complex of structures and associated internal and external spaces which provide accommodation for the museum and its activities. Where permanent structural work is concerned, this need is normally the subject of architectural design expertise, with assistance from environmental designers to consider the interior spaces. However, the museum's particular function of presenting, exhibiting and interpreting the collections requires design skills which may in part be environmental (and, to some extent, possibly architectural) but must also include the range of disciplines associated with communication design and possibly other areas of industrial and product design as well.

At a time when museums were becoming more aware of the potential of design, Sir Hugh Casson, in his address to the Museums Association (1961), reminded museum staff that it was not only museum exhibitions which needed to be well designed. He said:

> Everything throughout the museum, however small, should be the best possible of its kind, from such small items as ashtrays, fire buckets, attendants' uniforms, even the quality of the coffee and sandwiches in the refreshment room. Your invitations and postcards, your advertising and lecture announcements are all visual projections of the cultural centre which your museum is set out to be. It is vital that they be of the highest quality . . .

Designing is a process which involves many considerations and decisions, most of which ultimately relate to a use of resources in the form of manpower and materials which make up the production costs of the design. Museum design, in particular, will also involve valuable and unique collections of artefacts and specimens which must not be put at risk. A good design may not necessarily be inexpensive, but it should be economic to produce. It should function efficiently and be reliable; it should be well made, safe and easy to maintain. It should also be pleasing to look at. Failure in any one of these can not only be costly in terms of inefficiency, repair or replacement, but may also result in other problems like injury to persons or damage to specimens and ultimately loss of public respect and support. The complexities of the design process, and all the factors which have a bearing on design such as ergonomics, psychology and, more obviously, a knowledge of materials and production processes and the capacity for original thought and creativity in problem-solving, suggest that, in a situation where time, money and satisfactory end product are essential, it is prudent to employ the services of a trained professional.

A checklist of work areas in which professional design expertise would particularly benefit the museum might include the following:

1. *The museum site.* Layout of gardens, grounds and public facilities. Location of outdoor exhibits. External appearance of building. External signing. Banners.

2. *Internal spaces.* Overall plan, layout, fitting and finishes to staff accommodation, workshops, studios, laboratories and stores. All public areas and facilities, including restaurants, cloakrooms, shops, etc.

3. *The presentation and exhibition of the collections.* Design and co-ordination of the environment in which objects are seen. Physical supports of objects. Permanent and temporary exhibitions. Lighting. Security and atmosphere requirements.

4. *Interpretive aids.* Design of exhibition graphics, including labels, diagrams, charts, maps, illustrations and photographs. Audio-visual presentations. Catalogues and leaflets. Interpretive computer programmes. Educational technology.

5. *Publications and souvenirs.* Design of guides, educational packs, books, wall charts, models. Stationery. Giftware, decorative items, reproductions.

6. *Museum image and publicity.* Visual identity as presented to museum public. Signs, advertising aids, including press advertisements, posters, leaflets, television commercials.

7. *Promotional activities.* Performances, demonstrations, festivals, fairs, parades.

The museum designer

Design has been variously described as 'problem-solving' and 'the arranging of elements to some purpose'. Good design is evident when a solution satisfies set criteria of function, aesthetics and economy in manufacture and operation—or simply 'fitness of purpose'. The designer, in order to practise successfully, should be proficient in the basic design skills of problem identification, analysis and solving. However, the range of work areas in which design expertise is particularly valuable embraces several separate design disciplines, and an expert in one area may not necessarily have the skills and knowledge to provide adequate design solutions in other areas.

The range of work areas relevant to the museum's needs may be broadly termed industrial design with an emphasis on communication design. It may further be divided into the two main categories of design, *two-dimensional* design, which relates mainly to graphic images in print; and *three-dimensional* design, which is concerned with the utilization of materials to form structures and environments. Exhibition design is almost unique in combining both two and three-dimensional design elements.

Those areas of two-dimensional or 'graphic' design (2D) which have application within the museum include: advertising design; audio-visual design; communication design; computer graphics; educational technology design; film, video and television; general graphics; illustration; information design; learning resources technology; photography; typography and lettering; visual communication. The range of work which may be termed 'three-dimensional' (3D) includes: architectual design; display design; environmental design; exhibition design; furniture design; landscape and garden design; lighting design; product design; spatial design; theatre design.

While these two are generally recognized as distinct design areas, some, like 'environmental design', embrace several others, and 'exhibition design' as a specialist aspect of environmental design embraces such elements as display, furniture, lighting and even, on occasions, theatre design.

The multi-disciplinary nature of museum design dictates that the 'museum designer' is not quickly created but, after an initial training in a relevant two or, more appropriately, three-dimensional discipline, will emerge only after considerable experience of working in a museum and of resolving a wide range of design problems. To date, it has generally been the three-dimensional designer who has held the most senior design post in a museum, and has acted as group leader. This is because the 3D designer is normally responsible for the overall design concept, of which graphics are only a part. Generally, the environment and structure of an interpretive exhibition come first as part of the initial concept and graphics follow or are a subordinate element within the scheme. Also, in terms of costs, the three-dimensional components of an exhibition tend to form the major cost factor.

In conclusion, it is worth noting what the eminent exhibition designer Robin Wade (1972) had to say about his role as designer:

> The designer is often thought of as being purely a visual man . . . I personally dislike being cast in this role, as it denies involvement in the really creative and enjoyable aspect of museum design, which is (or should be) caring for the organisation and interpretation of the complete idea, story, concept or whatever you like to call it, of the exhibition. To my mind, this is at least as important as the proper display of the individual objects. The designer has an interpretive role.

Part two.   Museum exhibitions: communication function, modes and types

4. *Exhibition as a medium of communication*

The dictionary defines 'exhibition' as a showing and in this sense all the world is an exhibition of one sort or another. The natural shows of sunrise and sunset, a flower in bloom or an animal prancing have fascinated man from the earliest times. Man, being exhibition-conscious, has also liked to participate and this soon became evident in his concern with his appearance and with make-up, dress and jewellery, and his home and its contents, with the built environment, and with his general love of the spectacular. However, in the context of our discussions 'exhibition' should be defined as 'showing for a purpose', the purpose being to affect the viewer in some predetermined way. And, as a medium of communication, the possibilities afforded by exhibitions are boundless—limited only by imagination, practical skills, physical possibilities and budget.

Velarde (1988) makes the point that exhibitions come in all shapes and sizes and categorizes them under headings which include trade fairs, world fairs, public trade shows, science centres, heritage and eco-centres, museums and art galleries, travelling exhibitions and portable exhibitions. Today the expansion of the leisure industry to cater for a population with more free time and disposable income, coupled with a greater awareness of topics such as heritage and conservation, has created new variations on traditional exhibitions. The science centres, heritage centres and eco-centres mentioned by Velarde are examples, and to them may be added those other fashionable 'buzz' words such as 'theme park' and 'exploratorium'. Whilst basically exhibitions, much of the novelty in these developments has, of course, been provided by the new technology of computers and the degree of visitor participation. As a medium, exhibition has always been such that the novel and new have found immediate application, and the rapid pace of technological developments assures exhibitions an exciting future.

Undoubtedly exhibition, as a medium, has certain unique qualities, and many are highly advantageous in the context of communicating and have established exhibition as an effective and successful medium. However, it does also have certain limitations and disadvantages. Thus, when contemplating a communications project, it is important to consider the advantages and disadvantages of each medium and select the one (or ones) appropriate to the task in hand.

The advantages of exhibition as a medium of communication

The most important and unique characteristic of a museum exhibition is that it facilitates an encounter between visitor and three-dimensional object. Other media, such as television or the printed book, can portray images, but they are not the prime source. Only exhibition provides a controlled contact with the real, authentic object, and this is what makes museum exhibitions so vitally important.

Furthermore, exhibition is not limited to the size of a television screen or page. It can work at scales appropriate to those of the objects to be shown and facilitate a 'bridging' function so essential to making viewing comfortable on a human scale. Small objects can be given some prominence and positioned in a way that enables them to be seen, and larger objects distanced or brought close to heighten visual interest as needs dictate.

In providing this contact with objects, the three-dimensional quality of exhibitions is important, for it can facilitate the 'all-round' viewing of many objects and enable the visitor to experience fully the three-dimensional qualities not only of the objects but also of the total exhibition by moving about around and within it. Bringing object and viewer close together is the most important function of museum exhibitions, and the medium can achieve this in a manner which is safe for both object (in terms of security and conservation) and viewer.

The exhibition environment in which visitors look and move can be developed to encourage the use of all the senses. To looking and moving can be added touching, hearing, smelling and even tasting, to complete the multi-sensory experience which exhibition can provide. Activating all senses can have a most satisfying and memorable effect on the visitor and enable communication to take place through the whole range of human receptors. This can have the effect of increasing the number of people with whom communication occurs, and the intensity of the communication, since many people find the senses of touch or smell more memorable, and therefore more receptive, than even that of seeing.

In appealing to the range of human senses, an exhibition will utilize many different media and approaches in order to achieve its aims. Thus the traditional static displays are not obligatory, and exhibits can take many forms. They can include the dynamic, the real and the replica, models of all sizes, graphics in static and animated form, and the whole range of environmental and visual effects used by modern theatre and made possible by modern technology. However, underpinning these are the basic design elements of colour, form, shape, line, texture and light.

By providing a multi-faceted approach, exhibitions can function simultaneously at different levels and in many different ways. In this manner a range of aims and objectives can be achieved in a single exhibition by the use of a variety of interpretive materials, and the exhibition can appeal to a wider visitor group made up of different ages, levels of knowledge and intellects. They can also be designed for very specific single audiences and possibly located accordingly, remote from a central location, at, for example, a site of special interest or in a specific area such as a school's history room.

Irrespective of the audiences for whom they are designed, exhibitions are essentially spaces within which visitors may move and progress freely. This has the advantage of enabling the visitors to proceed at their own pace, and of allowing them to linger on that which interests them and bypass that which does not. For, unlike the ephemeral images of film, which, unless videoed, cannot easily be frozen or replayed, an exhibition exists to be viewed constantly. This permanence also means that visitors may leave and return to it many times, and it is therefore not necessary to attempt to see, read and assimilate everything in one visit. Indeed, a return visit is to be encouraged, as often the experience is more selective, and more penetrating and rewarding than the first.

The existence of an exhibition in time and space can enable it to be highly effective and economically viable. In the period of its existence the experience of visiting may be shared by vast numbers of people and, with a continuous throughput, many can visit simultaneously. Undoubtedly the experience is such that the public are prepared to pay an entrance fee for their entertainment, education or information, and to this end some exhibitions can be not only commercially viable but highly profitable.

Exhibition, therefore, has considerable advantages as a medium for both promoter and visitor. To the former it offers an effective, and even profitable, way of communicating information and ideas and of providing an opportunity to show objects in a controlled environment. For the visitor it can provide a very exciting multi-sensory experience with the opportunity of a first-hand encounter with real objects and the resultant pleasure, entertainment, satisfaction and acquisition of knowledge.

The limiting factors related to exhibitions

Good exhibitions do not come easily, nor do they generally come cheap. The production process of a major exhibition is normally complex, extensive and resource-intensive, drawing, in particular, on specialists' time and skills. Furthermore, the physical structure of an exhibition—its flooring, walling, ceilings, showcases and lighting as well as such items as graphics, photographs, audio-visuals and computers—are all very costly. And whereas it would be misleading to suggest that the quality of an exhibition is always directly proportional to the finance available, it is certainly true that adequate funding is essential.

In addition to finance, space and time are two other prerequisites. An exhibition needs to be in place and open for sufficient time to enable it to be seen by worthwhile numbers of visitors. Accessible locations and prime time are valuable commodities which can command a high premium in the open market. The location of an exhibition is important, as it can have a dramatic effect on attendance figures. The fact that visitors have to journey *to* an exhibition is a limiting factor which immediately becomes an obstacle for anyone reluctant to travel. Inconvenience, time and finance all become considerations in this respect and can limit the effectiveness of an exhibition.

An exhibition is located remotely from its audience, and so it is entirely dependent on other media for communicating information about it to prospective visitors. Although word of mouth is recognized as one of the best ways to disseminate information about an exhibition or event, initial contact on a large scale must be made by the use of posters, press advertisements, leaflets and media coverage, which also serves to promote and publicize. It was James Gardner, the eminent exhibition designer, who wrote, '. . . an exhibition does not in fact exist until it is crowded with people, and what really matters is how these people react to what they see' (Gardner and Hellar 1960). It is a salutary thought that attendance figures alone can be little more than a reflection of the extent and effectiveness of the advertising.

Exhibitions, by their very nature and by the way in which people are obliged to experience them, have a tiring effect on visitors, and, generally, the larger the exhibition the more exhausted the visitor becomes. Those responsible for the preparation and design of exhibitions need to be aware of this and take as many steps as possible to minimize visitor fatigue and also encourage visitors to return. Another limiting factor is the ergonomic problem of enabling the visitor to do certain tasks whilst standing, moving and being distracted by other visitors and possibly competing exhibits. Probably the most frequent tasks for the visitors will be looking and reading. Unless the items to be regarded are well positioned, neck and back ache may result, and even when the text is well written and well presented, with due attention paid to type size, length of line and layout, only a limited amount can be assimilated comfortably.

However, not only should the expectations of the exhibition organizers of what visitors might gain from a visit be tempered by a knowledge of the physical limitations of humans, the organizers should also be aware of possible mental barriers and of the fact that visitors may not respond in the way they wish. Indeed, there is no compulsion for visitors to look, to read a label, to learn, to enjoy themselves or to respond in any other predetermined way.

Often the visitor, therefore, needs to be encouraged, and one way to do this is by making the exhibits attractive. However, the very fact that exhibits *are* designed to attract, places them in competition with one another for attention.

If exhibitions are exhausting to the visitors they can be equally distressful to the objects, for, unless sufficient safeguards are taken, to put an object on display can mean exposing it to a whole range of hazards. An unsatisfactory environment is perhaps the most common, where light levels are too high, ultra-violet light is not adequately filtered, and both temperature and humidity levels fluctuate greatly. Theft and physical damage are other risks. Obviously the responsible exhibition organizer will take every reasonable precaution to ensure the safety of the objects in his charge. And this will need to be done at every stage of an exhibition's life—preparation, duration, maintenance and disassembly. However, complete safety is probably not possible, and is not compatible with the aims of showing and making material accessible to the public. Unfortunately, accidents do occasionally happen and it is certainly not possible to provide complete protection against the most determined and the insane, particularly if they are equipped to carry out an act of destruction.

In every exhibition project, the limitations of the medium need to be recognized. This awareness should help to minimize the adverse effects through careful planning and design, so that the medium can be used honestly to greatest effect.

Exhibition as an art form

The previous discussion has emphasized the functional qualities and limitations of exhibition as a medium of communication. Indeed, exhibitions *are* pieces of functional design, with the purpose of doing a specific task. However, at their best they also satisfy the most generally accepted criteria of an art form. A frequently used definition is that a work of art should elicit an emotional response in the viewer. Undoubtedly an exhibition is capable of this. By the nature of its design (quite apart from the objects within it, although they obviously form an integral component), a mood is easily created—but the feelings generated by a powerful exhibition go beyond this.

In his classic work *The Meaning of Art* Herbert Read (1931) considered the form of a work of art. He described it as that almost indefinable quality which, in that moment when someone in an open state of mind turns a corner and confronts an artefact for the first time, has the instantaneous effect of making him gasp for breath, dilating his eyes and captivating his attention. He notes that we say a work of art 'moves' us, and regards this expression as accurate. An exhibition can do this. It can elate and excite, arouse and satisfy, anger, shock and depress. Indeed, it can play havoc with the emotions, and the skilled exhibition 'artist' (i.e. designer) can so charge the exhibition that it elicits the response desired.

Exhibitions are conceived as sculpture. They are three-dimensional compositions which recognize the importance of solids and voids and strive for satisfactory spatial relationships. It is sculpture which people are encouraged not only to look at but also to walk in and explore. It is environmental art, which offers a whole range of experiences which may stimulate all the senses. Some art is visual; some is tactile; some may be heard. An exhibition can combine all these. It utilizes not just form and space but shape, colour, light and texture as well, and maybe even sound—and indeed, all the basic elements of art and design. It may also utilize imagery and semiotics. But this, in itself, is not enough. Simply combining the various components of a recognized work of art does not necessarily make another. Two additional elements are required. First there must be an intention on the part of the creator to produce something more than that which will just do its job; second, there must be originality of thought and creativity to produce something which is quite exceptional, for the mundane and the ordinary do not qualify as works of art. It is then for the viewer to respond in the way Read described.

Like the accepted art forms of sculpture and painting, exhibition is also subject to the various vicissitudes inherent in a dynamic, evolving medium which has its roots in the historical, social, economic, educational and political structures of society—all of which may be reflected in the very subject matter of the exhibitions. Thus, as Marshall McLuhan once noted, 'the medium becomes the message' and exhibitions may be considered for their own worth, as well as for the worth of the message they convey. In his paper 'Form, composition and contents in Museum Exhibitions' Jerzy Swiecimski (1978) wrote:

> The presence of the aesthetic factor means that in consequence the function of scientific-informative museum exhibitions *extends* far beyond strictly scientific or, even, didactic-informative aims. The artistically composed museum display becomes in a strict sense a *cultural creation* which acts not only through its *scientific content*, but also through its *aesthetic eloquence*. The *action* of this eloquence is directed towards the recipient's *emotional-impressive* sensibilities. In this way, the displays approach the plane of action of *works of art* and some of them (I mean here the best solutions) factually achieve the quality of *genuine* art; it happens especially, when *besides* scientific content the exhibition presents features which may be qualified in such categories as 'dramatism', 'lyricism', 'peacefulness', 'harmony', etc.

There are many exhibitions which, by virtue of their impact may be regarded as examples of the exhibition as art. They may be of either the permanent or the temporary mode, but it is those of the latter category which, because of their more adventurous nature, have succeeded more often. Arguably some of the 'blockbusters' which were mounted in London during the late 1960s and the 1970s at the Victoria and Albert Museum, the Royal Academy and the British Museum achieved this; as have, of course, many others. However, not unlike a theatre performance, these shows were ephemeral, capitalizing to some extent on the mood of the time, and, as temporary exhibitions, have long since been 'struck'. Nevertheless, something of their artistic quality can be gleaned from photographs.

Possibly the constraints on 'permanent' exhibitions and the need for stylistic restraint in an attempt to secure longevity have reduced the impact of most of these. Also, some of the design elements, such as imagery, are generally less pronounced, and many 'permanent' solutions can rightly be termed 'ordinary'. However, there are, of course, exceptions. Europe abounds with them, and the work of Italian architects such as Carlo Scarpa, who had a strong influence on exhibition design in the United Kingdom, comes readily to mind. In Britain, some of the permanent galleries at the British Museum are distinctive; so too is the presentation of the Burrell Collection in Glasgow and parts of the Museum of London, to name only a few. It is interesting to note that, in the latter two examples, the new architectural environment has contributed much to the overall effect. Exhibitions mounted in new museums, or in new architectural treatments of old buildings, are often exceptionally exciting. But unlike temporary exhibitions, permanent shows have rarely shocked their audience, and have relied more on providing a pleasurable aesthetic experience. They have tended to 'play safe', occasionally being a little thought-provoking, but generally remaining comfortable examples of the art. All rely on the skilful use of space, light, colour, shape and form to achieve their effect. Those with that added dimension of originality and a successful approach to the presentation of the subject matter do indeed have visitors enthralled as well as informed and entertained, and so the visual spectacle, as an art form, maintains its traditional ability to attract the crowds.

5. Exhibition modes

Exhibitions may be categorized in various ways and in the museum context it is perhaps simplest to examine first exhibition modes and their characteristics, and then to consider other aspects such as approach and style.

Permanent exhibitions

In Victorian times, when so many museums were established and exhibition galleries set up, it is clear from the way in which display cases were built into the architecture that the layout was intended to be permanent—that is, it was intended to last the life of the building. Today, however, the term 'permanent' is used more to distinguish intended long-term exhibitions from those intended to be temporary or short-term. The word 'intended' is deliberately stressed, as in practice what so often happens is that 'temporary' exhibitions are repeatedly extended and the 'permanent' are either extensively changed or subject to curtailment.

However, for planning and design purposes it is important to know the intended life of an exhibition, as it will certainly affect decisions made on virtually all aspects of the design and content. The aims and objectives of a 'permanent' exhibition may also differ from those of a short-term exhibition, although the basic communications functions will remain. In this context 'permanent' has come to mean a minimum life of about ten years. Addressing the Royal Society of Arts on the subject of museum design when director of the British Museum, Pope-Hennessy (1975) made the distinction that permanent exhibitions were to be absorbed through repeated visits whereas temporary exhibitions were aimed at the non-recurring visitor. This is an interesting distinction, and may well be appropriate to situations where access to the permanent collections is free and a charge is made for access to the major temporary exhibitions.

Any proposal for a 'permanent' exhibition must be considered in relation to a museum's overall communications policy and plan, an important factor in which will be the exhibition budget. This may be sufficient to provide the funds necessary to develop exhibitions of quality which will last many years or possibly be generous enough to facilitate change—or indeed both. Alternatively funds may be inadequate to do either and an exhibition may simply evolve and undergo modifications to extend its usefulness. This is not necessarily a bad thing, for even the most 'permanent' of exhibitions should be capable of change if needs dictate. However, funds need to be adequate to do the job properly, and, while it is often possible to raise money for a 'one-off' initial project, it can be more difficult to guarantee sufficient funding for an on-going programme. Furthermore, once completed, the 'permanent' gallery should not only be capable of undergoing, if required, the change indicated above, but also have the necessary finance allocated to it which will keep it maintained to a satisfactory standard. Nevertheless, sponsors providing finance for an exhibition often like the idea of contributing to something which has a degree of permanence.

The type of museum, its collections and the story it wishes to tell will also affect any proposals for permanent exhibitions. For small museums with limited material and some specialized museums with a straight-forward or even just a single story to tell, a permanent exhibition is probably the best answer, especially if what is done is very successful. Change for change's sake is not, in itself, defensible, for unless it is backed by sound intentions of improved performance, extending the coverage, attracting a wider and continuing audience or commercial viability, it cannot be justified.

Some types of exhibition lend themselves to longevity more than others. Exhibitions of quality art objects, for example, when sensitively displayed and well documented may successfully remain on view for a very long time (provided, of course, conservation needs are also met). The traditional hanging of pictures in many art galleries is a good example, particularly where the style of the interior (possibly Victorian or Edwardian neo-classical) is a major influence on the design of the presentation.

Currently there is a move to go beyond mere stylistic influence on the design of the presentation of some art exhibitions, and to restore accurately many nineteenth-century galleries to their original deco-rations and exhibition style. This concept of maintaining a period building in its original state (whilst making some concessions to modern standards of lighting, heating and security) is an interesting one which has validity in showing how the building originally appeared and how collections were presented at the time (Clifford 1987). Fortunately public taste is now more appreciative of the decorations of the Victorians and Edwardians (thanks in part to the commercial undertakings of such companies as Laura Ashley and the trend of nostalgia promoted by popular television programmes), and this approach is more acceptable today than it might have been some ten or even twenty years ago. However, there are still dangers in this approach as communication techniques and the expectations of visitors today are very different from those of a hundred years ago.

Other types of exhibitions which work well over long periods are those which need little updating in terms of the information given, or few changes in content. Finite and historic collections which are not likely to be added to come into this category, especially when they are shown in their entirety, or when a good representative selection can be made and a decision perhaps taken to show the remaining material in temporary shows or consign it to study collections or store. Those galleries which are often termed 'primary' or 'definitive' can also, if well designed, give good service for many years almost irrespective of discipline; here 'Roman' or 'Transport', 'Ceramics' or 'Ecology', 'Costume' or 'British Natural History' can all work well. So can the more thematic exhibitions, which perhaps are multi-disciplinary or have a strong story line. Indeed, as stated above, the subject is not the critical factor; it is the aims and objectives, the approach and style, and the museum's resources that determine the longevity of its exhibitions.

Exhibitions which incorporate showcases and extensive interpretative aids need to be designed along fairly restrained 'classic' lines if they are to withstand the 'dating' which affects so much ephemeral 'contemporary' design. Since 'new' things generally command the attention and interest of an audience (and marketing strategies are always taking advantage of this), museums, too, need to capitalize on the fact. They may do so perhaps once every ten years or so in respect of their 'permanent' exhibitions unless these are opened in rotation with perhaps one every other year, and must do so considerably more frequently if they intend to mount an effective temporary exhibitions programme.

For an exhibition to assume permanence, it must be designed to standards and in a manner which will last. It must also be made from materials and include components which will withstand continual wear and tear, and can be maintained or easily and economically replaced. Good design is arguably timeless in its appeal. To achieve this quality there are, perhaps, four distinct approaches from which the designer, guided by the requirements of the brief, must select but one. The alternative approaches are:

1. To design it very much in the style of the day, and incorporate many of the design clichés, e.g. this year's fashion colours, the currently popular typeface, the latest high street display spotlights, etc., and make it very much a statement of current popular or 'trendy' design. Inevitably this will be and will always appear to be what it is—an exhibition produced at a particular time and in the (possibly exaggerated) style of the day. It will be noticeably so from the moment it opens and as next year's colours, typefaces, light fittings and wallpaper designs supersede it.
2. To provide a design which is very much in the 'modern' idiom, but taking care to avoid the design clichés (as above) and design extremes. Use 'classic' simple design elements; select colours which have a modern 'flavour'; select and use decorative elements with restraint and use all materials honestly with a generous inclusion of natural materials such as wood and stone which have a timeless quality. This approach, whilst appearing 'modern', will be less easy to date precisely, and will therefore be seen to have lasting freshness.
3. To attempt to provide a truly original solution. This might anticipate a style or even create one which others will follow. It can be an exciting if difficult approach for the designer who, although trained to be innovative, is nevertheless a person of his time and as such inevitably

influenced by the present and the past. Furthermore he is obliged to use the materials and equipment of the day, albeit in new guises, or to engage in the expensive pursuit of product development. To try consciously to anticipate what style will be fashionable in, say, ten years' time is indeed difficult. Even the fashion industry, which has considerable resources with which to influence trends, if not bring them about, finds predicting even a year or two hence hazardous. And although the museum world is arguably slower, at present it also lacks the arbitors of style which (essentially for commercial reasons) the fashion industry has in abundance.

4. To design in an acceptable style of the past, but incorporate certain modern technical refinements such as lighting. Clearly this approach can be used only when relevant either to the objects to be shown or to the architectural environment. However, it could provide the opportunity to work in the style of Art Nouveau, Art Deco or whatever, and be assured it will not become *passé* as far as fashion is concerned, but remain true to the time of the objects or the building.

The design approach selected must clearly be in sympathy with the material to be exhibited, the environment into which the exhibition is to be placed and be developed in response to the aims and objectives as defined in the brief.

Temporary exhibitions

If 'permanent' means a life of up to and around ten years, then 'temporary' means something less. The intention of how much less needs to be stated in the design brief but in practice will often be determined by events. However, if it is helpful, temporary can be qualified by 'short', 'medium' and 'long'-term. *Short-term* could be a day, a week or a month or two, depending on the museum's exhibition programme and events. *Medium-term* might be three to six months—perhaps an annual major summer exhibition running from Easter until the autumn, again depending on the programme cycle. *Long-term* tends to be a designation applied when a space is to be filled without certain knowledge of the time when it is to be brought into a schedule, and so is 'temporarily' filled pending further developments. Unfortunately the funding of many museums, with the annual uncertainties of budget allocations and occasional cutbacks, often makes medium and long-term planning difficult and frequently means that too many projects are undertaken on a temporary basis and then assume an unintended permanence.

Advantages of temporary exhibitions

Planned temporary or short-term exhibitions have several distinct qualities and should serve both the museum and its audience well. For when space and time are limited and there is an abundance of material to be shown, the mounting of changing exhibitions of short duration ensures that the utilization of the resources is maximized. Furthermore, the effect of a lively exhibition programme is to stimulate interest from different sections of the public whilst, at the same time, encouraging regular visitors.

One of the most important qualities of the temporary exhibition is that it affords the ideal opportunity to be innovative and daring without placing too much at risk. Thus obscure subjects can be featured— particularly those which, because of their esoteric nature, may not be included in a permanent gallery. Also new ways of encouraging the visitor to see things can be tried—for example, through the juxta- positioning of objects—and countless original themes can be pursued. Indeed, no concept should be excluded from consideration if the aims and objectives are valid, the safety of the objects is assured and its relevance to the overall programme satisfactory.

Yet another strength of the temporary exhibition is its capacity to be topical and controversial. For by the use of suitable structures and the inclusion of available material (even if it is largely graphic), a museum may respond, almost spontaneously (if adequately resourced) to current events. This is an important capability if the museum wishes to promote an image of being up-to-date and concerned with the present and future as well as the past.

And if the approach to the concept and content of the exhibition can be fresh and experimental, so too can the methods of presentation. The very impermanence of the exhibition means that new approaches can be made, new materials used and new techniques tried out. Indeed, risks can and should be taken (but not, of course, with the objects) which would be entirely ruled out in a permanent situation. Furthermore, it should be an aim of every temporary exhibition to test and evaluate a new aspect so that knowledge is gained. This could be in light fittings or any other exhibition element—for only in this way will the body of knowledge in relation to exhibition techniques be conveniently and economically advanced.

Such have been the achievements of the temporary exhibition in establishing a standard, that, on visiting such an exhibition, the public now have certain expectations. This is so much so that, should an exhibition fail to delight, entertain, surprise and inform, the public may well depart disappointed and even disillusioned.

Temporary exhibitions programme

It is obviously not possible in this work to provide a comprehensive list of all the topics which are suitable for inclusion in a museum's temporary exhibitions programme. An encyclopaedia is perhaps best equipped to do this, and it is surprising the possibilities which come to mind when idly thumbing through the relevant sections of such a publication. A 'brain-storming' session is yet another method by which ideas may be generated.

However, a brief checklist of some of the main subjects and sources which might be relevant to a multi-disciplinary museum is given below.

1. Anniversaries of the birth or death of relevant worthies who have achieved local, national or international significance in their field.
2. Suitable anniversaries of notable events. These may include inventions and discoveries, battles and disasters, achievements, etc.
3. Anniversaries of local happenings—such as the founding of a town or its church, or the opening of the museum.
4. Material from the museum's various departmental collections which is not normally on show.
5. Material which is already on show, perhaps in different locations, but which may be brought together to illustrate a particular theme.
6. Material which may be assembled in conjunction with a national event, nationally organized festival or similar campaign.
7. Material which may be borrowed from other museums or exhibition circulating agencies.
8. The work of local societies, organizations and educational establishments.
9. The work of artists and craftspeople living or working in the region.
10. The work of the various departments of the museum.

This list forms something like the staple temporary exhibition diet of most regional multi-disciplinary museums in the country. However, exactly how each museum devises its programme must depend on its policy on communicating with its public—its aims and objectives—and the material it has on permanent exhibition. A further consideration must be the resources it has available to mount the exhibitions, in terms of space, manpower and money. A major national museum may have the capacity to mount several temporary exhibitions concurrently - one perhaps in each department, and a major one in a specially resourced gallery. While a multi-disciplinary regional museum may lack the resources to do this, it may instead feature in rotation the subject matter of each of its departments within the programme. Clearly the expertise and enthusiasm of departmental staff are a rich resource for use in the provision of temporary exhibitions.

However, although resources to provide in-house temporary exhibitions are restricted because of financial limitations or other priorities, incorporated within a programme will probably be exhibitions circulated by other museums or agencies. Those producing such exhibitions include many of the major national museums, the arts and crafts councils and the area museum services. Yet another source is the commercial sector, where many companies produce exhibitions illustrating their history or the history of their products. Although there is often a fee involved in hiring these exhibitions, undoubtedly most are good value when compared with the cost of providing an 'in-house' exhibition or commissioning a similar exhibition from outside contractors—provided, of course, the exhibition is relevant to the museum's aims and objectives.

Having more than one venue available in which to house the exhibitions in the programme should enable there to be at least one exhibition open at any one time, for turn-round time (the time taken to dismantle, or 'strike', one exhibition and mount another) must be considered, and will obviously vary, depending on the size and complexity of any particular exhibition and the staff available to work on it. For the more straight-forward, this could be as little as a week, whereas for large-scale productions, up to two or more months would not be unreasonable. Here prefabrication techniques and detailed planning can help reduce the 'fallow' periods which clearly do not benefit visitors and can lead to counterproductive reactions of disappointment and even dissatisfaction. Good venues, which provide easy access to services and good security are therefore important if the exhibition programme is to operate smoothly, with the changes effected rapidly.

Decisions relating to when exhibitions should be open and when it is sensible to be 'turning a space around' will come partly from an awareness of the museum's visitor pattern. For most, the year is punctuated by the major holiday periods of Christmas, Easter and the long summer break. Each will doubtless warrant a particular temporary exhibition, possibly augmented by other activities such as lectures or participative events. Christmas is perhaps a time when, because the lead-up period is often quiet, such events can be provided. In contrast, Easter and summer are times when the population is more mobile and major tourist centres can expect a large influx of visitors. In between these holiday periods are the academic terms when exhibitions can be timed to coincide with school or college teaching programmes. It is a sad truth that at times when the population at large is not at work and might perhaps like to visit a public museum, for example on a Sunday morning, a bank holiday or a summer evening, most are closed.

A knowledge of how visitors will respond to any given exhibition will help to determine its optimum showing period. This is important, for to keep an exhibition on display after all those who want to see it have done so is a waste of valuable time and space. In a small local museum this 'saturation' point might be reached in a relatively short time—perhaps as little as a week or two. Indeed, a period of not much more will probably also enable all those intending to do so to see an exhibition in a regional museum—especially if the exhibition has limited appeal. Often it will be the exhibition opening or private view which will attract a large percentage of these people—particularly if the museum has a good mailing list! However, the pattern may change if the museum, in addition to its local resident population which provides the regular visitors, also attracts a substantial number of tourists (or, in term time, students). For these may well enable a good level of attendance to be sustained virtually throughout the year.

Many of the London museums fall into this category—particularly the major national museums which attract visitors from their locality and from all over Britain and abroad. Attendance, therefore, at a major temporary exhibition in a national museum may, after an initial burst of enthusiasm, be maintained at a fairly constant and satisfactory rate, and sustain this almost indefinitely. However, the familiar attendance pattern for most well advertised exhibitions is that attendance is greatest immediately after the exhibition's opening and again just before it closes.

Estimating the number of people who might attend an exhibition is important for several reasons. The first is simply the economics of the venture. If admission charges are a consideration it is important to have an idea of the potential income and indeed to set targets. These can be used in determining the exhibition budget and included in the design brief in relation to the practical problems of crowd flow within the exhibition space. Admitting too many people at any one time results in congestion, an uncomfortable environment, overheating, and few of the objects being properly seen by any of the visitors. Conversely, limiting the number can create congestion elsewhere, necessitating special queueing facilities. Unless a museum is used to handling large numbers of visitors, it will need to seek special advice on the servicing and transport implications. Yet another reason for estimating visitor attendance is to enable an assessment to be made of the likely requirement for publications. In particular, the print runs of such items as catalogues need to be determined and also possible sales of souvenir items. Gauging these numbers accurately can be crucial to the economic success of the project.

Other modes of exhibition

Special exhibitions

While the term 'temporary' is apposite for use within a museum, and occasionally may create a sense of urgency to view if used in publicity material, a word used frequently, if rather arbitrarily, in relation to exhibitions is 'special'. The dictionaries give several definitions: 'of a particular kind, peculiar, not general'; 'for a particular purpose, especial, exceptional in amount, degree, intensity, etc.', and all these have application in relation to the exhibitions which may be included in this category. Clearly the word 'special' implies consideration and purposefulness, and something out of the ordinary. Coming into this category are those most special of special exhibitions which have been dubbed 'blockbusters'.

Although some exhibitions have success thrust upon them, that achieved by a blockbuster tends to be anticipated and worked hard for. Fundamental to success is charismatic, high-quality material, but this in itself is not necessarily enough (our national museums are full of such items). It is also necessary to bring the material or the subject to the attention of the public, and that can be achieved only through extensive promotional work in both the quality papers and colour supplements and through radio and television coverage. The support of a powerful and effective backer in such an enterprise is essential.

Subject matter has generally related to the fine and applied arts and archaeology, and among the most memorable have been 'Treasures of Tutankhamun' (1972) at the British Museum, 'The Genius of China' (1973) at the Royal Academy and the major exhibitions of such artists as

Constable, Turner, Renoir, Chagall and Monet. One characteristic of this type of exhibition is the uniqueness of the occasion, which tends to offer a 'once in a lifetime' opportunity to see groupings of objects which are brought together, possibly from all over the world.

The importance of such exhibitions is clear. To the scholar they offer the opportunity to see works conveniently in one venue and make comparisons which might otherwise be impossible. Thus, for example, the progression in an artist's work might be traced, the influences explained and the range and volume demonstrated. They may also prompt the production of useful catalogues and other publications which can not only serve as a permanent reminder of the exhibition but also exist in their own right as vital reference which will help the advancement of knowledge long after the exhibition is over.

But blockbusters owe their name not to the service they provide to academics but to their ability to attract the crowds. People come to see objects they have heard about, and to experience the spectacle for themselves. For a large number of visitors the reasons for this are probably twofold. The first is a genuine desire to see work which interests them. The second is more complex, and comes about as a result of a mixture of advertising and social pressures. Rather like the opening of the Summer Exhibition at the Royal Academy, which traditionally marks the beginning of the new season of social occasions, and where, for some, it is important to see and be seen, the blockbusters have acquired a similar social elitism and basic 'snob value'. Not to have seen the current blockbuster might mean the same exclusion from dinner-party conversations as not having seen the latest West End play or not having read the Booker prizewinner. In some circles to attend the private view (when it really is 'private') is certainly 'one-upmanship'.

If there are benefits to the scholar, to those interested in the subject for its own sake and those interested in it for what it might represent, there are also benefits to the museum and the sponsor. For the former, it can provide publicity and a central role on the museum and gallery stage, both nationally and internationally, thus enhancing its professional and popular standing. For the sponsor it can bring the benefits associated with being known to be actively supporting the arts and thereby giving pleasure to a large number of people whilst at the same time assisting the pursuit of scholarship.

However, planning a blockbuster requires special attention to be paid to the scale of the operation and, in particular, to the large number of visitors expected to attend. A useful case study is given by Coutts in 'Profile of a blockbuster' (1986), in which he discusses the very successful exhibition entitled 'The Emperor's Warriors' which was mounted in Edinburgh City Art Centre in 1985. In particular, he stressed the fact that the visitor pattern reflected the power of the media coverage. He reported a large attendance in the first week of 27,121, followed by a drop of about 25 per cent in the second week. However, owing to television advertising, a documentary and extensive coverage of a stunt to provide a free trip to China for the 150,000th visitor, an attendance figure of 31,331 was achieved in week five. This, owing to what Coutts describes as 'Warrior fever' then increased to 41,505 in the seventh week. It is interesting to note average daily attendances of visitors at some of the major blockbusters. Coutts quotes a 'league table' which rates the top four as (1) 'The Genius of China', Royal Academy, 1973/74: 6,600, (2) 'Tutankhamun', British Museum, 1972: 6,228, (3) 'Manet at Work', National Gallery, 1983: 5,000, and (4) 'The Emperor's Warriors', City Art Centre, Edinburgh: 4,559. Numbers of visitors of this order mean that good planning is essential. Decisions will need to be taken on visitor flow throughout the exhibition, on how many it can accommodate at any one time and the through-flow rate, and also whether this can be accelerated in any way by limiting viewing time at peak periods. Indeed, every aspect of a museum's resources will need special consideration if it is to cope with a project on the scale of a blockbuster.

Travelling, circulating or touring exhibitions

Exhibitions designed to be mounted in several venues are variously described as travelling, circulating or touring exhibitions. Preparing an exhibition in this mode can have certain advantages which could justify the initial decision to undertake the project, for, given the considerable amount of work which goes into the research, preparation and production of an exhibition, it is clearly sensible to maximize the benefits to be derived from such labours.

Some of the possible advantages of preparing an exhibition which can be circulated are:

1. The exhibition can be seen by larger numbers of people and in different locations.
2. The costs of production can be shared by those museums who are to show the exhibition. There is the possibility of charging a hire fee to help offset production expenses or even produce a profit.
3. The enterprise can operate on a scale which would justify the production costs involved in the publishing of ancillary material such as catalogues, publicity material and souvenirs, all of which involve high initial start-up investment, and depend on quantity production to reduce unit costs.
4. There is the possibility of a reciprocal arrangement with museums to whom the exhibition is circulated whereby they produce and circulate exhibitions of similar quality.
5. There is the opportunity to promote the museum more widely and enhance its reputation in every centre which hosts the exhibition.
6. In certain circumstances there are also political pressures to make collections more widely available or meet the needs of communities some distance from the museum. Certain national museums have found themselves in this position, some benefiting by providing such a service and others being fiercely criticized for not doing so.

The disadvantages of travelling exhibitions also need to be appreciated. Probably the overriding concern of the museum originating the exhibition is the safety of the objects. Second, the museum may be inconvenienced, and its visitors likewise, by not having the objects available for study or display purposes.

Travelling exhibitions need to be conceived as such and designed accordingly. In particular, special consideration should be given to the structure to ensure that it is erectable and demountable with minimum difficulty, robust enough to function efficiently, and sufficiently flexible to adjust to the requirements of different venues.

For these reasons, travelling exhibitions are often designed as 'core units' with optional supplementary units which may be incorporated if space permits. The approach needs careful consideration at every stage, and in particular the copywriting and selection of objects if a coherent exhibition is to result, without obvious omissions or gaps.

Before embarking on a circulating exhibitions programme it is worth undertaking a thorough feasibility study. This should assess the market and consider the financial and resource implications of the venture. In particular it is important to determine who will be responsible for exhibition assembly, dismantling and re-erection, packing and transport, security and conservation, insurance and maintenance, as well as administration. Some organizations which circulate exhibitions have their own technicians who are responsible for moving the exhibition from one centre to another, with all that this entails. This is clearly sensible if the size of the operation warrants it, since the staff concerned can be suitably trained and will become experienced with all aspects of the task. Other aspects which warrant particular attention are security, conservation and object packing. Here too staff need to be made aware of the needs of each type of object. Insurance is relatively straightforward, but necessitates forethought and clearly defined written agreements prior to any material circulating. Responsibility for maintenance also requires consideration, and, since it can be an area for disagreement, it is wise to produce guidelines as to who should be responsible for what, and in particular any damage or fault which occurs whilst the exhibition is in progress.

In fact it is wise for the museum producing exhibitions for circulation to draw up written details of all aspects of the scheme. These should include information on the following:

1. The exhibitions: titles, themes, content lists.
2. Space requirements: weights, etc.
3. Service requirements: power, etc.
4. Conservation and security requirements.
5. Maintenance schedules and responsibilities.
6. Insurance details.
7. Draft terms of agreement.
8. Transport.
9. Fees.

In addition to any general information on the scheme a separate manual should be provided for each exhibition. This should contain information on all exhibition components (even down to the last nut and bolt), and provide sequential instructions on unpacking, assembly, dismantling and repacking and list all objects. Also included should be separate checklists which can be signed by the host museum and act as receipts for the material.

Much of the foregoing discussion has related to the museums which originate the material. From the point of view of a museum seeking temporary exhibitions for its programme they are ideal, particularly if resources are limited and do not permit much in-house development. Furthermore, a wide range is often available, so museums can be selective and ensure that what they 'hire' is relevant to their temporary exhibitions policy or programme. Some organizations which circulate exhibitions (such as the Arts Council) grade them in accordance with their security and conservation needs and inspect venues to ensure that they comply with their requirements. Organizations in Britain which are involved in the organization and funding of exhibitions include area museums services, the Arts Council of Great Britain, the British Council and the Crafts Council and also many of the major national museums. Several of these also produce regular lists of the exhibitions available, together with useful documentation.

Portable exhibitions

Generally 'portable' exhibitions are regarded as those small, self-contained exhibitions which may be transported to a site, erected and, after a period of display, removed and probably brought back to base for use again if required. Possibly the main features which distinguish them from travelling exhibitions are those of scale—portable exhibitions are generally quite small and may comprise as little as a few graphic panels. They may even be contained in a protective carrying case little larger than a suitcase. Portable exhibitions are useful, since they may enable museums to extend their coverage to such events as local fairs and county shows and similar one-day events. They may also be used as short-term displays in library foyers, as tourist information/promotional events or may even be placed in the display windows of local building societies and banks, etc. Generally their function is to create interest in the museum, its work and its collections, i.e. to promote the museum service and attract visitors to the museum.

Portable exhibitions may also, of course, be 'tailor-made' for specific occasions. Given a basic structure, they may be 'dressed' in a variety of ways as needs dictate. However, because of their size and their need to be easily transported, care must be taken to ensure that no items of great value are included in the exhibitions, since it is often impossible to provide adequate security.

Mobile exhibitions

Mobile exhibitions can be defined as those self-contained exhibitions which operate independently of a fixed site. They have their origins in caravans and trailers but now include quite sophisticated purpose-made units, buses and even trains. The limited and confined space available in such vehicles obviously presents particular design problems, and inevitably places limitations on the quality and type of material to be included. However, this does not mean that they are ineffective. Quite the contrary, in fact, for they have the unique capacity of being able to bring the museum directly into the heart of a community, and to where people live, shop, work or play, or to where some action, like an excavation, may be taking place. Indeed, the mobile exhibition provides an ideal way for the museum to be present at a whole range of 'happenings', including fetes, fairs and shows—and virtually anywhere people are meeting in large numbers.

Units such as these can be comprehensive in their coverage of the museum service. They can include objects from the collections, interpretive material and facilities for the sale of publications, etc. They can also accommodate staff, which may enable visitors' enquiries to be answered, objects to be identified or even facilitate workshop-type demonstrations to take place. Often it is possible to design the unit in such a way that a basic module (probably the vehicle) may be extended by means of awnings and similar tent-like structures. To these may be added flags and banners to create an exhibition which can command considerable visual impact.

Loan exhibits/exhibitions

Items in the museum's collections which may be borrowed by outside organizations or, occasionally, by individuals are termed 'loan' exhibits or exhibitions. Normally they consist of either one or a group of items which is cased for transport and then opened and even handled by the recipient in what will normally be a teaching or studying situation in schools or colleges. Whereas this type of material often has minimal documentation, to allow the teacher to interpret it in a variety of ways relevant to his/her particular teaching needs, it may also be presented in a way which provides the type of support material which would suit different teaching situations. Thus historical objects may well be complemented by photocopies of maps, illustrations and documents which are ideal for group projects. This 'work-box' approach has proved very popular and is used extensively by many museums operating 'schools' loan services'. Whereas some exhibits are intended to be opened, others are designed more as free-standing 'mini-exhibits' which may be displayed as sealed units in schools or colleges or similar venues. They are still of considerable importance in providing the opportunity to examine real objects and specimens in the place of study but stop short of enabling the observers to handle the material as well.

Nevertheless, care must go into the selection of objects for use in this way as 'loan exhibits', since they will be exposed to considerable risk. Therefore duplicate, unprovenanced and indeed almost expendable material should be used. Notwithstanding this, the impact such material can have is considerable. The thrill of handling genuine Roman coins or mosaic tessera should not be underestimated, nor should the sensation of touching the scales on a snakeskin or feeling the feathered head of a bird for the first time. However, the thrill of touching something in this situation can be an added bonus to the more standard didactic presentation, which can have clearly defined educational objectives and relate closely to a specific teaching programme.

Yet another scheme, more concerned with individual objects than exhibitions, is the picture loan service which is operated by many art galleries on similar lines to a lending library. However, instead of books, members of the scheme may borrow original works of art for periods of several months of even longer. Once available mainly to schools and colleges, this scheme has been extended by some local authority art galleries to cover art in public places (such as hospital reception areas, etc.) and even to private individuals requiring an original work of art for their home.

6. Types of museum exhibitions

In 1890, at the first Annual General Meeting of the Museums Association, the president, the Rev. Henry H. Higgins (1890), in his presidential address said:

> The conclusion cannot be far away—that the highest aim of work in Public Museums is not—however ingeniously—to multiply facts in the memories of visitors, but to kindle in their hearts the wonder and the loving sympathy— THE NEW KNOWLEDGE—called for by every page in the remotely-reaching annals of Nature.

This romantic notion of the aim of a museum exhibition is but one of many which, over the years, have been put forward to support or otherwise a particular approach to the presentation and/or interpretation of objects. For exhibitions, in addition to being categorized by mode (as in the previous chapter), may also be distinguished by type. Whereas the mode relates to aspects of the exhibition's longevity and location, type is concerned with the concept of the exhibition and the response it is intended to elicit from its audience. This gives it a character which might be described in one of three ways—emotive, didactic or entertaining. These categories are not, of course, mutually exclusive and an exhibition may well comprise elements of each. Indeed, it might be argued that all exhibitions, almost by definition, are educational and contain elements which are didactic. It might also be hoped that all would at least be entertaining. In the circumstances it is unfortunate but not surprising that a word has been devised (by the Americans) to cover the dual functions—'edutainment'!

Nevertheless, the three broad descriptions do relate to particular types of exhibition. Some objects obviously lend themselves more to one approach than another. Traditionally art objects, particularly paintings, have formed the mainstay of the type of emotive exhibition which is termed aesthetic. The effect an art object has on its audience is clearly an emotional one (Read 1931: ch. 4) and because of this paintings have tended to be presented in a particular way. They have been hung on a wall, together with a discreet label which provides minimal information, little or no attempt being made to interpret the object in the belief that, as an art object, the work should speak for itself. Conversely, there has been a recognition that the abstract concepts of science need explaining. How things work in terms of processes and cycles—whether technological like a steam engine or biological like photosynthesis—are difficult to under-stand by simply looking at the relevant object, and so interpretive material is generally provided. But, of course, it all depends on the message to be communicated, where the emphasis is to be placed and the response required of the audience, for the techniques, imagery or concept of a painting can also be explained (and often need to be), and an object such as a steam engine may have as much aesthetic appeal as many a traditional 'art object'.

Setting aside traditions, it is possible for virtually any object to be the subject of an exhibition conceived in one of the three main character types. It will be for those who write the *brief*, in conjunction with the designer who has the task of providing the solution, to decide what character type, or character types, any given exhibition will have. This decision must, to a certain extent, arise from ethical perceptions relating to the way in which the museum's collections are used and the changes that are to be brought about in the visitor. It should, of course relate to museum policy. Over the years, different people at different times have had their own perceptions of what museums should be doing, and in this context it is worth mentioning that most opinions are based on the largely nineteenth-century premise that the acquisition of knowledge through education is morally good and beneficial. This is education in its broadest sense, summed up by D.A. Allen (1949), then Director of the Royal Scottish Museum, in a remarkably perceptive paper which he gave to the Royal Society of Arts, London, on 25 May 1949:

> Museums and Education—Museums *are* education. They exist only to further it: they can be neither provided, maintained, nor utilized without it. Education is the preparation for living, and for living, if possible, the good and complete life; it aims at understanding and appreciation leading to the application of what has been learnt to the art of living.

Allen's view of museums, embraces, rather like Higgins, all exhibition types, and not just the didactic.

Emotive exhibitions

Exhibitions which are designed and produced with the intention of having an effect on the emotions of the viewer are termed *emotive*. Broadly they fall into two types, the *aesthetic* and the *evocative*, the former concerned with the effect a confrontation with an object of beauty can have on the viewer, and the latter with romanticism.

Aesthetic exhibitions

Dr. Peter Pott (1963), Director of the National Museum of Ethnology at Leiden, in the Netherlands, considered that the aesthetic approach 'required a well thought out presentation which uses a quiet but neutral background to do justice to a limited number of objects of artistic value, arranged in the most effective way possible.' This expression of good taste is not entirely what aesthetic exhibitions are all about today, since many would disagree over the necessity for 'a quiet but neutral background' as an aesthetic requirement. However, that said, in the early 1960s in Europe, this was the aesthetic approach and the concept remains valid today.

'Aesthetic' may be defined as relating to the theory of the perception of beauty. Although it is most frequently applied to things which are appreciated for their visual appearance, it may be applied equally to any sensed phenomenon, be it listening to a piece of music, touching something exquisite, tasting a marvellous gâteau or the like. When the aesthetic quality is judged to be good, the term 'beautiful' may be applied. Judging what constitutes 'beauty' is often a matter of considerable debate. On the one hand, beauty is said to be 'in the eye of the beholder' and people do indeed know what they like and find a remarkable range of things, including other people, attractive. This particular and often idiosyncratic view has little application beyond a worth to the individual concerned, who, without rational argument and accepted criteria, might find it difficult to justify his assessment to others. A consensus on what is or is not beautiful derives from agreed and accepted criteria applied by an informed and recognized group of experts, the arbiters of good taste. In a sense the curator may well play this role, for it is he or she who decides the selection of objects against accepted academic and philosophical ideals of beauty and requires them to be presented in an aesthetic manner to become an aesthetic exhibition, with the intention that those who come to it will also respond to the objects, and experience beauty. From a design point of view, in an aesthetic exhibition, objects will need to be presented sensitively, and in such a way that their particular visual qualities can be fully appreciated. This may well require an environment which is also aesthetically pleasing, thus heightening the emotive response in the viewer.

To summarize, the main characteristics of an aesthetic exhibition are that:

1. The aim of the presentation is that the visitor should appreciate the beauty of the objects, which are selected for exhibition on that basis.
2. In order to achieve this aim, there is a minimum of 'visual interference', and graphics and other interpretive aids, such as there may be, are generally kept to a minimum, or are subservient and discreet, and in no way compete with the objects.
3. The design of the presentation, i.e. the exhibition environment and all the components, is compatible with the aim, and an aesthetic 'ambiance' is created.

Evocative exhibitions

The other main type of emotive exhibition is the evocative or romantic, which is about arousing emotions in the visitor by creating an atmosphere and possibly a 'theatrical' style of presentation. Dr. Pott (1963:6) said of the 'romantic' approach that it:

> requires that a series of pieces that are interesting for purely human reasons be presented in such a way that they, as it were, invite participation or identification with the society that they represent. In such a setting the human figure should be present, and it should be portrayed as naturalistically as possible.

Pott's reference to the presence of the human figure is worthy of note. The human factor is important in that it forms the bridge between the viewer and the scene viewed. People identify with other people, wherever and whenever they were or are, whether it is people in England relating to people in Africa, or people today relating to people in Roman times, and this is particularly true if they are doing the everyday things of life such as eating, working or playing. These activities take on a particularly human interest. This romantic approach assumes that it is beneficial (and indeed often pleasurable) to share human experiences. It suggests that although societies differ in respect of their cultural background and although they change as they evolve, life is relatively static in the sense that people change very little.

However, the actual presence of figures, helpful though it may be, is not absolutely essential, for the visitor with imagination can still transport himself into a scene—another place or time—if the scale is correct. The credibility of a modelled, reconstructed environment diminishes in direct proportion to its scale. Full-size, and done well, it will be accepted and believed, but once a reduction occurs an uneasy feeling is created in the viewer, and disbelief sets in which affects the quality of the experience.

The most successful evocative exhibitions, therefore, tend to be those which recreate a total environment. While a 'peepshow' approach will have some success (as in a theatre), by far the most effective approach is the full open diorama which allows the visitor to enter it and become part of the scene. This approach has been undertaken with particular success in museums such as Milwaukee Public Museum in Wisconsin, which pioneered this style of exhibition. It is also an approach which has seen recent popularity and proliferation in Britain with such theatrical presentations as Jorvik at York and the 'Blitz Experience' at the Imperial War Museum, London. These specifically aim to take visitors back in time through a form of presentation which has its origins in the old 'tableaux', which often incorporated wax figures. Today, with sophisticated animation techniques, these sorts of presentations, once silent and static, are now capable of being extremely realistic. Movement may be introduced to the figures, and the whole production may be extremely authentic, even to the inclusion of real objects. This may even reach the point of being confusing for the visitor who, aware of the 'make-believe' concept, cannot distinguish between what may be real and what is false. Margaret Hall (1987) summed up what this type of exhibition is about when she said that:

> In an 'evocative' exhibition an atmosphere of an era, a country, a particular art

style, or a scene is created in a theatrical way. This scene-setting aids understanding by evocation and association, and not necessarily by the display of informative texts.

Didactic exhibitions

Exhibitions which are intended to impart information are generally termed 'didactic'. Their aim is to instruct and to educate. They encourage the visitor to engage in a learning, if not a thinking, process where intellectual stimulation is important. Gilman (1918) provided an apt interpretation of education in a museum context when he said that:

> It conveys the general idea of a modification of personality in three senses, which may be called respectively a loose, a broad, and a narrow sense. In the loose sense education is synonomous with influence, in the broad sense with improvement and in the narrow sense with teaching.

Although, as has been suggested, all exhibitions are broadly educational, characteristically, in a didactic exhibition, the instructional and educational functions are not left to the objects themselves but are undertaken by the interpretive media.

Dana (1927) wrote, 'Objects are silent. They must tell about themselves, their origin, purpose, their relative positions in the development of their kind and countless other details through labels, guides and catalogues.' Not everyone would agree that objects are silent. Cameron (1968) considered that 'The museum as a communications system . . . depends on the non-verbal language of objects and observable phenomena. It is primarily a visual language, and, at times, an aural or tactile language'.

However, even Cameron (1968) noted that this presentation of reality may be sampled and structured by arbitary models of reality. Cameron's apparent underestimation of the importance of the 'aids' to communication was seized upon by Knez and Wright (1970), who, in assessing Cameron's view, commented:

> In order to bring maximum clarity to the verbal message, an exhibitor also employs such supplementary means as diagrams, maps, photographs, models, all of which are interwoven with the carefully selected museum objects to provide a satisfying message. By means of design and art skills, the impact of the message—its intellectual cognition and its emotional force—is significantly enhanced . . . Dr. Cameron has by no means ignored these verbal or cognitive adjuncts . . . but he has relegated them to a minor role.

This may be seen to take the argument back to Brown Goode (1891), who thought an 'efficient' educational museum was 'a collection of instructive labels, each illustrated by a well-selected specimen', a definition which, today, could be applied to a thematic-style exhibition. However, if one accepts that the visual language of the objects themselves is not enough to provide an explanation of what they mean, then it follows that aids to understanding are necessary and that the language and secrets contained in the objects need interpreting. This mixture of objects, text and other interpretive aids has often been likened to a three-dimensional essay or book, whose prime function is to inform and educate.

Even a brief discussion of didactic exhibitions would not be complete without reference to the work and interest in educational exhibitions and their effectiveness shown by a group of researchers in the USA. Their work, begun in the 1960s, has had widespread influence on many concerned with the development of new exhibitions. In particular, the work of Shettel, Screven, Nicol and Borun has advanced our knowledge of the behaviour of visitors when confronted by educational exhibitions. And many of the ideas contained in the initial research of these individuals have been considered and developed in the UK by staff working in the Natural History Museum (see Miles and Tout, 1979). A good example of the type of work undertaken in the USA is Screven's (1974) paper 'The Measurement and Facilitation of Learning in the Museum Environment'. In it, many pertinent issues in relation to finding out how the museum visitor learns and what devices can be used to make the experience more meaningful are discussed. It details the use of instructional technology in museums, and points the way forward for more research.

From the various studies undertaken, the application of the principles of educational technology to the museum situation becomes apparent, and the typical stages in the preparation of an educational exhibit are:

1. State the objectives of the exhibition, ideally in measurable terms.
2. Identify the characteristics of the group to be taught.
3. Analyse the learning task or message of the exhibition.
4. Design the instructional sequences and didactic materials.
5. Test the design with a representative visitor group sample.
6. Modify and produce.

However, those who seek a wholly effective educational technology for exhibitions are not without their critics. Indeed, some would argue that they overlook the fact that a large number of visitors do not enter museums to be coerced, however subtly, into learning. They want to see objects, and there is a marked tendency in the educational technologist to declare the traditional strength of museums, i.e. the objects, redundant and to replace them with teaching machines.

Perhaps the last word on this topic should go to Professor Jacques Barzun (1969), who, when participating in a seminar held in New York on the 'Exploration of the ways, means and values of museum communication with viewing public', reacted against the extreme commitment of the twentieth century to education. He said:

Having lost religion as a means of saving our neighbour, we have substituted art and knowledge as supreme good, which we want everyone to possess willy-nilly . . . Thrusting art and knowledge on the unwary is an invasion of privacy—same as that of thrusting religion. The twentieth century is committed to education, and that effort is often the chief cause of our unhappiness and despair, for education is the worst game of chance ever invented.

Exhibitions as entertainment

Since the late nineteenth century museums have been uneasy about their role as entertainers. While few museum professionals would disagree with the idea that an exhibition should be enjoyable, the understanding has generally been that this should, in some way, be subordinate to or even a by-product of a more 'worthwhile' pursuit such as education and the quest for knowledge; 'sugaring the pill', as someone once described it. Over the years the arguments have, of course, been well rehearsed. Museum academic staff are charged with responsibility for research, for collecting and for the care of objects, and they have rightly considered that the task of interpretation should be undertaken to the same professional standards and have broadly educational aims. Museums are about scholarship and the interpretation of real objects—not about entertainment, but, if some people find this entertaining, all well and good. Curators have worked hard to dispel the 'showmanship' image of the museums of Bullock and Barnum. Popularization is not thought of highly in academic circles.

However, this is, to a certain extent, to ignore the visitors' perception of the museum and market research which suggests the visitors want to be entertained. It was Dr. D.B. Harden who, in 1965, pointed out that, for most people, a museum is essentially a place of entertainment and amusement—a view which many visitor surveys have since endorsed, but much of the entertainment does, of course, for many, come about through being informed or educated. Verlarde (1984(1)) noted, 'In essence, however, museums are places of what might be termed "higher entertainment". They are places to which those who delight in knowledge resort . . .'

However, for many others the entertainment value will not be dependent on these activities. Theirs will be entertainment in the form of amusement. The dictionary defines 'amusement' as 'pleasant diversion', and an 'amusement arcade' as a place of recreation with automatic game machines—a description which could well be applied to some museum presentations where push-button and computer technologies are extensively employed: the 'funfair' approach. Indeed, a recent study of science communication through exhibitions (Castillo 1989) comes to the conclusion that the philosophical basis of many science centres is not well founded and that their educational aims are seldom being met. Thus the terms 'amusement arcade' or 'funfair' are perhaps apt descriptions. However, since the displays in these exhibitions are generally based on scientific principles, there is always the chance that—through enjoyable play—something may be learnt, for, as any educational psychologist will afirm, creative play is important in developmental terms, and learning can and should be fun!

Why shouldn't museum exhibitions simply entertain? To provide people with good entertainment is not an unworthy motive. If it is done well an exhibition may well attract large numbers of visitors who will be very satisfied with the experience. They may also become interested in other types of exhibitions. The answer lies in the definition of a museum, and the requirement to interpret objects, and inform. Although not a museum, Disneyland, for example, has succeeded by giving visitors what they want—and by doing it well. It may not interpret real objects, but it provides, like a growing number of 'leisure attractions', an experience based on historical or literary themes. Nevertheless, for the most part it stops short of the emotive experience of the evocative exhibition. If any emotional response is sought it is—happiness. This type of presentation represents the point where the scholarly pursuit of recreating environments and the leisure industry's interest in providing entertainment overlap. 'Entertaining' exhibitions may therefore be varied in their style, and range from the 'funfair' approach, through the humorous to the theatrical style presentations. They differ from other types of exhibition in that their aim is quite simply to provide recreation and amusement.

Miscellaneous categories

In addition to the relatively straightforward categorization of exhibitions into mode and type, various terms have been applied to particular sorts of exhibitions or exhibits, which put them outside these two categories. Some of the terms frequently used are discussed below.

Interactive

Among various, and often misleading, definitions of an 'interactive' exhibit, possibly the most acceptable is that put forward by Hill and Miles (1987), which states that 'Truly interactive exhibits are those which can vary their presentation according to the designer's perception of the response of the visitor.' The important factors in this definition are the responses of the visitors, which have an effect on the presentation. Thus pushing a button to start a sequence is not, in this one act, 'interactive'. Only an exhibit which involves the visitor in a series of related activities that involve intellectual as well as physical action, and which come about as a result of some sort of feedback from the exhibit, can be called interactive. A good example is the interaction between a visitor and a computer programme which facilitiates a 'dialogue' between the two in the new range of computer-based exhibits which are now being widely introduced. Most interactive exhibits, by their very nature, work on a one-person-to-one-exhibit basis, and are generally not designed for group audiences.

Responsive

Verlarde (1984(2)) defines 'responsive' exhibits as 'those which automatically respond to the arrival of the visitor'. This is an apt description of an exhibit which, for example, switches on and lights up as a visitor approaches.

Dynamic

This term may be applied to any exhibit which moves, and is especially relevant to those which are powered by mechanical or similar means, but can be applied to visitor operated displays.

Object-oriented

This, in effect, means what it says—the exhibition is reliant upon objects which form the basis of the concept, and which take precedence over any form of interpretive media. By their nature they may defy presentation in a systematic or thematic way and quite simply be a number of objects deemed worthy of display in an exhibition. Many exhibitions of art objects fall into this category.

Systematic

This term implies an arrangement of objects according to an accepted system. It might be taxonomic (if biological material is involved), or whatever method of classification is applied to the type of objects in question. It has advantages in that those familiar with the system can find their way easily, and those unfamiliar can learn how the material is ordered by experts. An approach favoured by those concerned with 'three-dimensional textbook learning', this type of display has a certain relevance to students undertaking sixth-form and university studies. Its starting point is with the group of objects.

Thematic

Unlike the systematic approach, the thematic exhibition starts with a story line and draws upon objects to illustrate the theme. Obviously, in practice, the two may well evolve together, for a thematic exhibition without objects would be a non-event. The theme is the linking element between objects which are strung along in linear sequence, like beads on a necklace. However, this approach does not preclude the interpretation of objects either within or in relation to the main theme.

Participatory

Not concerned solely with passive viewing, participatory exhibitions are those which actively involve the visitor in using his/her sense of touch as well. They range from interactive computer-based displays to the 'do it yourself'-type events where visitors are encouraged to participate fully and produce drawings, prints, ceramics or whatever. They are based on the old educational adage: 'I hear and I forget. I see and I remember. I *do* and I understand.'

Part three. *Exhibition policy, planning and brief*

7. *Museum exhibition policy and planning*

The parameters of an overall museum policy have been outlined in a previous chapter. A part of this policy is museum communications, and exhibition policy forms a subdivision, with further information being included in both the communications strategy and plan. In formulating statements on exhibition policy cognizance will also need to be taken of other decisions on museum policy which are relevant to this issue. These may relate to such topics as the collections, education and design. Like other policy papers, details of the museum's exhibition policy should be accessible to both museum staff and outside agencies and individuals, and should seek to clarify the whole basis upon which the museum undertakes its exhibition activity.

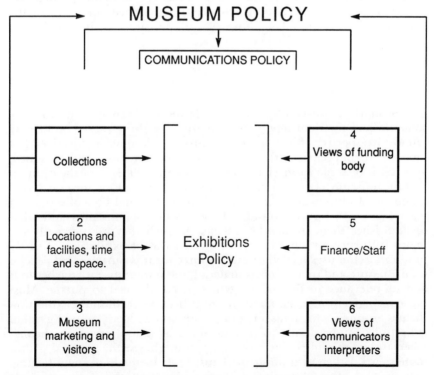

Figure 7.1 Factors which affect museum exhibition policy

Factors that affect museum policy

In any museum situation, there are a number of factors which will have a bearing on the formulation of an exhibition policy. Not all will exert equal influence, and much will depend on an individual museum's circumstances. Figure 7.1 indicates the main factors which affect policy. The two-way flow system should be noted, as each factor exerts an effect on exhibitions and also needs to be responsive to change and provide feedback in order to modify overall policy if necessary. For example, 'space' is made available as a result of museum policy and, once provided, acts as a factor in determining what can or cannot be done. Any proved inadequacies (or unused surpluses) are communicated back from the exhibition policy to the overall museum policy-makers in order to effect change. Thus policy at all levels should be seen not as inflexible but as capable of responding to changing situations and needs, and, certainly, as subject to periodic review.

The greatest influence on a museum's exhibition policy should come from its overall policy, and any detailed exhibition policy must be in accordance with the general philosophy of the museum. Thus such issues as the nature of the museum's approach to communicating, the image the museum wishes to project, the type and content of material to be communicated, and the people with whom the museum particularly wishes to make contact should have been determined, and it is for the exhibition policy to relate those overall decisions to the exhibition situation.

Collections

Traditionally a museum's collections have also been its exhibitions— sometimes in their entirety, with virtually everything placed on display (almost irrespective of its relevance to any specific aims or objectives) but more often, and particularly as far as the larger museums are concerned, as a result of some form of selection. Cameron (1968) is of the opinion that the museum as a communications system 'depends on the non-verbal language of objects and observable phenomena', and the collections of real objects are rightly considered the essence of museums and what distinguishes them from other media. As such they are normally the major influence on what is communicated via the exhibitions. Exactly how a museum uses its collections resource for this purpose will depend on the nature and quality of its material, the importance it attaches to it and its relevance to the themes which it has decided to pursue. Most museums, given important and strong collections, will build exhibition themes around them. Thus a regional museum with, say, good Egyptian collections might decide to include them as one of its main themes, whereas, had the collection been sparse, it might use the material within more general themes dealing, perhaps, with methods of manufacture, materials or other comparative themes. Alternatively, if the museum decided that Egyptian material had no place in the themes of its permanent exhibitions it might use the collection in occasional temporary exhibitions or place it on loan to another museum keen to augment its own holdings. There are, of course exceptions to this approach. A good example is the decision taken by the British Museum (Natural History) in the 1970s to develop an exhibition on human biology when it had no collections whatsoever to exhibit (Miles and Tout 1978).

It must be stressed that where objects are selected for exhibition to illustrate an idea and communicate a specific message, it must be done with care and exactness. Displaying irrelevant objects, or the right objects in the wrong relationships, will only confuse the visitor, whilst displaying too many objects of similar type will lose the attention of all but the most dedicated specialist.

Whilst the collections form the main resource to be used in relation to the majority of museum exhibitions, omissions and weaknesses can be overcome if loans can be negotiated or if sufficient finance exists to purchase suitable new material. (Failing this, the exhibition organizers must resort to using either two-dimensional representations of the objects or replicas if the topic has to be included as a visual representation.) But where there is richness and variety, these will be the factors which will determine how comprehensive the exhibitions may be, and will provide the opportunity for a variety of approaches, including systematic, comparative, and so on, and will also determine the extent to which a museum may, within its own resources, be capable of implementing change. The need for change is important if visitors are to be encouraged to revisit the museum, and if the museum is to attract visitors with new interests. Equally, whilst certain objects will justify permanent display, others will not, and should be identified as such and used, perhaps, in temporary displays.

Locations and facilities—time and space

There is clearly a need for an overview of museum and exhibition facilities at local, regional and national level if material is to be made accessible to centres of population on a geographical basis. Planning is essential to ensure that resources are maximized and that there is an equitable, or at least a rational, provision of museum services. This overview may well extend to include the increasing number of developments such as interpretive centres, historic houses, parks, gardens and zoos, demonstration farms, and so on. However, historical accident will, to a large extent, have determined what a location has at its disposal, and it is then a matter of policy as to how this resource might, or might not be developed and augmented. Those areas which have been particularly fortunate in what they have inherited may have the opportunity to become centres of provision, and attract visitors from far afield. If such is the case, access and transport will be important considerations, together with a policy which ensures that the resource itself is safeguarded, and is not over-used to a point where the sheer number of visitors puts at risk the very material which is preserved for people to appreciate.

A locality or region will want to see that it is adequately provided for, to take stock of its existing provision of museums and to be prepared to modify and develop this resource as necessary to meet perceived needs— not only in terms of preservation and collection (and response to new opportunities as they occur) but also so that the public may see objects in which they are interested. Equally, at institution level, each museum needs to determine its role as a provider of exhibitions with regard to its location and the policies and the activities of other neighbouring (and probably competing) organizations. This should help identify opportunities, encourage complementary and collaborative ventures and, at the same time, help reduce wasteful duplication.

An encouraging development in recent years by certain London-based national museums has been the policy decision to display sections of the national collections outside the capital. In various collaborative ventures between the museums concerned, government departments, local authorities and other agencies, a number of significant developments have occurred. Among these are the National Museum of Photography, in Bradford, and the National Railway Museum, in York, as two 'outstations' of the Science Museum, the collections of the National Portrait Gallery on display in the National Trust property of Bessingborough Hall, North Yorkshire, and the new 'Tate of the North' in Liverpool. The creation of these museums of national importance in areas outside London has been beneficial in several ways: first, by making important collections easily accessible to large population groups outside London; second, by helping to develop those locations in which the museums are situated as important cultural centres, with all the economic benefits this provides; and finally by helping to reduce congestion in the capital, but still enabling the material to be accessible through good communication links.

It is the combination of location, and the quality, type and extent of collections, which determines whether the museum is destined to play an international, national, regional or local role. Certainly the large, multidisciplinary museums which are located in regional town centres should have their role fairly clearly defined and may wish to adopt an exhibition policy which enables them to act as a regional centre and, at the same time, integrate the museum with the local community. Often museums develop branch museums to meet specific needs. The neighbourhood museums piloted in America in the 1960s were introduced specifically to meet local community needs, and their exhibition policies were devised accordingly. Some museums can obviously do little about their location, particularly if they occupy historic buildings. However, what is important is that they should have an awareness of the significance of the location, of the advantages and the disadvantages and their effects on the visitors and their needs, and should use this information in developing the exhibition policy.

Since both time and space are limited, their use needs to be maximized, and the apportionment of space in respect of permanent or changing exhibitions is one of the most difficult decisions which has to be made. For many museums, change is important to sustain visitor interest and attract new visitors. The possession of sufficient space to enable a viable temporary exhibition gallery to be created, and the setting aside of areas within designated 'permanent' exhibitions for such things as topical displays or recent acquisitions, will not only reflect a museum's positive approach to exhibitions but will also indicate a concern for the visitors, and their interests. The timing and duration of exhibitions are also complex issues and it is perhaps unwise to generalize when so much will depend on the size and topic of the exhibition, the type of the museum and its visitor pattern and communications policy. A national museum may well be able to sustain fairly constant visitor attendance at a 'temporary' exhibition even after several years (should it run that long), whereas a small local museum, especially outside any tourist season, may reach exhaustion point—when all those likely to want to visit the exhibition have done so—in only perhaps a fortnight. Irrespective of size, the typical attendance pattern is high at the beginning and again towards the end of the exhibition period.

In an attempt to get the best out of all worlds, many larger museums, in addition to their 'permanent' exhibitions, provide various types of temporary exhibition. These include a 'major' show, possibly running throughout the summer 'peak' visitor/tourist season, regular smaller temporary exhibitions, perhaps changing every four to six weeks, and topical, weekly or even daily displays of suitable material.

Other factors affecting the longevity of an exhibition are the environment it creates and the physical durability of the structure and equipment in respect of the use it receives. Clearly the safety of objects must be an overriding consideration, and conservation and security requirements must be satisfied. Indeed, they may well be the determining factor in deciding the period of the exhibition and the length of time the object is exposed. Failure to meet minimum environmental standards for certain categories of objects, particularly when they are on loan from other sources, could mean that permission to exhibit them is withheld. Exhibition materials and components which go to form the structure and physical environment also vary in quality and durability and need to be specified with a particular 'life expectancy' in mind. However, irrespective of the intended duration of the exhibition, it must be adequately maintained, especially if electrical, electronic or mechanical elements are incorporated. Communication time should not be lost by component failure.

Museum marketing and visitors

Mention has been made elsewhere of museum marketing and the need to undertake a programme of market research in order to obtain information on 'customer' needs and the service the museum might provide.

Table 7.1 Popularity of exhibits, Milwaukee Public Museum, 1952

Subject	Summer visitors	Winter visitors
Indians	155	97
Mammals	110	72
History	37	45
Guns	34	32
Insects	5	–
Minerals	5	–
Telephone	–	5

In a market-led institution the needs and preferences of the customer or user group will have considerable influence on exhibition policy. And even a museum which is not overtly responding to customer demands would nevertheless be prudent to take note of visitors' views, lest it find itself without any. Fortunately, in recent years, museums have gradually become more interested in their customers, the visitors to their exhibitions, although they have seldom regarded them as such. Many surveys have now been undertaken to find out who visits museums and why, and a few to find out who does not visit museums and why. This type of information is very relevant to the formulation of an exhibition policy.

Milwaukee Public Museum in Wisconsin was among the first to take an interest in audience reaction to exhibitions. In his surveys conducted in 1952 Arthur Niehoff gained a considerable amount of information on the age, sex, occupation and so on of the museum visitors, and on their preferences as regards exhibitions. He surveyed both summer and winter visitors, for whom some of the most and least popular exhibits with their score are shown in Table 7.1. Many museums have undertaken similar popularity polls, with fairly predictable results, although the extent by which one exhibit topic exceeds another can be surprising. Nevertheless, it should not be too difficult for a museum curator who is alert to what is going on—not just in the museum but on television, in the press and in the world generally—to gauge what subjects will make popular exhibitions.

Visitor characteristics and behaviour are other factors which have been well researched and which have a bearing on exhibition policy and design. (Chapter 12 deals with this subject in more detail.) Most studies agree that the visitors consist of a heterogeneous group with numerous variations, including age and sex, intelligence and knowledge, social and economic grouping and, of particular importance, motivation. Motivated visitors derive more benefit from exhibitions than those who visit casually and wander aimlessly round the galleries.

The various studies which have been made of visitor characteristics and behaviour provide much detailed information which should be considered in relation to exhibition policy and planning. However, care must always be exercised in the interpretation and application of the data. For example, it is known that the average time a visitor spends before certain displays is between twenty and forty-five seconds (Neal 1965; Shettel *et al.* 1968). Coles (1982) reports that people walking round a large exhibition of paintings spend on average five seconds in front of an individual picture. However, Alt (1982) rightly makes the point that the concept of an average time may not be very useful, since it does not necessarily describe many people. Indeed, in a situation where some visitors study a few pictures for several minutes and ignore others completely it can be seen that an average figure may be very misleading indeed. Where studies are specific, and objective, the data obtained can be most useful. Alternatively, such information as 'visitors seldom come alone' and that 'there is a high incidence of family groups' can also be useful, since it has implications for the provision of exhibitions, their design and the supporting facilities required.

In studies of the behaviour of visitors, anthropomorphic data are also important, particularly when ergonomic factors are being considered. In addition to this type of information, it is also useful to have available the market research data and know what visitors—both actual and potential—are thinking, and what expectations they have. For example, visitors returning to a museum for a second visit may expect to see new things as well as renew their acquaintance with established favourites. They may also expect high standards of presentation (comparable to those of shop displays or a commercial exhibition) and the use of modern technology (as might be seen in various television programmes). To deny them this may mean that they will become dissatisfied with the museum. Borun (1977), it may be remembered, recognized the importance of knowing what visitors were thinking and the need to monitor their response 'so that the museum becomes a flexible, self-correcting institution in touch with the desires of its public'. Many aspects of the cyclic approach of museum marketing with its concern for visitor opinion are also linked with the important topics of exhibition evaluation and effectiveness. This search for the 'ideal' product in the form of the successful exhibition is explored in more detail in Chapter 13.

Views of funding body

Generally speaking, the views of the funding body will have been taken into account in the overall museum policy and will therefore be applied to the exhibitions policy via the communications policy, for it is inevitable that the body which funds an organization, or which is charged with the financial responsibility for it, will have a view—even in very general terms—on how the resources should be deployed. Trustees, governors, local authority representatives and industrial sponsors will all need to be satisfied with the exhibition policy pursued, as will national and regional funding bodies such as the Arts Council and regional arts associations if support from these bodies is to be successfully sought.

However, in the current economic climate, when commercial sponsorship is becoming commonplace, the views of the funding body may exert excessive influence on exhibition policy. Sponsors, not surprisingly, want to be associated with exhibitions which are popular and spectacular in order to derive the maximum benefit from the high public profile, so exhibitions which feature the less popular subjects or are of a more academic nature may not easily find sponsors, a fact which could have serious implications for a museum's exhibition policy.

Yet another aspect of sponsorship is censorship and the limitations which might be imposed on the freedom of the museum to provide the information which it feels to be appropriate, especially if it is intended to give a balanced view on a particular topic. The inclusion of excessive advertising or promotional material could also lead to disagreements between museum and sponsor. In situations where the views of an external funding body might be incompatible with a museum's philosophy, it is important that areas of possible disagreement should be clarified, preferably before they become a problem, and that each party proceeds with a knowledge of the other's viewpoint and intentions. However, if ethics do become a consideration the museum will need to defend its professional integrity.

The museum also has an obligation to its public (as tax and/or admission fee payers) and, although representatives of the public are frequently elected to committees charged with the oversight of museums, those elected or appointed do not necessarily reflect the views of the public in general, or of the museum audience, and while they may 'care' in a very general way about museums they may know very little about them. In the controversy surrounding the reorganization of the Victoria and Albert Museum in 1989 the issue was debated in the House of Lords and reported by Davies (1989). He noted that Baroness Birk drew attention to this problem when she stated 'there is no one among the trustees who has any experience of working in a museum'. In this context, therefore, the specialist advice and opinion of the professional museum staff are also important. However, it should be remembered that it was this very group of professional individuals who, earlier this century, were responsible for isolating museums from the public, and that among their number many extreme views are held, while certain individuals have the seniority to implement their viewpoints. Thus opinions need to be canvassed widely and notice must be taken not only of the funding body but also of professional colleagues and visitors before a decision is taken.

Finance and staff

Adequate finance is a prerequisite of any effective exhibition programme. Pearson (1981) makes the point that public art galleries have suffered in the past from the idea that exhibitions can be run on the cheap, and the same, of course, can be said of museums. Money buys staff—and staff need money in order to function effectively. Materials, equipment, transport charges and insurance all have to be paid for even if the manpower is available.

What can be achieved in any one exhibition will depend, inevitably, not only on the total resources available but also on the way in which they are deployed. Money spent on creating a suitable environment in which objects can be viewed, for example, can so heighten the experience for the visitor that it is money invested wisely. The most memorable exhibitions tend to be those in which special consideration has been given to the exhibition space. Where funds are restricted, it may be that exhibitions are smaller, less well produced and less frequent. Financial considerations may also determine whether the items displayed are two or three-dimensional (cases being more expensive than wall space), and whether the environment can be changed to relate to each successive exhibition. A consequence of limited finance and the ensuing restrictions could be a falling-off in visitor interest and museum attendance, particularly at a time when other branches of the leisure industry are investing heavily in order to attract custom. Indeed, it is worthy of note that some museums, because of lack of finance, have had to close to the public on one day a week when previously they would have been open.

Views of the communicators and interpreters

Few should have a greater input in the debate regarding the formulation and implementation of a museum's exhibition policy than the communicators and interpreters themselves. The subject specialists, designers and educationalists should form the nucleus of this group. It may well be this group, who, by virtue of their expert knowledge, decide on the topics for exhibitions and how the collections will be interpreted. Almost certainly it will be for them also to decide what the specific objectives of exhibits will be and by what means they can be attained. The qualities which distinguish the good communicators from the mediocre are difficult to define, but are those which enable the attention of the intended audience to be gained, held and then satisfied. Much, therefore, depends on the skills, experiences and preferences of those charged with the task of communicating. Communicating through exhibitions is not an exact science, and although exhibitions are designed for a purpose, they nevertheless remain a plastic art form, and as such they can be fashioned by their creators to impart their own personalities and knowledge, and to elicit specific responses from the visitors.

Where professional staff are not available, one solution is to have exhibitions produced by others. Obviously this can be an excellent way of benefiting from the expertise and collections of others, and may not always be expensive. However, Pearson (1981) also draws the useful distinction between art galleries and exhibition spaces, regarding the former as active and the latter as passive. It is not enough for a gallery (or museum) merely to receive exhibitions from others. It needs to initiate its own policy, and implement it through selective exhibition programmes and other organized events. If hired exhibitions fit into this scheme, all well and good, especially as a museum also needs to fulfil a social role, to stimulate and educate, and to have an active relationship with an involved public.

The exhibition team

In order to fulfil its functions, a museum requires many skills to be brought together in its staff. The same applies to producing an exhibition, which, by its very nature, is a team or group activity where each member contributes his or her particular expertise, knowledge or talents to the benefit of the project. The concepts of a common goal and shared responsibility are important in teamwork, and help overcome some of the problems associated with jealousy, possessiveness and status. In a medium-size museum those with a significant contribution to make in the production of an exhibition might include:

The museum director. To initiate the project; to obtain the necessary approval and authorize resources to be committed in line with museum policy and plans. To receive progress reports, monitor the project and be available to act in the case of disputes or in any unforeseen situation which requires intervention at senior level.

The curator. To provide specialist information on the subject matter and undertake any research necessary. To be the major contributor to the brief. To identify, locate, select and if necessary negotiate the acquisition and/or loan of material. Prepare lists of exhibits and information. Provide draft copy for labels, references for illustrations, etc. Possibly write the catalogue. Above all, to be enthusiastic about his/her subject, and understanding of the designer's role.

The designer (exhibition). To contribute to the brief and undertake any preliminary programming and/or feasibility study. To undertake research into exhibition methods, materials and solutions. To answer the brief and produce a design solution to the problem. To produce/ supervise the production of working drawings, specifications, tender documents. To co-ordinate the project, oversee contractual arrangements and, in effect, act as project manager in the absence of a specialist appointment. To evaluate/maintain the exhibition in the absence of specialist staff. To work with tact and sensitivity.

Designer (graphics). To work with the Designer (Exhibition) on graphic elements of the exhibition, e.g. logo, caption panels, etc. To design publicity, the catalogue, invitations, etc.

Conservator. To prepare objects for display as selected by the curator. To advise on environmental conditions within the exhibition and other factors in relation to the care of objects, including, if appropriate, supports and fixings.

Security officer. To work with both curator and designer to advise on all aspects of security—both for the final exhibition and throughout the preparatory stages when objects are moved.

Education officer. To contribute specialist knowledge on educational aspects of both the subject and the exhibition to the brief. To undertake research as necessary. To advise on aspects of educational psychology and technology. To plan for the educational use of the exhibition (if appropriate) and devise associated teaching materials.

Editor (if appointed). To provide the exhibition text, including labels, and possibly to edit the catalogue—all from information provided by the curator. This will involve close liaison with the curator to ensure factual accuracy, and liaison with design staff to ensure the compatibility of copy with the design concept.

Production staff. To take the project from the design proposal stage to reality. The skills involved may include draughting, photography, electrical, model making, taxidermy, joinery, metalwork, audio-visual, computer, etc. In most instances production staff will work to the designer's instructions.

Maintenance staff. To advise the designer on maintenance methods and costs. Once the exhibition is completed, to clean and maintain it in full working order and good appearance. A range of specialist skills may be involved including lighting and electrical, electronic and audio-visual, display and graphic as well as cleaning.

Marketing officer. To advise on the marketing and publicity aspects, working in conjunction with the designer. Unless specialist staff are appointed, to liaise with the designer on evaluation and market research.

Consultants. It is often a good idea to engage the services of an outside consultant to review an exhibition proposal. Objective advice from an experienced practitioner can help prevent mistakes and lost opportunities. A museum which lacks a particular specialist on the staff (e.g. editor, designer, etc.) may employ the services of a consultant for the duration of the project, or on a longer-term retainer.

To enable the group to function effectively, it is advisable that each member should have clearly defined terms of reference, with stated areas of responsibility. The decision-making process, too, may need to be clarified, and an officer nominated who will retain executive control of the project. Of paramount importance is that a good rapport should be established between members of the team, and in particular between the curator and the designer. Regular group meetings will help keep individuals informed and involved and unite the group in attaining its goal.

Stages in the preparation of an exhibition

Producing an exhibition can be a very complex operation involving many people in the planning, design and manufacture of hundreds, if not thousands, of components. Because of the complexities it is sensible to utilize some form of management tool such as bar charts or critical path analysis. These systems tend to itemize the various stages and relate them to a time scale. In critical path analysis the critical stages, which need to be completed prior to the commencement of the next stage, are identified. These visual systems can demonstrate the whole complex scheme in a graphic way, and are particularly helpful in showing activities which are undertaken concurrently by different specialists. To be of real use, however, they need to be prepared with care and to incorporate realistic estimates of the time needed to undertake each task. They also need to be updated as necessary, and constantly monitored. To facilitate this, it is a good idea on a major project to hold regular progress meetings and possibly employ a clerk of works or project manager.

The main stages in the preparation of a typical museum exhibition are set out below. Some projects will require additional stages, whilst others may have fewer. Not all the stages are finite and sequential. Some activities may be undertaken in parallel. A useful network system identifying the various stages in detail was produced by Howell (1971), and the reader is also referred to this.

1. *Awareness of the need.* First must come an awareness of the need for the exhibition. It may emanate directly from the museum's policy statement, communications strategy or plan. Alternatively it may come about in other ways, but will nevertheless be consistent with museum policy. For example, the need may be discovered through research or it might be an 'inspired' idea of an individual which, on assessment, is found to be worth pursuing. Other ways in which the need might become apparent include the evaluation of existing provision; growth in collections; the outcome of excavations or gifts; suggestions from visitors or as a result of anticipating future developments.

2. *Preliminary consideration of proposal.* If the project is to proceed beyond the awareness stage it will need to have some preliminary consideration. A proposal should therefore be formulated which states the need, and the ways in which the intended exhibition will meet that need. Consideration can then be given to the proposed theme and its relevance to the museum's exhibition policy, and also to its suitability as an exhibition. Other aspects to examine will be the intended audience, a possible location and timing, and some indication of the resource implications. If it seems to be a good idea the proposal can proceed to the next stage.

3. *Feasibility study.* This is a more thorough examination of all aspects and implications of the proposal. It will, therefore, first define the project and its aims and objectives, and then include an outline brief, the feasibility of which will be examined. Important considerations will be the priority given to including the proposal within the exhibitions programme; the availability of objects and their conservation/security needs; staff involvement and availability; location, timing and the overall cost.

4. *Consideration of feasibility study.* Acceptance of the feasibility study and the decision to proceed should be coupled with the appointment of project staff— possibly the setting up of a working group or steering committee and, if necessary some preliminary work to secure resources or interest sponsors.

5. *Further research.* The curator, designer and possibly others will need to undertake research into aspects of the exhibition prior to the next stage. They may also wish to visit other institutions to see how similar problems have been

solved. Additionally, expert advice may be sought from outside the museum and consultants appointed.

6. *Formulating the communication.* As a preliminary to writing the full brief, the curator may develop the outline brief given in the feasibility study into a more detailed conceptual plan and make a preliminary selection of objects for inclusion in the exhibition.

7. *Conservation.* Once items have been identified for possible inclusion in the exhibition, work can start on preparing them for display.

8. *Preparation of brief.* The brief is the document in which the exhibition's aims and objectives are set out in detail and which contains all the information necessary to enable the designer to understand the problem and commence work on a design solution. This is a most important stage, and the ultimate solution to the problem may well be dependent on the quality of the brief. Inadequate, incorrect or misleading statements will inevitably be detrimental and possibly waste both time and money. Normally the brief is written by the curator, consulting other specialists as necessary. It is, however, desirable that the designer should make a contribution and discuss the nature of the problem and ways of approaching it. Also he might advise on the viability of spatial allocations, etc., and ensure that the brief does not set out a problem which is impossible to resolve. At this stage the designer may also undertake a detailed site survey.

9. *Exhibition design.* On receipt of the brief the designer will undertake further research and commence work on the design solution. Preliminary ideas will be generated and tested. Probably the first concern of the designer will be a concept of the total environment, the allocation of space for each section of the exhibition, a circulation pattern and the type of structure envisaged. Once these are established, more detailed work can follow, including the development of the exhibition graphics. Initially preliminary ideas may be explored by means of rough 'ideas' drawings and conceptual models. These will be developed into visuals, presentation models and even 'mock-ups' at full scale for approval before further work is undertaken. Estimates of cost may also be required at this stage to ensure the design is within budget. Once the designer has a knowledge of the design solution, he may consult colleagues to revise the critical path analysis of the project for submission to the approving authority.

10. *Formal approval.* This is an important process and may involve several separate approvals. Ideally the designer will want to be sure that the proposal has or will have the agreement of any planners or fire officers before proceeding too far. The museum director may also need to give his approval to the proposal, together with the museum's governing body if items of this nature are submitted to it. Sponsors, too, may need to give their approval if they are to be involved. It is, of course, quite possible that, as a result of making these submissions, revisions will be required to the proposals.

11. *Finalizing the proposal.* Following approval of the design scheme, additional work is required prior to production. This will include finalizing the selection of objects and, if appropriate, concluding loan agreements; completing the exhibition text, even to individual labels, and selecting illustrations, etc. Working drawings also will need to be prepared, together with any necessary detail drawings and graphics layouts. Mock-ups may be developed into prototypes and tested, and, if necessary, modified and retested. A written specification will be prepared. This is a period of intense activity and decision-making. Anything left unresolved could create problems later on. Similarly,

any errors made at this stage could be expensive to correct once the project has moved into production.

12. *Tendering.* If the work (or even a part of it, such as audio-visual programmes or models) is to be produced by outside contractors, tender documents will need to be prepared together with specifications and drawings for each item. These will be circulated to those invited to tender. Depending on the size and complexity of the project, this stage may take several weeks. On receipt of quotations, some adjustments may be required in order to meet budget targets. Once agreement has been reached on costs, delivery dates and the like, orders can be placed.

13. *Production.* Once production starts, it is normally the designer's task to check and supervise all stages of the work in order to reduce the possibility of errors or misunderstandings. It should be a busy time, with the many activities such as building on and off site, the production of models, typesetting, production of artwork, etc., being undertaken concurrently. On completion of the structure, services such as lighting, security and environmental conditions will need to be tested. When they are satisfactory, objects may be installed. Some minor adjustments and 'touching up' may be required prior to hand-over, when formal responsibility for the items passes to the museum (subject to guarantees, etc.).

14. *Opening, on-going monitoring and maintenance.* Arrangements (including the preparation of printed material) for the opening will need to be put in hand well before the opening date. These may include advance publicity, invitations and press view material. Also to be prepared well in advance of the opening will be schemes to evaluate the effectiveness of the exhibition. Maintenance teams, too, should be formed and ready to go into action as soon as the public are admitted, to ensure that the exhibition is always in good order. Among the various end-of-project requirements, such as completing the files and the accounts, it is also a good idea to hold a debriefing session so that as much as possible may be gained from the project for possible application on the next. A photographic record of the exhibition should be made.

8. *The exhibition brief*

A good brief is a prerequisite of any successful design solution achieved by a systematic, methodical approach to the problem. Yet, surprisingly, the importance of the brief is often underestimated and, as a consequence, projects are often ill considered and superficial, and this is reflected in a troubled developmental stage and a less than satisfactory end product. Indeed, it has been said that the final solution can only be as good as the brief.

It is the brief which should define the exhibition problem, and this initial stage, when there is concentration of thought on the exact nature of the project, should clearly be important for all concerned. Indeed, since there may well be several ideas as to the definition of the problem, it is necessary to clarify thinking. Margaret Hall (1987) wrote:

> A brief for an exhibition is a starting point for the design process. It is the culmination of the first stage of work on an exhibition, the outcome of the dialogue between the curator and the designer, of the consideration, discussion and agreement between all the parties involved.

It should therefore be the vehicle which brings together an agreed (or, in some circumstances, imposed) set of clearly defined problems which need solutions. As such it is important that it takes the form of a written paper to which reference may be made, if necessary, at various stages throughout the project. Writing the brief is normally the task of the curator or subject specialist. However, others, including the designer, may also contribute and would certainly need to be consulted frequently as the nature of the problem is defined. In particular, these specialists may be able to ensure that the brief is realistic, and does not set out a problem to which no physical design solution is possible.

The brief serves several functions, the most important of which is to provide the designer with a definition of the problem to be solved. A secondary function is that it enables or requires those initiating the project to clarify ideas and commit themselves to making firm decisions as to the nature of the project. It thus serves both designer and curator. Max Hebditch (1970), when speaking about the curator's role in briefing the designer, said:

> Successful briefing of the designer, pre-supposes a number of things.
> Firstly a clear idea of what museum exhibitions are for, namely to assist the visitor to understand the language of real things;
> secondly, a clear idea of what roles the curator and designer play in creating the exhibition;

thirdly, curatorial staff who must be able to imagine the whole purpose, content and text of an exhibition in advance and present this to the designer in a way he can interpret visually.

Time spent in considering and formulating the brief is normally time well invested. Thinking through a project before expensive design work and yet more expensive production work are undertaken only makes sense, and can help obviate mistakes. It can also help prevent those associated with the project from feeling that their opinions do not matter, or, later, that changes to the agreed definition of the problem can be made on a whim. Thus it can also help prevent frustration, resentment and loss of morale. The successful setting-out of the nature of a problem, the exploring of its parameters and the determining of the approach to be used in its resolution are an achievement which should rank as at least equal in significance to the solution itself. Unfortunately, the creative aspect of writing a good brief is often overlooked by some curatorial staff, who see only the selection of colours, forms and textures as the truly 'creative' aspect of preparing an exhibition. Good practice shows that the production of an exhibition is a creative experience to be shared by the contributors, and not the sole prerogative of the designer. All associated with a project should have a contribution to make within their respective area of expertise. Martin Elliot (1977), rightly stressed that:

> Of prime importance in any museum design work is the rapport between curator and designer. The designer will need to know what is intended by the design or display and the curator must accept responsibility for communicating this orally or in written form. It is his task to give instructions and information to the designer and these instructions form the basis of the briefing procedure.
>
> The design problems in need of a solution can be isolated in a brief and solutions to the brief put forward. The designer is often in a position to advise on the problems as well as the solutions.

The relationship between the two principal contributors and their responsibilities has been discussed earlier (Chapter 7), but it is worth restating that each must respect the other; honour their agreed areas of responsibility, but not be afraid to give advice and take it as professionals working together in pursuit of a common goal.

Formulating the brief

In most museum situations it will be a subject specialist, that is, a curator or keeper, who is charged with the task of writing the brief. However, it could be a collaborative effort, with staff within a specialism working together, or, if multi-disciplinary, could involve several specialists. Others who might be involved would be the specialist exhibition organizer, the education officer and, indeed, the designer. Those museums which now have a lively marketing policy may like the apparently non-academic but nevertheless important marketing side to be included, especially as by doing so the consumer's interests may be said to have been considered. These could, for example, be represented by an input from the 'Friends of the Museum'. As many people as are considered helpful should, therefore, be consulted and have an input to the briefing document, for which, in these circumstances, the curator may act as convenor or editor. In this role, in addition to a knowledge of the exhibition subject, the curator will also need tact and firmness. Those contributing to the brief should be aware of the museum's communications policy and remember that the decision to mount an exhibition should not be arbitrary, but should emanate from a defined and agreed policy. On completion of a draft brief it may be helpful to circulate it to those with a possible interest in the project and who, perhaps, have not had the opportunity to contribute to it so far. By inviting them to comment upon it the curator may gain the benefit of their views, and in making their views known they will feel a part of the project.

The briefing sequence (checklist)

The 'lead-in' time for a major project can be considerable and is often underestimated. A typical briefing sequence might be:

1. A need is identified and/or an idea for an exhibition is informally discussed by interested parties.
2. After discussion, first ideas are committed to paper as an exhibition proposal, outline brief or draft proposal. The basic information will include: provisional title; purpose; theme and content; proposed audience; timing; location and possibly an indication of the resource implications.
3. The proposal is circulated to a wider circle of interested parties and comments invited.
4. Proposal reviewed by museum exhibitions committee, the officer responsible and/or the director.
5. If the proposal is acceptable, a feasibility study is commissioned to explore the proposal in depth.
6. On acceptance of the feasibility study the briefing document is commissioned.

(For a further account of stages in the preparation of an exhibition see Chapter 7.)

The brief: form and content

The brief should take the form of a well considered piece of instructive writing, written for ease of reference. It may well be prepared to a standard size (such as A4), be typewritten or produced on a word processor and it should have a title page and list of contents, with each section suitably coded and paragraphs numbered. It should not be as 'glossy' as a feasibility study or prospectus where the intention is to persuade or promote. Above all, it should be a purposeful, functional, workmanlike document. Supplementing the main brief may be appendices giving details of location and listing exhibits and draft text, or this information may be available in card index form or as computer print-outs. However, whatever the form this information takes, it should be regarded as a part of a single, comprehensive and all-embracing document. Although all concerned should strive to produce a complete and definitive brief, some revisions may be necessary, but obviously they should be kept to a minimum, and should be capable of being absorbed into the brief document.

The brief should include statements on each of the following topics:

Title and nature of the project

Ideally the brief should be headed by the project title, if it has been decided; otherwise a working title should be given, pending a decision being made early in the work sequence. This may be once the designer has considered the problem and proposed a title which might relate to the corporate identity of the programme. A good title will help promote the exhibition.

The statement on the nature of the project should describe the type of exhibition envisaged, with particular reference to the approach, which might be aesthetic, evocative, didactic or simply entertaining—or a combination of each. Main features such as the nature and extent of the material to be displayed or proposals relating to reconstructed environments or facilities required for practical demonstrations might also be mentioned in order to give an indication of the whole nature of the project and all that it embraces.

Purpose of the exhibition

The need for the exhibition should be stated in general terms and its purpose made clear in a series of aims and objectives. These should make reference to such topics as educational role, promotional role, commercial significance, political aspects, prestige, etc., or whatever is particularly relevant. Possible lines which should be developed in relation to the particular situation are: 'The exhibition aims to benefit visitors by . . .' 'The exhibition aims to benefit the museum by . . .' 'The exhibition aims to benefit museum staff by . . .'

These aims could be developed into specific targets against which the effectiveness of the project could be judged. Such targets should be carefully considered in order to be realistic, particularly as they will almost certainly involve design considerations. The types of targets which might, in some cases be appropriate include: 'The exhibition aims to attract n visitors, who on average should spend x minutes in the exhibition. After this they should, on average, spend £y on souvenirs related to the exhibition.'

There should be a similar statement of aims and objectives in relation to each section of the exhibition and indeed, each individual display.

Audience

The brief should provide information on the audience for whom the exhibition is intended. Those aspects which will have a particular bearing on the design include:

1. *Age of the audience.* Each age group has its own physical and psychological characteristics which may affect the design approach. In particular exhibitions for the very young and the elderly will differ in style, content and facilities.
2. *Ergonomics.* Age also has a bearing on ergonomic factors and the need for displays to be functional. Such things as the average eye level of visitors are important, and visitor size if seating, etc., is to be provided.
3. *Anticipated visitor numbers.* Estimates of the number of visitors who might be in the exhibition at any one time and the duration of their stay will be of use to the designer in specifying the exhibition layout, such things as gangway sizes and, if necessary, queueing arrangements. If visitors are to be encouraged in family groups or parties of, say, ten or twenty, this too will have design implications.
4. *Motivation.* Targeting the exhibition at a group of visitors which is already interested in a topic and is therefore motivated will require very different considerations to those which apply when trying to interest an apathetic audience.
5. *Level of knowledge.* Communicating with a well informed audience requires a different approach from that adopted when the audience is ignorant in the subject.
6. *Intelligence.* An aspect which is less easy to gauge without formal testing. Intelligence, as distinct from knowledge, will have a bearing on the mental agility which can be expected of visitors.
7. *Reading age.* Allied to both level of knowledge and intelligence, the reading age of the intended audience will affect all written text.
8. *Gender.* Apart from the ergonomic factors which relate to all-male or all-female audiences, there may be circumstances in which the gender of the audience will be a consideration in relation to exhibition content and interpretation.
9. *The handicapped.* Facilities such as wheelchair access and viewing will be a consideration. Also, communicating with particular handicapped groups will need special consideration.
10. *Origin of visitors and language.* The language/s used in the exhibition should be those with which the intended audience is familiar. Cultural characteristics and customs may also be a consideration.

Policy and context

The general context in which the exhibition is to be presented should be stated. This may include reference to museum policy statements, and in particular how the project relates to the museum's communications plan. Thus the relationship of the exhibition to other exhibitions, publications or services needs to be explored and links identified. These may be philosophical, subject-oriented or physical.

In addition to the internal museum context, there is also the wider context of the community which it serves to be considered. Competing institutions or 'rival products' need to be identified, and an approach similar to that which a commercial organization about to launch a new product might adopt could be considered. The intended role of the exhibition in the museum, in the locality and in the region and beyond needs to be explored.

Design

Many museums have an identifiable 'house style' which has perhaps evolved through tried and tested solutions. The style may simply relate to the typeface used on captions or the design of showcases or go further to include the design concept of entire galleries and the 'total' design 'image' the museum wishes to project. The degree to which the new project should adhere to or depart from existing design will need to be stipulated.

Longevity and reuse

An indication of the intended life span of the exhibition needs to be given, as this will affect the selection of materials and structural details. Additionally, if the exhibition is to be reused in other venues, this too will have design implications.

Location

In addition to the context explored under 'Policy and context' above, details of the physical context and location need to be given. Items to be covered will include the site in relation to the museum's circulation pattern; location of proposed/existing entrances and exits; floor loading; access for large items; electrical capacity and services.

Regulations

Any regulations which relate to the site/museum in terms of fire, buildings, planning, conservation, health and safety, etc., should be noted.

Security

The brief should include general statements on the security requirements envisaged, in addition to information which might be provided in relation to specific objects. Some systems, such as CCTV or the extensive use of security staff will have particular design implications.

Conservation

As with security, there will probably be a need for general statements on environmental conditions as well as specific specifications for individual objects or types of objects.

Maintenance and servicing

Information on the resources available for exhibition maintenance should be given, together with any special considerations in respect of such things as lighting, computer equipment, etc.

Evaluation

Mention may be made of the procedures and criteria to be applied in evaluating the project. These may, as indicated under 'Purpose' of the exhibition above, relate to the general purpose of the exhibition or deal with specific issues or the evaluation of particular displays.

Programme

An outline programme should have been provided in any feasibility study. However, the programme included in the brief may be more considered, as more detailed information has become available.

Administrative procedures

It may be helpful to clarify administrative procedures in relation to the project, indicating areas of responsibility and channels of communication in an effort to avoid misunderstandings as the project proceeds. Should the brief be given to a consultant designer or a design group working outside the museum, this information will be essential. However, in these circumstances it may well form part of a separate contract document. If this is the case, it will no doubt stipulate exactly what is required of the designer, i.e. the type of presentations required at various agreed stages in the project, the fee and other contractual arrangements.

Theme and concept

The exhibition theme should be stated and a conceptual plan given showing the relationships of the main topic areas to one another. This may be done diagramatically (figure 8.1) but should not, at this stage, be a plan of the actual physical layout of the exhibition.

Exhibition contents

Accompanying the theme and concept paper, and using the same reference system, will come a proposed list of contents. Section by section, it should list the main aims and objectives of each, the individual exhibits proposed and their aims and objectives, right down to lists of every object to be displayed. These may well be individually numbered for reference and coded to indicate, for example, object type, e.g. 'original specimen', 'facsimile', 'model', 'photograph', etc. Accompanying this schedule, coded for cross-reference, will be the draft exhibition text, again right down to individual item labels.

The way in which this information is presented will depend on the type of project. Also, depending on circumstances, captions for individual items or possibly details of more significant elements might not be included in the initial brief but follow as the project progresses. This may be particularly appropriate for 'self-contained' elements such as audio-visual programmes and similar items.

Related items

The brief may well extend to such items as exhibition catalogues, leaflets, posters and publicity; educational material; signage and souvenirs.

Design methodology

Designing may be described as the solving of an identified problem or need by the purposeful use of creative thinking which leads to the production of a solution or artefact. In recent years designing, as an activity, has become more considered and, as a consequence, more complex. Possibly because of its close relationship with art, designing was, not so long ago, popularly considered to be largely intuitive, relying not just on the taste of the practitioner but also on some type of inspirational process which he experienced. Earlier than this, the designer's role was thought of in terms of the craftsman who would choose the right material for the job and specify how it might meet the functional need whilst, at the same time, making it look pleasing—and do this within a set budget and take into account the means of production available.

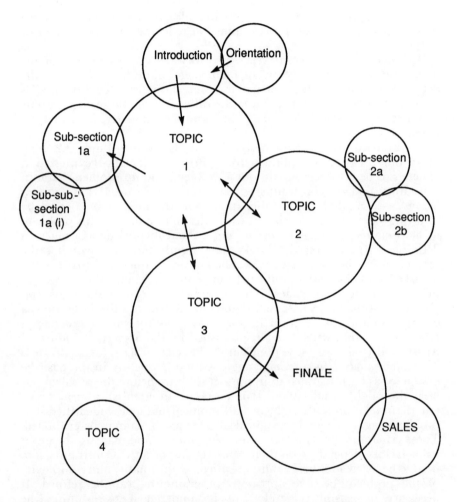

Figure 8.1   Example of a typical conceptual planning diagram

Designing today still embraces these processes, but they are set within a far more complex and systematic approach to problem-solving which relies less on intuition and more on selective methodology. Bruce Archer (1964) in his paper *Systematic Method for Designers*, identified no fewer than 229 distinct events within the structure of the design act. However, the effect of this process is not to reduce the need for creativity and original thought so much as to ensure that ideas evolve and are tested in a more logical way. It is a process aimed at reducing the risk of error or failure.

Designers have, in recent years, put forward various models of the design process. Most agree on the main stages but differ slightly on the detail, depending on their particular design specialism, for the demands on a product designer, for example, are different from those on a graphic designer or a theatre designer. That said, the underlying principles remain the same.

A simplified model of the design activity is given in figure 8.2. First must come an awareness of the need. As Bruce Archer (1964) expressed it, 'There can be no solution without a problem; and no problem without constaints; and no constraints without pressure or need. Thus design begins with a need.' More often than not, the need is discovered by someone other than the designer, who calls on him to share his problem, to help clarify it (stage 1, *preliminaries*), and to provide assistance in defining it (preparing the brief). The significance of involving the designer at the briefing stage is that he knows the questions that need to be asked and the sort of information that will enable the project to progress to the next stages. This will help to clarify the aims and objectives of the project. A useful guide to the type of initial questions a designer should ask is given in *The Study of Professional Practice in Graphic and Industrial Design*, published by the Society of Industrial Artists and Designers, now the Chartered Society of Designers (1974).

Problem analysis is a crucial stage. All too frequently in the past the designer has been tempted to jump to a solution before the problem has been thoroughly understood. It is necessary to establish a clear set of criteria in relation both to the overall problem and to any identified sub-problems, against which design ideas and proposals may be evaluated. These criteria may be ranked in order of priority and may also be given value factors, depending on their perceived importance. Constraints, too, need to be listed and their validity verified. As the totality and complexity of the problem become apparent, programming can be refined. If necessary, a feasibility study can be undertaken to examine the possibilities and explore the parameters of the project. Data collection becomes an important activity. The designer will want to see how others have solved similar problems and seek published research data and other information relevant to all aspects of the task. This should be a receptive and acquisitive period for the designer, who works with an 'open' mind and yet with direction, collecting ideas and information, and analysing and assessing their worth.

Synthesis is the putting together of conceptions or propositions related

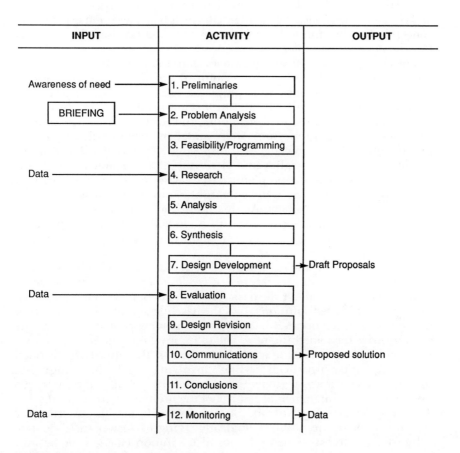

Figure 8.2   Model for design activity

to the problem. It is when the designer searches his mind, ponders the data, and deliberates on the reference material he has acquired in a quest for elements, or even fragments, which he thinks (rationally) or feels (intuitively) might have application in the project in hand. This is the abstract, creative thinking stage and as such is very complex.

In particular, the designer will again consider previous solutions to similar problems and how he has resolved problems of this type in the past. He will refer back to the problem in hand, and its sub-problems, and consider the elements and fragments he has isolated, and decide how, conceptually, they might be augmented and modified in order to satisfy the dictates of the problem.

The *design development* stage moves from the abstract to the concrete. Ideas, having been notionally examined in theory, are developed, modified and redeveloped into proposed solutions. This stage can be approached systematically. It might for example, involve proposing and then manipulating structures or colours, and working through a range of combinations; or of proposing a shape and then methodically varying the proportions of each element, or transposing elements, until a 'unique' combination appears 'right', and is worthy of being tested against the criteria established at the problem analysis stage and the requirements of the brief. Some ideas may well be thought to satisfy certain aspects of the problems better than others. At this point the application of the rank order of priority must apply, and will include the degree of importance attached to such things as function, aesthetics, manufacture, costs and maintenance.

On the one hand, the designer will seek a solution which will work well and do its job in a functional way. This, in itself, will determine certain parameters, and, if the basic problem is not new, may be deduced from tried and tested solutions. It is the baseline and provides a solution which can be relied upon. But on the other hand, he will almost certainly want to strive for something new, and to improve on what has previously been achieved, or to meet new needs. In the past this approach has often resulted in rather superficial 'styling', involving merely the changing of the outer appearance of something which was basically the same. To overcome this, a fundamental rethink of the problem is often the answer. The designer can work in one of two ways. He may begin from the starting point of the problem, logically trying to answer each separate sub-problem almost sequentially, until a solution emerges; or he may work by proposing an answer (the intuitive way) and then adapting and modifying it until it meets the requirements of the brief. Each is valid, because each involves systematic development.

The outcome of the *design development* phase is a series of draft design solutions which, the designer has adjudged, meet the demands of the brief. These may well take the form of models or prototypes or 'mock-ups'—convenient ways simulating the proposed solution which, in the next stage, are evaluated. The criteria for *evaluation* will be those previously applied as ideas were being developed. The evaluators will need to know how well the proposed design solutions satisfy the requirements of function, manufacture, cost and maintenance, and any other requirements, including aesthetic standards. To obtain this information, a whole range of tests might be undertaken depending on the nature of the project. They might include the physical and behavioural sciences, test marketing and so on. The data obtained are used in any *design revision* work found to be necessary and then the revised proposal is re-evaluated, redesigned and re-evaluated until it is satisfactory.

The *conclusions* stage is concerned with bringing all aspects of the project to a satisfactory close and ensuring that the documentation is complete: it is about tying up loose ends. Project records—the systematic recording of each stage—are of considerable use, not only as points of reference as the project progresses but also afterwards in relation to a future project. They may also assist in the evaluation of project methodology and form the basis for refinement or improvement. Although it might be pleasant to close the files completely on a project, in practice that which has been designed and created generally lives on; and its progress in life justifies *monitoring*.

Part four. *The exhibition environment*

9. *Orientation and environment*

Orientation

Orientation is concerned with relative positions. Cohen (1974) summed it up as 'the logical relationship of one situation to another already familiar'. For the visitor to the museum it is of considerable importance. In physical terms it is about his/her progress from home, through the remote external and internal environments, to the point where he/she comes face to face with his/her chosen museum object. In contextual terms it is concerned with the mental preparation which can and should be undertaken prior to experiencing an exhibition or confronting an object.

Winkel *et al.* (1975), in a study undertaken in the Smithsonian Institution, Washington, was of the opinion that:

> the availability of a comprehensive orientation system is absolutely essential if the museum is to ensure that visitors comprehend and appreciate its goals and purposes. The absence of an integrated approach may very well lead to inefficient strategies for viewing the exhibit halls with a resultant increase in frustration, boredom and fatigue.

There are four distinct types of orientation which affect the visitor: geographical; intellectual; conceptual and psychological.

Geographical orientation is concerned with having a knowledge of the geographical layout of a particular place and of its relationship to other places beyond, and being able to locate oneself within a given layout. This form of orientation is clearly important, as people need to know their whereabouts if they are to get to places efficiently and avoid getting lost. It is also important psychologically, because people who know where they are, and who are on familiar territory, tend to be more confident, more relaxed and receptive than those who do not. When people are disorientated, and lost, it is natural for them to feel agitated and tense, with an inability to concentrate on anything other than finding their bearings. Probably the first geographical orienteering task for the museum visitor is to locate the museum. Once this is done, getting to a particular exhibition in what could well be a large and complex building will probably be the next. Although regular visitors may well know the location of the museum, strangers to a town may not; and, while frequent visitors should know the geography of a museum building, occasional visitors and first-time visitors almost certainly will not, and so the need for aids to facilitate geographical orientation is great.

Intellectual orientation is concerned with preparing the mind so that it can progress from the known to the unknown in a learning process. In the museum context, it is about the visitor acquiring the basic information on a subject in order to maximize the benefits to be gained from experiencing an exhibition. Providing an introduction to a topic, 'familiarization', and 'advance reading' are all facets of intellectual orientation. Preparation of this kind has definite advantages; for example, acquiring knowledge before a visit can free exhibition viewing time so that the visitor can concentrate on studying the objects rather than reading the background texts. Also, time can be used selectively and purposefully, and having a knowledge of a subject before seeing objects related to it should make for a greater understanding of the exhibition and make the experience more meaningful. In this way the material, instead of being the substance of an initial stimulus which the brain may well struggle to comprehend, becomes reinforcement, explaining and developing topics with which the visitor is already familiar.

This type of orientation is particularly appropriate for organized, educational visits, and many teachers would regard it as crucial to the success of any such visit. It is often included in a museum's 'outreach' programme as it extends beyond the physical boundaries of the museum.

Related to the intellectual content of the exhibition is conceptual orientation. This deals not so much with the content (as does intellectual orientation) as with the ideas which the exhibition is trying to convey and their organization, that is, the concept. For the visitor, an understanding of this aspect may well be vital in facilitating comprehension of the whole, because facts in themselves are of limited value without a knowledge of how they relate to each other through some process of synthesis. If this can be accomplished before the visit takes place, then the visitor will be prepared for the experience—particularly if it is combined with intellectual orientation. Not only should this prevent any confusion occurring when the visitor is actually in the exhibition, it should also make for a planned and comprehensive visit, and so one less stressful and more enjoyable.

The fourth type of orientation, psychological, is about being in the right frame of mind and having the right attitude. In the same way that an athlete needs to prepare mentally for a competition, so a visitor needs to adopt a positive attitude towards a forthcoming visit to a museum. There are many facets to this type of orientation, which should encourage anticipation, excitement and receptiveness. The willing visitor, going of his/her own accord to a museum, will have a very different attitude from that of a visitor who is being coerced to attend, whether in a family group or in a school party. Research has confirmed this, for it has been established that motivated visitors derive more from their visit than those who are not, and psychological orientation plays a key role in creating the positive attitude necessary.

The museum orientation system

The museum should assist the visitor by providing aids which relate to each of the four types of orientation. Although many of these will overlap or be a part of other areas of the museum's activities, such as its publicity and image, nevertheless orientation should be regarded as a distinct system. It should have its own clearly defined aims and objectives and be subject to periodic evaluation and review.

Elements of the system are discussed in more detail elsewhere in this chapter, so below is a brief checklist of items as they relate to each type of orientation.

1. *Geographical.* 'How to get there' information included in the museum leaflet; signs to the museum; the museum should be included in town plans, tourist maps, etc; plans of the museum should be available to visitors as hand leaflets and on display throughout the building. Internal signing system in museum and exhibitions.

2. *Intellectual.* Introductory and subject leaflets, publications and reading lists; catalogues; educational packs; introductory panels to exhibition topics, lectures and videos.

3. *Conceptual.* Guides and leaflets on the organization of the museum and individual exhibitions; educational packs; explanatory panels; numerical sequences; orientation areas.

4. *Psychological* Museum and exhibition promotional material. Exhibition worksheets and educational packs.

Additionally, general orientation facilities such as a museum visitor centre, information desk, and a museum plan and exhibition listing board will form a major part of the system, and complementing these physical resources will be staff specially selected for their ability to help the visiting public.

The museum environment

Radiating from the object and its immediate environment within a display are a series of environments which the visitor must traverse in his/her journey from home to the object. These environments are important, not least because of the effect they can have on the visitor in directing and preparing him or her for the ultimate experience of confronting the museum object.

The management of this experience is not easy, since so many factors are outside the control of the museum. Nevertheless, an influence can be exerted which should intensify dramatically as the visitor enters the museum environment. How the museum approaches this problem will depend on circumstances, museum policy and in particular its concern for orientation. For example, the strategy employed in preparing visitors to experience a site museum, where a Roman villa has been *in situ* for nearly two thousand years, will differ in approach to that employed to

prepare visitors to a multi-disciplinary regional museum. Such a
regional museum may well acknowledge the incongruity of collections
culled from distant places and times, and brought together completely
out of context within a city museum building.

The extra-remote environment

A museum's general influence on the extra-remote environment such as a
distant region or town is normally limited to some promotional and
publicity work, backed up perhaps by a touring exhibition or an
occasional lecture. National museums have attempted to promote themselves in the regions through circulating posters and leaflets which
advertise and provide information on current and forthcoming exhibitions. These are generally mailed to 'key' locations such as local
museums, libraries, colleges and schools, and occasionally, for major
exhibitions, they have been supplemented with 'orientation' packs which
have contained sample exhibition material as well as introductory text,
and have been 'targeted' at selected audiences of teachers and lecturers.
    Another means of extending the boundaries and influence of museums
has been through the use of circulating exhibitions and occasionally
mobile exhibitions. Although these generally act as exhibitions in their
own right, they are also extensions of the museum which prepared them,
and generally they serve to promote the image and identity of the parent
museum. Occasionally they can be used to extend a particular exhibition,
and feature a small selection of the type of material on display in the
main show. Given the need to travel from the extra-remote environment
to the museum, the points of departure—travel agents' offices, bus, train
or air terminals—all make logical and productive places to display
material relating to the activities of the museum. The same is true of
tourist information centres, which attract a high proportion of people
seeking places to visit. Advertising in the buses and trains themselves is
also effective but can be comparatively expensive.
    These are ways in which a museum can deliberately raise its profile in a
particular area, but it can also consider more general methods. They
involve nationwide/regional advertising campaigns, but there are also
more subtle methods such as involvement in radio and television
programmes and general publicity. For example, a 'spin-off' from a
museum's publishing programme may well be the availability of a range
of its publications in public libraries beyond the region in which the
museum is located. These serve not only to educate, inform and entertain
but also to promote.

The remote environment

The town in which a museum is situated may be regarded as its remote
environment. Remote it may be, but important it undoubtedly is, and the

visual presence of a museum in its surrounding town or district should be considerable. A lively, outward-going, inviting museum will make its presence felt well beyond its four walls, in a whole range of 'outreach' activities. The experience of Sir Frank Markham (1938), noted in his report on *The Museums and Art Galleries of the British Isles*, still holds a message for museums today:

> Time after time my colleagues and I, on our visits to museums, have arrived at some station or market square and have asked a porter or a policeman the way to the museum, only to be met by the assertion that there was no museum in the town . . . It follows, therefore, that if the general public are completely ignorant of the existence of the museum in a town, they must also be unaware of the service that it can render and totally uninterested as to whether it is adequately financed and cared for.

In its own town or region, the ways in which a museum promotes its existence could include the following areas, to which we must now turn.

Adequate signposting is probably the most neglected of aids to the prospective museum visitor, and yet it is one of the most vital and cost-effective. As a means of assisting those seeking to find the museum, good signposting is essential. Also, if they are well designed, signs can serve the dual functions of acting as directional devices and advertisements, and will certainly help those who were previously unaware of the museum's existence to know in which direction it lies, even if they are not initially persuaded to visit it.

Signing should be available from the town's main travel centres. These will normally include the coach, bus and railway stations and should ideally be mounted in association with other information about the museum. This could include times of opening, details of admission and the nature of the collections. A map showing the main museum and any branch museums should be a minimum requirement in a town of any significance which is concerned about promoting its museum services. The route from the main travel centres to the various museums and galleries should be indicated and signs located especially wherever the configurations of roads and pathways makes it necessary. Ambiguous signing is infuriating! If appropriate, additional signs should be provided to ensure that the way to the museum is made clear from the main public buildings such as the town hall, library, university or colleges and from busy areas such as shopping precincts.

Simple signs, possibly incorporating the museum logo or designed in the museum house style (if permitted by the local authority) are ideal. Those indicating distances, e.g. 'Museum 150 m', provide additional helpful information.

The above recommendations relate mainly to pedestrians. Those using their own transport also need to be directed, and in this some local authorities are less than helpful, since they do not like a proliferation of signs, and a museum is but one of many organizations seeking the facility. This is unfortunate, for greater problems are often caused through failing to signpost a popular institution than by providing good signing in the first place. Other local authorities are very aware of the problem and have done much to raise the level of awareness of visitors to a town of its amenities and have signposted and promoted them accordingly. In an ideal situation the museum would be signposted from the main approach roads to a town as well as from the town centre. Also of help to the traveller by car would be an indication of convenient parking facilities. For particularly popular museums located in old towns with narrow streets, coach routes should be indicated, with setting down points and coach parks. A visitor who has arrived at the museum after a pleasant journey will be more receptive to the museum than the visitor who arrives tired, frustrated, and bad-tempered, having been unable to find the museum or a parking place for his vehicle easily.

Adequate advertising is clearly crucial to this whole process. As an indication of its liveliness, a museum needs to maintain a 'high profile', and keep in the public eye. One way of achieving this is by undertaking significant advertising campaigns. As a minimum, the museum should be advertised by posters in all libraries, colleges, schools, other museums, information offices, tourist centres and similar places. Additionally a museum might usefully take poster sites around a town, including, as mentioned above, main travel centres and the modes of transport such as buses, trains and taxis.

Posters may be of two types: those relating to the museum in general and to the permanent collections, and those which advertise specific events such as a temporary exhibition or concert. However, even the first type should be changed and updated every year. The poster has been tried and tested as a means of advertising and has proved to be a most cost effective means of medium to long term general advertising.

Another most effective way of reaching a large audience is by placing an advertisement in the press. This can be done in a general way, where the notice may compete with a wide range of other advertisements, or in a particular way, under a listing of events. Often special rates are offered to advertisers who are regularly included in the listings, and such is the importance of these lists that many organizations cannot afford not to be included. This is particularly true of 'arts listings', where galleries need to maintain a presence in what is becoming a very competitive field. Keeping the name of an institution in the forefront not only helps to promote it but also ensures that it is seen as an active, dynamic organization where things are happening. Here museums can take advantage of human nature—for if something is going on people like to know about it, and few care to be left out if everyone else is in the know.

Actions speak louder than words, and in addition to telling the public how active the museum is via the media, the museum also needs to be seen to be active. It can do this by participating in as many events as possible. The sort of promotional work the museum can undertake will depend on its status and location. Representation at national, civic and local events should be considered, and this includes events which might range from national exhibitions, or the provision of a float in the annual 'mayor's parade', to attending school careers conventions to advise young people on careers in the museum field. Whatever the event, raising the profile of museums in general or one museum in particular can only be to the good.

Some museums have benefited by such simple actions as mounting a small display at local shows and staffing it with museum curators prepared to comment on items brought to it by members of the public. This, modelled on the popular television programme *Antiques Roadshow*, has often benefited the museum by locating interesting or important objects. Indeed, there is no end to the type of events in which a museum conscious of the benefits of promotional activities can become involved.

Although predominantly concerned with intellectual orientation, a museum's education department can contribute much to the other forms of orientation as well. By working through established links in schools and colleges and endeavouring to develop new ones, the departments can undertake a wide range of activities. These may well include the loan of objects, the publication of specific material for educational purposes and the provision of a programme of lectures. But it would be wrong to suppose that educational activities are concerned only with schools and colleges. Outreach activities should be available to everyone, particularly informal events such as field trips.

There are, of course, numerous ways in which the museum can reach the public by going beyond the confines of the museum building. In addition to fulfilling a specific function, these activities will serve to advertise the museum service and provide something of a foretaste of what might be expected in the museum itself. Ideal projects are those which involve an element of interpretation and can direct those interested to specific material in the museum's collections.

In this respect, both town trails and nature trails are ideal, or indeed the interpretation by visual or audio means of any interesting feature of the natural or man-made environment. Additionally, displays placed immediately outside the museum or in shopping precincts, libraries or other public areas introducing the themes of the main exhibitions in the museum work well provided they are secure, or house relatively expendable or reproduction material. Depending upon the interests of the museum, an introduction to local natural history or local history are topics which may be undertaken without too much difficulty.

Without doubt one of the most important things a museum must do, if it is to enjoy a high public profile, is to establish good relations with the media, and in particular the press. To this end the museum needs to appoint a suitably able communicator, who is both enthusiastic and tactful, to act as spokesperson and liaison officer. Large museums may well be able to appoint a full-time public relations or press officer, while in smaller museums it will probably have to be a part-time role.

Maintaining a place in the media requires much effort. Information and 'newsworthy' items need to be sought and prepared and fed to the press in the form of press releases together with appropriate photographs.

For the most part, gaining reportage and having exhibitions reviewed in the press are free, but the placing of advertisements can often facilitate matters too. Good contacts are vital, and the publicity-conscious museum will work hard to develop links with all forms of the media, including the press, radio and television and possibly advertising agencies as well.

The media are powerful and effective communicators. Most media people, especially at a personal level, are very approachable and receptive to information, particularly those concerned with local events. However, the ways in which the media use the information they are given, and the degree of accuracy they accord it, may not always be to the liking of a museum. Nevertheless, in the hands of professional public relations and promotional personnel the media can be used advantageously to extend the base of the museum.

The immediate environment

The immediate surrounds of the museum are regarded as its external environs and as such are of vital importance, for it is here that the public meet the museum. People who have read the literature, reacted favourably to the advertising, followed the signposting, participated in the extra-mural activities and sampled the tasters have high expectations and should not be disappointed.

First, the museum needs to be clearly identified. Signs need to be employed which give the name of the museum: how often are museums lost amid a host of buildings all of which look as if they *might* be the place one seeks? Once the museum is signposted from all approaches— and this is particularly important when it is set amidst other buildings or extensive grounds—directional signs should again be employed, as necessary, to locate the entrance or, if appropriate, ticket office.

At the entrance, and also at the perimeter entrances to museum grounds, details of the opening hours and admission charges should be given. This information should be provided conveniently, in order to prevent a would-be visitor from making an abortive trek only to find that the museum is closed or is charging more than he/she is prepared to pay. The practice so often employed by stately homes and commercially-minded country houses of not divulging the admission charge until the prospective visitor is confronted by the ticket seller is to be despised, and is in the interests neither of the visitor nor the organization concerned. In addition to this standard information, the displaying of a banner, pennant or flag can indicate the presence of a particular event. It can also add a festive, active and friendly air to the most sombre of facades.

If the argument for bringing the museum beyond its site into the 'remote environment' is strong, the argument for bringing the museum out of its building into its grounds is—subject to the normal safeguards regarding security and conservation—even stronger. Certainly there can be no better signs than large specimens suitably displayed. Spectacular examples which come readily to mind are the rocket outside the Museum

of Science and Technology in Washington, D.C., or the military equipment outside the Military Museum in Cairo or the National Army
Museum in London. Some objects, indeed, were designed to be seen in an
external environment; a tank, for example, does not look right in a plush
interior, and nor does a Henry Moore sculpture, which was created for an
natural outdoor setting, necessarily fit happily in an internal display.
The potential for using the museum grounds and precincts as extensions
of the internal exhibition spaces is considerable.

An out-gallery, an outdoor sculpture garden, or a courtyard can add a
new dimension to the displays, and be an appropriate setting for objects
designed to be seen in an outdoor setting, in naturally changing light, in
variable weather conditions and perhaps against natural foliage. Areas
can be gravelled or paved and suitable enclosures built. Even simple
structures may be considered, possibly as permanent units or on a
seasonal basis to protect exhibits from the weather or offer them security
from the visitor. Alternatively the structures could be to protect the
visitors from the elements. In either case, there is an opportunity for the
creation of some visually exciting structures. Those museums fortunate
enough to have enclosed courtyards, such as the Victoria and Albert in
London, have also been able to use these spaces as oases within the built
environment. Here visitors may be relieved of any possible claustro-
phobia, and be refreshed by a breath of the outdoor, in a beautiful setting
which can be fully appreciated from without and anticipated from
within.

The provision of showcases outside the museum is yet another way in
which a museum can extend beyond its immediate area. This is, of
course, by no means new, and was another aspect to which Sir Frank
Markham referred in his 1938 report. He wrote (p. 111):

> Possibly the most successful way of appealing to the British public is through
> the combination of Press articles and the museum window, this latter being an
> external window or windows arranged like a shop window so as to attract the
> passer-by.

Effective as the provision of showcases can be, it is not without problems,
and the museum must consider the risks involved. Concern for security
and conservation will be paramount and will determine the way in which
the cases can be used and whether any original material can be displayed.
Producing a case which is secure and vandal-proof as well as weather-
proof is not easy, particularly as condensation can also be a problem.
Nevertheless, with the aid of toughened glass and double glazing,
temperature controls and security alarms, some of the technical problems
can be overcome, and, used sensibly, these showcases can do much to
promote the museum. Even if real objects are not used, replicas and/or
promotional graphic material can still attract and interest the public.

A museum or gallery blessed with good grounds and gardens can, in
addition to using them for static displays, also consider them for use for a
whole range of activities which may be related to the aims and objectives

of the museum. The possibilities are endless, and include the more obvious lectures, demonstrations and workshops as well as craft fairs, traditional fetes and performances of music, dance and drama. Involving large numbers of people in activities takes particular skills and resources but can be very rewarding for all concerned. For example, the Yorkshire Sculpture Park, Wakefield, in the mid-1980s held an 'animal sculpture day'. Visitors were encouraged to come and, under the guidance of a resident sculptor, make animals from the natural resource of the park—wood, augmented with string, nails, and so on. The response was overwhelming and the sculpture produced outstanding!

Irrespective of whether the grounds or precincts of the museum are used as an extension of its exhibition function, they must be given careful consideration, and be well maintained. Everything, from the perimeter railings, the paths and garden beds to the buildings themselves, must give the appearance of being well cared for. A litter-strewn garden overgrown with weeds, and buildings with flaking paint, graffiti and an uncared-for aura are no advertisement for a museum. Further, they are inconsistent with the very ideals of an institution dedicated to preservation and conservation.

The psychological effect the external appearance of the building can have in conditioning a visitor to what lies within can be considerable. This is easily demonstrated when one visits a house for the first time, or different sorts of shops, or official or religious buildings—the appearance of the facade gives one an expectation of what lies within. It is therefore a false economy to cut back on essential maintenance of the museum's exterior and immediate environment, for these should be seen as an extension of the museum, and treated as such.

The museum internal environment

When he crosses the threshold of the museum building the visitor enters the internal museum environment. Ideally, he should enter full of hope, optimism, enthusiasm and excitement, having had his appetite suitably whetted along his journey. Indeed, he should not have been able to get as far as the museum entrance without having encountered at least some tangible evidence of the museum's active existence. Hopefully, too, the preliminaries to his arrival, including literature and publicity, will provide a sense of purpose to the visit, and he will come with a clear idea of what he wishes to accomplish.

What confronts the visitor when he first arrives is therefore of vital importance. The internal environment should be designed to be welcoming and to cater efficiently for the visitor. Orientation needs will be paramount. The entrance is a functional space and one in which the visitor should be able to come to terms with what is probably an unfamiliar environment. Reassurance is important and the welcoming, friendly face of a member of the museum staff will do much to get the visit off to an encouraging start, especially if the staff member is more a receptionist than a guard, and in ordinary clothes rather than official uniform. A reception and/or enquiry facility is therefore a prime requirement, preceded only, perhaps, by such geographical orientation devices (like plans and a signing system) as are necessary.

A problem for many museum entrance areas is that they have to cope not only with individual visitors and family groups but also with whole coachloads of visitors. If these larger groups can be served by a separate entrance it can be very helpful, and particularly so if the entrance is located so as to enable coaches to set passengers down conveniently. Entrances must also be capable of receiving wheelchair visitors.

The entrance often serves several competing and contradictory functions. It is a thoroughfare for visitors, both entering and departing, a waiting and meeting area, and a space where people are seeking orientation information, and possibly purchasing admission tickets and souvenirs as well. As if this were not enough, some museums insist on having exhibits in this area too. Therefore, in order for the entrance area to function effectively, the various groups, and in particular those which are predominantly static and those which are mobile, need to be separated.

A checklist of some of the facilities which might necessarily or usefully be located in the museum entrance areas includes:

1. *An admissions desk* for the issuing of tickets.
2. *An orientation area* providing layout plans, signing and possibly incorporating an information desk.
3. *A reception area* with seating where visitors can wait for and meet friends.
4. *A cloakroom facility* to deposit coats and baggage.
5. *A lavatory facility* with washrooms and toilets.
6. *A mothers' room* where young children can be attended to.
7. *A medical room* with facilities for the unwell.
8. *A pushchair bay* where pushchairs are available for the young, old and/or disabled visitor.
9. *Telephone facilities.*
10. *Sales facilities* for the complete range of souvenirs and informative publications.
11. *Catering facilities* to cater for a range of needs, including light refreshments and main meals.

In planning entrance areas, particular attention needs to be given to the sequence in which facilities are provided for those entering and those leaving the museum. Furthermore, the physical constraints of the architecture may dictate or suggest certain solutions. Yet another consideration could be how to make a limited range of facilities available for special functions whilst securely closing others off. Use of the museum for evening activities and the growing practice of hiring out museum facilities often create this problem, which requires careful analysis if it is to be resolved successfully.

How the entrance areas are treated in terms of interior design, whether antique splendour or modern functionalism, will, to a certain extent, be dictated by the architectural style of the building and the environment the designer creates in response to the requirements of a brief. But the effect the design has on the visitor will be significant. It will help set the 'mood' of the visit. The entrance area is a transitional space, a conditioning area between the real world whence the visitors have come and to which they return and the worlds of the objects, which may be far removed in time and place. It is transitional, too, in another sense. It is an acclimatization area. Outside is the bright sunlight or night sky, the rain and the cold, but beyond the entrance lies the controlled environment of the exhibition galleries with constant temperature, controlled relative humidity and subdued levels of lighting. Because of this, lighting, in particular, needs special consideration, for if a gradual sequence of different light levels is employed the eyes of the visitors can be helped to adjust in comfort to what otherwise might be drastic contrasts.

Transitional space is not just that which is located at the entrance of the museum. It is also the function of those areas which connect one exhibition with another. Such spaces have an important role to play not just as circulation routes but also as areas which relax and prepare the visitor for each new exhibition experience. Bernado (1972) remarked that 'The actual capacity of a museum to handle people efficiently is a function not of the area or volume of the museum building, but of the width of its corridors and aisles'. (See Chapter 12).

If they are to function effectively, the temptation to line the walls of these areas with exhibits should be resisted, since people stopping to view get in the way of those walking through. This in turn has the effect of discouraging people from stopping to look at the exhibits, making it pointless to locate them there in the first place.

Circulation is related closely to the concept of 'pacing', which is about providing the visitor with a variety of experiences as he/she progresses through a given space. It is therefore as applicable to the museum as a whole as it is to a specific exhibition. Too much of the same creates boredom. Maclagon (1931) was aware of this over fifty years ago:

> There is no doubt whatever that the ordinary visitor to one of our great museums is apt to emerge from it exhausted rather than stimulated. Museum headache is a recognised ailment, although, like a common cold, no effective cure has yet been devised for it by the medical profession, and I am persuaded that the people who can best help sufferers from the distressing complaint are the architects of the future.

It is, as Maclagon suggests, up to the architects (or environmental designers) to resolve the problem, and there are a number of devices which might be used to do this. The most obvious is to provide, in between galleries and conveniently located off the circulation routes, suitable rest areas.

These areas may be serviced by light refreshments, or simply be areas where visitors can sit quietly. If the areas are fenestrated, with a view to the outside world, this too can be very relaxing. In some, quiet music might be played with perhaps a fountain of water acting as a gentle distraction from the concentration levels and physical energy required in the exhibition galleries. Other devices which have the effect of relaxing and recharging are environmental changes. These can include changes in temperature, changes in floor surfacing from soft to hard (and vice versa) (which helps stimulate the feet), and changes in the treatment of wall surfaces, either in colour or in texture. Movement from enclosed areas with low ceilings and from dark areas to more brightly lit spaces has similar effects. If access can safely be given to external areas such as gardens, courtyards, balconies, terraces or roof gardens, this too is particularly pleasant and helpful.

The local exhibition environment

The local exhibition space is that in which a particular exhibition is contained. It is normally a room, hall or gallery but may equally be a physically defined area within a larger space which has been given over to a specific exhibition. Signs may be employed to direct visitors to it, but little acts better to draw people than interesting sounds like animal noises, an engine getting up steam, or music and chanting, and some eye-catching feature at the exhibition entrance.

This latter approach is not new, and an earlier writer, D.B. Major, (1837), recommended that:

> at the entrance of the collection the visitor's eye should be caught by a few conspicuous specimens, such as a crocodile, a stuffed bear, tiger or lion, a dried whale, or some other objects that would impress people by their 'splendour', 'venerable character' or 'ferocious looks'.

Undoubtedly visitors are attracted to dramatic objects and there is a substantial amount of recent research to support this. Lakota (1976), for example, found that visitors responded to exhibits which were primarily object-oriented, and that materials such as graphics were found to deter visitation, particularly for family groups.

For the entrance area the ideal solution could be the use of a replica or model. These have the advantage of being capable of being made in lightweight materials and can be located in positions where, for reasons of security or safety, the use of real objects might be unwise or impracticable. Also, in the case of models, they may be dramatic enlargements of reality, so increasing their capacity to attract attention.

Once beyond the entrance there is a need for orientation support. This should include an introduction to the topic, details of how the exhibition is arranged (ideally incorporating a plan or diagram) and its concept and purpose. The entrance area is also the place to provide any information which will assist the visitor when in the exhibition. This might include such items as catalogues, guide sheets or audio guides, but also exhibition regulations on photography or re-entry.

Once in the exhibition, visitors spend a disproportionate amount of their visit time near the entrance, and progressively less and less time on exhibits as they move towards the exit. This was observed by Melton (1935) in his early studies on how visitors behave in the exhibition space, and is generally known as the 'exit gradient effect'.

If an exhibition is to function efficiently, and if visitors are to respond as intended to the stimuli provided, the exhibition environment must be well organized. Fundamental to the organization of the space are two closely related elements—the individual displays and the circulation routes to them and around them. There are, of course, endless ways of organizing these in design terms, and, in most circumstances, the layout will emanate from the brief. However, circulation routes increase in importance in relation to the number of visitors attending the exhibition. Most circulation routes are based on the premise that visitors circulate in the direction in which they read, i.e. from left to right. However, except in the case of a simple 'linear' exhibition this will not always be possible (or necessarily desirable), and it is for the designer to devise ways of encouraging, tempting or ultimately physically forcing the visitor by means of barriers to follow what is deemed the appropriate route. Some of the more subtle methods which can be used include the use of light, colour and sound as attracting elements, or, as has already been stated, the glimpse of an exciting object. Another device is numbering—much underrated by curators and designers alike but nevertheless of consider-able assistance to those visitors who seek this form of guidance.

A number of writers have addressed this issue (Lakota 1976; ROM 1976; Hall 1987) and have given an indication of the infinite number of variations possible. One of the basic problems is to overcome Melton's 'exit gradient effect'. In fact Melton himself suggested a simple way of doing this which has been endorsed by others (Coleman 1950, Lakota 1976). Exhibition spaces should be considered as cul-de-sacs with a single entrance/exit, and not as through routes, where visitors accelerate towards a visible exit. In his model the use of an alcove arrangement, each dealing with a single concept or topic, offers an effective layout, provided the spaces are of a comfortable size in proportion to the whole. This arrangement prevents the gallery from being used as a thoroughfare to another part of the museum. It cannot therefore expect to pick up 'passing trade', and is very dependent on good signposting and an attractive entrance in order to encourage the visitor to enter.

Lehmbruck (1974) evolved a typology of circulation patterns and identifies five basic types: arterial; comb; chain; star and block (Fig. 9.1). The term *arterial* may be applied to a continuous path, whether straight, angular or curving, which offers the visitor no alternative route. As such it is suitable for linear sequences. Its main limitation is its rigidity. There is pressure on visitors to move in one direction only. If a visitor wishes to refer back to something he has already seen it can cause congestion, and so can the crowd which congregates around particularly popular exhibits. Ideally, exhibits should be located only on one side of the route, and if this is not done increased congestion could occur in crowded exhibitions, with people moving from side to side, with the added likelihood that they would miss something.

The *comb* pattern consists of a main path supplemented by optimal alcoves. This arrangement has the advantage of providing areas off the main traffic route where visitors can study without being jostled, and, if space permits, may even allow a two-way flow. Each alcove ideally lends itself to a particular topic, and need not, of course, be of equal size but can be adjusted to the needs of the exhibition.

The *chain* is similar to the arterial scheme, in that it is linear, but it is more complex in that it consists of a series of self-contained spaces, each of which may have a more varied path within it. This form of inter-connecting gallery is frequently used in art galleries, and although congestion can occur at interconnecting doorways it allows considerable freedom of circulation within the spaces.

A system which presents the visitor with a series of alternatives radiating from a central point may be considered a *star* or *fan* formation. This has the advantage of separating topic areas, and can create a very busy central area, which can be a pleasant feature if not over-stressed.

The *block* is in a sense a non-system in that it provides free random circulation, dependent on the whim of the visitor or the attraction power of individual exhibits. This self-directing space is conditioned only by the location of the entrance/exit and the exhibits.

The five basic patterns described above may be used individually or in combinations to cover most situations. For the most part, the exhibition presentation with its subtleties and points of emphasis may well disguise the underlying circulation structure. However, the most significant factor in any pattern is whether or not the space is enclosed (i.e. a cul-de-sac) or forms a through route. If the latter, the problem will always be to ensure that the visitor sees as much of the exhibition as possible, and this means overcoming the pull of the exit gradient, and the natural reluctance of the visitor to pass an exit in order to see further exhibitions when he knows that he must double back on himself to leave by that exit later. If a museum wishes to accommodate a succession of temporary exhibitions, it is sensible for it to equip certain areas to receive them. These may include special galleries, or spaces within the 'permanent' exhibitions which, for one reason or another, particularly lend themselves to the purpose. This might be because of their proximity to facilities such as 'rest' areas, or their relation to the content of the main exhibitions. If this approach is adopted, particular attention should be paid to adjoining areas and displays, access for both the public and exhibition materials, the effects any disruptions caused by erecting and dismantling exhibitions might have on the surrounding areas, and the security of the space.

Ideally, however, a museum should have at least one self-contained temporary exhibition gallery. This should be purpose-designed as a versatile space and incorporate all the necessary services. These may include power grids to floor and ceiling and possibly some form of adaptable lighting system such as that afforded by lighting track. If the space is devoid of any architectural feature so much the better, as each

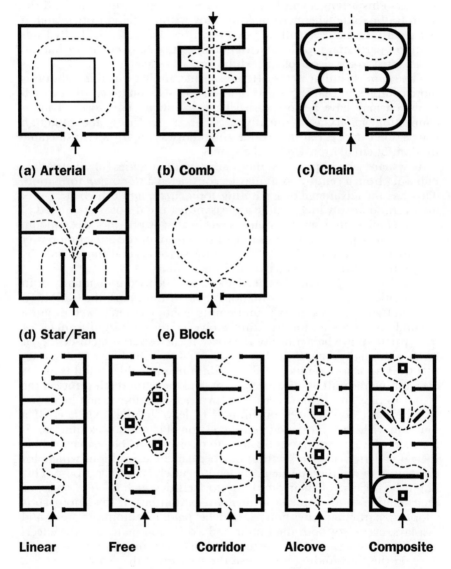

(a) Arterial   **(b) Comb**   **(c) Chain**

(d) Star/Fan   **(e) Block**

Linear   Free   Corridor   Alcove   Composite

Figure 9.1   Examples of typical circulation patterns (after Lehmbruck 1974)

exhibition will want to create its own visual identity. The space will therefore need to be of reasonable proportions, with a ceiling height which will allow for the showing of large objects, and a floor loading capacity capable of taking heavy ones. Additionally, the area needs to be able to be made secure whilst exhibitions are being erected and dismantled, and of course when they are completed and open.

Environmentally the space needs to be designed for the types of exhibitions it is intended to receive. For example, if it is intended to stage exhibitions of major works of art, then the highest standards of environmental control are required, including full air conditioning, satisfactory levels of ultra-violet light and round-the-clock security. Many lenders of exhibitions, including the Arts Council of Great Britain, grade their exhibitions according to their environmental needs, and museums unable to meet them are not eligible for consideration as suitable venues.

Particular care should be taken in selecting the location of such a gallery. In all probability it will need to be accessible for special viewings after normal opening hours, and this could present security problems for the rest of the museum. A location close to an entrance may therefore be preferred where cloakroom facilities are also available. Access to the gallery for both exhibits and exhibition units is also an important consideration. A level route from delivery bay to gallery with wide passageways is obviously ideal, but if the gallery is to be located elsewhere it needs to be serviced by an adequate goods lift. Also important are conveniently located storage and servicing facilities. A store where showcases, screens, lights and packing materials can be kept is ideal, and the service area should be kitted out to undertake minor production and maintenance work without constant recourse to the main workshops.

Safeguarding the exhibits—and the public

The exhibition climate

Displaying objects in an exhibition places them at risk, and risks arise not simply from a security viewpoint, where theft and physical damage are the main considerations, but also from a conservation viewpoint, where uncontrolled environmental factors can be equally destructive. Light, heat and humidity can all, in certain circumstances, be damaging, and so can pollutants, various chemical reactions which display materials can induce, and attacks by various living organisms.

Assessing the environmental needs of any particular object is normally the responsibility of the conservator. He/she will work closely with curatorial colleagues and design staff, and is therefore a vital person in the exhibition team. Information on the environmental requirements of the objects when they are displayed should be provided in the brief, and the designer needs to be aware of these design implications from a very early stage in the development of an exhibition scheme. A requirement for particularly low levels of lighting, for example, can be a major influence on the final appearance of the exhibition. The importance of conservation in relation to the exhibition environment means that it is essential for the designer to have at least a basic knowledge of the climatic requirements of the different types of objects and how they may be achieved. Additionally he/she must be prepared to seek and take expert advice.

Ideally all exhibition areas should be environmentally controlled and, if they contain important material, they should be air-conditioned. This facility enables both temperature and relative atmospheric humidity to be maintained at appropriate levels and can also provide for pollutants, including dust, to be extracted. However, where it is not possible to provide such a comprehensive system, special consideration needs to be given to the problems of temperature and relative humidity control.

Both relative humidity and temperature are of vital importance in relation to the exhibition climate; in fact the two are interrelated, as the ability of the air to retain moisture increases as the temperature rises. *Relative humidity* is the ratio between the actual amount of water vapour present in the air and the saturation amount expressed as a percentage, for example:

$$RH = \frac{\text{Absolute humidity}}{\text{Saturation humidity}} \times \frac{100}{1}$$

where absolute humidity is the amount of water vapour present in a given volume of air at a given temperature, and saturation humidity is the amount of water vapour required to saturate the same volume of air at the same temperature.

Relative humidity is an important consideration, as objects which contain moisture-sensitive materials such as paper, wood and textiles react to changes in the relative humidity of the surrounding air by undergoing dimensional changes. If not quickly checked, these can result in some materials cracking and fracturing. Furthermore, if the relative humidity is too high (above 68 per cent) mould growth may occur. Relative humidity levels are measured with a hygrometer. Low readings indicate dryness; high, excessive dampness. An acceptable level for general exhibitions is between 50 and 55 per cent at a temperature of between 60°F and 65°F, although this temperature is set more for the comfort of visitors than for the benefit of the objects. Provided the levels are kept constant, they should be satisfactory for the majority of objects. It is important to emphasize that in most instances it is the *changes* in levels that are responsible for the most serious damage. Switching systems off at night (including lights which provide a heat source) or failing to adjust to day and night conditions and to climatic changes can have serious consequences for the objects.

In order to monitor relative humidity in sensitive areas a self-recording type of hygrometer should be used. It records relative humidity on a graph related to a time scale, so that fluctuations over a period of time can be noted. Also useful for observational spot checks is the small paper hygrometer. In order to meet the recommended levels of relative humidity and temperature, suitable systems or items of equipment must be installed. Where there is no air conditioning, control of the climate may be achieved with the assistance of humidifiers and dehumidifiers, in conjunction with a heating system.

Humidity control in showcases will be assisted by the use of moisture-retaining materials such as wood and textiles in their construction or in display supports, as these will act as buffers against relative humidity fluctuations. Should strict control be necessary, chemical dessicants such as silica gel may be used and can be preconditioned to effect the desired level of relative humidity.

Light is damaging to the surfaces of many kinds of museum object. Only items of stone, metal and ceramics are normally unaffected by it. Particularly sensitive are works on paper (especially water colours), textiles, natural history specimens and, in fact, all organic material whose surface colour is important. The harmful effects of light are difficult to eliminate entirely but may be significantly reduced in three ways: by eliminating as much ultra-violet (UV) radiation as possible; by reducing levels of illumination to the minimum necessary to view (i.e. about 50 lux); and finally by reducing the time during which objects are illuminated.

Daylight is the most serious source of UV radiation, but by the application of suitable filters to the windows most of this can be eliminated. Also, by reflecting daylight off UV-absorbent surfaces, much of the harmful effect can be reduced. Ultra-violet is also emitted by most fluroescent tubes and these too should have protective filter sleeves fitted if they are to be used in sensitive areas. Alternatively the special UV-filtered type may be used. Recommended minimum light levels for various categories of material, which should not be exceeded, are 150 lux for bone, horn, ivory (where there is surface colour), lacquer; leather (undyed) and oil paintings; 50 lux for dyed leather, furniture, manuscripts, natural history specimens, prints and drawings, stamps and textiles (including costumes and tapestries).

In addition to a concern for light levels, the heat associated with the light source needs to be considered carefully. Principal sources are tungsten lights, low-voltage spotlights and the starter units of fluorescent tubes. In all instances these are best physically separated from the space in which the object is enclosed, not just in order to reduce heat but also because maintenance work on light fittings can represent a serious hazard to objects.

Probably the pollutant which poses the commonest threat to museum objects is dust. Ideally, general levels should be reduced and kept in check by an air-conditioning unit. Failing this, and if necessary in addition, cases should be dustproofed. This can be done to varying levels, depending on the methods employed. In critical situations cases can be pressurized, sealed, or objects can be kept in an atmosphere of nitrogen. Dust contains atmospheric pollutants, and substances like sulphur dioxide and hydrogen sulphide can be particularly damaging to the surface of some objects.

Pollutants may also be present in some of the materials used in display work or may occur as a result of chemical reaction between materials and gases or other substances in the atmosphere. For example, certain woods, like oak, have a high acid content which, in certain circumstances, can cause a chemical reaction to occur which may result in the tarnishing of silver. Similarly, certain textiles (especially velvets) are 'dressed' with sulphur-containing compounds which again can have tarnishing effects. Acids may also be present, or may occur as a result of reactions in certain adhesives and lacquers.

The chemicals used in the manufacture of many common materials such as plywood, cork, textiles and adhesives are very diverse and are varied from time to time without notifying the consumer. It is therefore advisable for the designer to discuss materials with the conservator and arrange for the suitability of any suspect materials to be tested prior to use.

Care should be exercised not to introduce living organisms into the exhibition without adequate precautions, and material likely to contain pests should be suitably treated. In particular, natural material such as bark, thatching, matting and even plants warrant special attention, as they frequently contain insect life. Open windows in galleries can also present a problem if they allow insects access to an exhibition. However, the most damaging living organism as far as objects are concerned is man.

Safety in the exhibition environment

The exhibition environment should be designed to be safe for both objects and people. In the United Kingdom the designer has certain legal responsibilities, together with his/her employer, under the Health and Safety at Work Act to ensure that any exhibition designed by him/her is a safe place both for museum employees and for visitors.

In order to achieve safety there are a number of regulations of which the exhibition designer must be aware. The exact nature of these may vary according to the type of museum and the nature of the exhibition. Some may involve submitting designs for formal approval, whilst others, where public performances or the sale of liquor are involved, may involve an application for a licence for the premises. However, the regulations which are likely to concern the designer most are planning and building regulations (especially for new, permanent structures), regulations relating to listed buildings, and fire regulations. These are of particular importance as they affect virtually all public exhibitions, because, in addition to making demands on the layout of an exhibition (e.g. width of corridors; doors; access to fire appliances and exits), the regulations as interpreted by the fire officer will almost certainly also require materials used in the exhibition structure to the fireproofed and/or conform to certain standards of classified fire resistance. Much will depend on where and how they are used and in what quantities.

In some situations it will be prudent for exhibition plans to be submitted to the fire officer for approval prior to production. It may also be necessary for the fire officer to inspect and approve the exhibition prior to its being open to the public. In other situations, depending on local agreements, it should be possible to design new exhibitions which comply with existing regulations and maintain access to fire exits, appliances, and so on.

In all situations where the designer is in any doubt as to whether regulations apply, the interpretation of regulations, or any aspect of public safety, advice should be sought from the appropriate authority. In many instances an informal chat with the right person at the outset of a project can prevent problems occurring later on.

A brief checklist of *some* of the items which may be subject to regulations or on which the designer may benefit from specialist advice include:

1. Building regulations.
2. Electrical work.
3. External work (siting of exhibits; signs; illuminations, etc.).
4. Fire regulations.
5. Floor loadings.
6. Health and Safety at Work Act.
7. Heating and ventilation.
8. Planning permission.
9. Security.
10. Structural engineering (structures, suspensions, fixings, etc.).
11. Use of hazardous materials.

Aspects of exhibitions which may present particular hazards to visitors include:

1. Accessible electrics and trailing wires.
2. Dark areas.
3. Doors and narrow passageways.
4. Large areas of clear glass into which people might walk.
5. Low barriers over which people might trip.
6. Over polished and slippery floors (especially when wet).
7. Projections and sharp corners.
8. Structures which are poorly secured and which may topple over if leant against.
9. Stands with protruding feet.
10. Uneven floors/loose carpet edgings.
11. Unexpected changes of level and steps.

The designing of exhibition environments to which the public have access must take into account the fact that unless they are particularly well supervised a few visitors will behave in a way not expected or intended. Children *will* climb, given the least encouragement. Weary adults *will* sit on anything vaguely flat 0.5m or less from the floor. And both children and adults may also eat and drink whilst doing these things. Additionally, many visitors of all ages are given to be light-fingered, and will touch and tug at any tempting element. For all these reasons, a wide safety margin needs to be given.

Unwanted occurrences in exhibitions can be reduced and/or their effects minimized if:

1. No eating or drinking is allowed.
2. No smoking is allowed.
3. Only limited numbers of visitors are admitted.
4. The exhibition is designed to be free of hazards and consciously attempts to meet the needs of all visitor groups, including the handicapped.
5. There is an adequate public address system.
6. There are adequate resources (first aid, etc.) to cope with an emergency.
7. Visitors are not allowed to carry large bags, umbrellas, etc.
8. Visitors are adequately supervised.

Exhibition security

Museum exhibition designers are faced with something of a dilemma—how to make objects as visible and as accessible to the public as possible whilst, at the same time, keeping them secure. Museum objects are, by definition, valuable. Some are overtly so, being celebrated, rare, beautiful or made of precious materials. For others, their value is perhaps less obvious to the layman, and lies in their uniqueness and the fact that they cannot be replaced and, of course, in the information they hold.

Working with objects of such value places a considerable responsibility on those concerned, and emphasizes the need to work to established codes of practice and seek the advice of specialists on matters which fall outside accepted areas of expertise. All museums have their own security procedures and these need to be adhered to strictly in respect of exhibitions. For example, when it is necessary to move objects from one area of the museum to another the correct procedures will need to be observed and the necessary documenting, checking and receipting of material undertaken. For most museum staff an awareness of security becomes something like second nature.

In terms of an exhibition, security arrangements should not be something applied after the exhibition opens, but should form a part of the initial exhibition brief and be developed like any other part of the design. For most objects the first line of security is the showcase, and this emphasizes the need for the designer to know what security is required at an early stage, in order that he/she may design a suitably protective enclosure. The difficulty is that, while it is relatively easy to make a secure case, to do so *and* enable it to be easily opened for the curator to gain access can be problematic. There are, of course, a wide range of local security devices available, from locks to alarms, and a museum needs to formulate a policy about what systems it is to employ.

For uncased objects on open display, security is no lesser problem. If touching is not to be permitted, then some form of barrier needs to be devised. The level of security required will determine the type of barrier selected, and whether it provides physical protection or simply acts as a psychological deterrent. If the former, then it must obviously be fairly substantial to be effective, and be designed to fit in with the design of the exhibition environment, possibly incorporating quantities of glass to become an 'open' showcase. If the deterrent is to be psychological, little more than a change of floor level or surface may suffice. Thus the provision of a low plinth could be appropriate, but it might simply provide a convenient sitting place for a school party to consume sandwiches, depending on the museum's audience and its regulations. Both systems may usefully incorporate graphics panels which can also serve to delineate a space and suggest the point where visitors should stop and consider both caption and object.

The decision to place an object on completely open and accessible display should come only after careful assessment of the security risks involved. Any part of an object which may easily be detached or unscrewed is likely to disappear, and will range from the last few vertebrae in a dinosaur's skeleton to the wheel nuts on a vintage car.

The use of restrictive labels is commonplace, so much so that it has become something of a museum cliché. Nevertheless, if they are not applied the visitor is apt to assume that, for example, objects *may* be touched. Thus some form of instruction is probably required, but care should be exercised lest it be too negative in its tone and effect.

In addition to all this, a surveillance system utilizing video or closed-circuit television may be employed, both to act as a deterrent and as a functional part of the system. Surveillance is an important aspect of security, and electronic systems can be very cost-effective. Ideally, however, they should be used in conjunction with security personnel who can add another dimension to their role. In addition to being a visible deterrent and surveillance unit, they can also help, advise and assist the visitor. The role of a museum warder, if it is to be achieved successfully, requires a subtle mix of authoritarianism and public relations skills, and certainly requires the staff concerned to be well informed about the museum's public exhibition galleries and services. In the past the public have often felt unhappy about the presence of too many uniformed 'guards'. Some museums have overcome the problem by the introduction of staff dressed in a more casual manner, to get away from the stereotype dark uniform. The introduction of more female staff in this role has created something of an 'air hostess' type of image which many visitors seem to appreciate. The visible emphasis should be on the provision of friendly, approachable assistance and information, and the primary role of security should be underplayed. By careful design, and by the provision of adequate security systems, the likelihood of theft, vandalism and accidents should be much reduced. However, preventing the most determined attacks on objects is virtually impossible. History tells of some notable disasters, from the smashing of the Portland Vase to the attacks on works by painters as different as Leonardo da Vinci and Salvador Dali.

10. Exhibition elements

The museum showcase

A necessary component of most museum exhibitions which display relatively small objects is the showcase. It has its origins in the early cabinets of curiosities and in the reliquaries which contained religious

evolved and developed in line with domestic furniture, and second, and on a larger scale, in both private and public museums, where its design has been influenced by the furniture of the day and by its architectural setting. Fortunately, the material on which the successful showcase is so dependent—glass—became available in pieces of large size and good quality in the latter part of the nineteenth century, just at the time when there was considerable expansion and development of the public museum. Innovations in science, technology and materials have continued to influence and benefit showcase design. Among the more important developments have been the advent of electric lighting and its incorporation within showcases, acrylic sheeting and 'invisible' glass cements, and the fabrication of light, strong, slim-line metal sections to form the structural elements.

To many visitors showcases are an irritant, creating a physical and psychological barrier between viewer and object, and filling a gallery with monotonous rectilinear forms. However, showcases fulfil a number of important functions. These can be summarized as follows:

1. To protect objects from theft and damage.
2. To provide a micro-climate in which constant levels of temperature, relative humidity and light can be maintained to protect objects from ultra-violet light, pollutants, dust, insects, etc.
3. To provide a 'setting' in which objects can be seen.
4. To support objects safely and position them in a way in which they may be viewed conveniently.
5. To act as a design element which will bridge the gap in scale between a very small object, say, the size of a coin, a person, and a room with a ceiling height of perhaps several metres.
6. To act as visual and physical components within a gallery, almost as 3D sculpture or furnishings within a room, having the capacity to interest and attract the visitor.
7. To be used as an element to assist in establishing a circulation pattern within a gallery.

In addition to the above, showcases must be designed in such a way that:

122

1. They are normally level, completely stable and do not vibrate.
2. They are adequately secure and incorporate any devices such as locks or alarms as are deemed necessary.
3. They are accessible when necessary, and permit objects to be placed within and removed both easily and safely, subject to the security precautions.
4. They are made of materials which do not directly or indirectly have a detrimental effect on any objects which may be displayed within.
5. They maintain good light levels.
6. They take into account both the nature of the object to be displayed—its shape, material, colour and the other characteristics to be observed—and the nature of the viewer, his/her physical characteristics and eye level, and ensure that the object is seen easily and comfortably.
7. The materials used and method of construction are suitable for the intended life of the case.
8. They are safe, without sharp corners or dangerous protrusions and capable of withstanding normal wear and tear from sometimes over-enthusiastic visitors.
9. They permit basic maintenance (e.g. for changing light fittings or cleaning) without putting their contents at risk.

Because of their function and nature, showcases form an important element in an exhibition, not least because they are visually related to the objects and help establish the context in which they are seen. Often the exhibition designer is faced with the dilemma of either making the cases as unobtrusive as possible, with the intention of enabling the viewers to focus their full attention on the contents, or of designing a case which forms part of an overall exhibition environment and which will enhance the objects and be visually strong in its own right. Occasionally both requirements can be met in solutions which are very satisfactory, at least in visual terms.

However, cases are not without problems. For the visitor viewing an exhibition, one of the most irritating attributes of the glass fronts is their capacity to reflect light. It can be reduced or eliminated by positioning spotlights with more care, by not having cases opposite each other, by inclining the glass, or by reducing the level of ambient light, depending on the nature of the reflections. Yet another problem is making a case dustproof whilst at the same time providing suitable means of access, and sliding glass doors can be particularly difficult in this respect. Whether access is to be gained from front, side, back or top, the points of contact of the moving parts need to be detailed in such a way that an effective dust seal is produced. When the air inside a case increases in temperature as a result of the heat from the lighting, or sunshine, it expands. At night, or when the lights are switched off, the case cools, and as the air contracts it sucks dust and other pollutants into the case through any suitable aperture. To counteract this, cases should be fitted with suitably filtered 'breathers'. Alternatively, they can be slightly pressurized by a constant supply of filtered air.

A further problem is the difficulties cleaning staff have when trying to clean beneath and right up to the edge of many showcases. To avoid aggressive knocks from cleaning equipment, the bases of showcases need to be suitably designed. It should be said that the practice of combining

storage accommodation under display cases in an exhibition situation
can present difficulties, especially in terms of access and security.

It is true to say that showcases come in all shapes and sizes: spheres,
domes, cylinders and pyramids. Cases exist in most basic geometric
shapes, but, for reasons of ease of construction, the vast majority are
rectilinear in form. We must look at some of the main types, discussed in
greater detail by Hall (1987).

Many museums have *traditional showcases* constructed perhaps
between fifty and a hundred years ago. Generally they are well made and
of good quality materials. Their doors tend to be close-fitting and fairly
dustproof, and their well seasoned timber components act as balancing
factors with regard to fluctuations in relative humidity. Unfortunately,
however, their style and proportions do not always allow them to take
their place happily in a modern presentation. In these circumstances,
rather than dispense with a functional if ungainly piece of exhibition
equipment, ways may be found of masking or adapting them so they may
be successfully incorporated in a new scheme. Many a museum has
regretted the speed with which it disposed of all its early showcases.

Today there are many *display and showcase systems* on the market,
some of which have been developed for commercial shop display rather
than for museums. Where they have been designed for museums the
specification reflects the higher degrees of security and environmental
control necessary for the display of irreplaceable objects and specimens.
Many systems utilize standard-size components which may be assembled
in a variety of different ways. This gives the flexibility necessary to adjust
to different environments and provide a range of case types, often to a
modular system.

No matter which style of showcase is available, they normally come as
standard cases or *wall cases*. The free-standing case, consisting of a base
unit and glazed upper portion, is generally known as a 'standard case'.
Variations are possible, and these include enclosed or open base units and
a variety of different tops, like 'upright' (the 'standard' version), or 'desk',
with flat or angled top, with a range of access arrangements from hinged
sides or tops to those which lift off. Upright cases can, of course, be glazed
all round or have backboards provided on one or more sides. Indeed,
endless variations are possible, depending on the range of the supplier
and manufacturer.

As the name implies, wall cases are cases fixed to a wall. They use space
economically, but of course, afford only frontal viewing. Generally
restricted in depth, they are nevertheless very suited to the display of small
objects which may be seen at close quarters. Being fixed, they lack some
of the flexibility of arrangement of free-standing cases.

A further range are the *suspended cases*. Although attractive in
concept, the suspended or floating case is, in practice, very difficult to
achieve successfully. This is because of the technical difficulties of
providing a fixing which is sufficiently rigid to prevent any movement
when it lacks anchorage to the ground.

There are as many approaches to the design of the interiors of showcases as there are to the cases themselves. Some will be 'open' in concept to allow all-round viewing of the objects, whilst others will be enclosed with backings and stands. The use of shelving is very common in general terms; the aim of the designer must always be to display the objects to advantage and produce an integrated design where object, physical support/backing and graphic elements (including label) combine to form a satisfactory composition.

For the display to function effectively, the whole composition must have the capacity to attract. To do this successfully may necessitate the inclusion of objects or motifs of sufficient size to enable them to catch the eye of the visitor when he is several metres away. Once his attention has been caught, especially if this has been by some device other than the case title, there is a need to establish quickly the name of the topic displayed. The composition should lead the eye from the main objects to the title, or vice-versa, and then in a logical sequence, running through title, introduction, objects and individual labels. Arranging the elements of a display in the order in which they are to be viewed clearly makes sense, and this may need adjustment or duplication of title and introductory panels if the visitor can approach the case from more than one direction. Having attracted the visitor, the elements within the display should be of sufficient interest to hold his/her attention long enough to communicate the essence of the topic, and ideally rather more.

Various materials may be used to provide a satisfactory surface on which or against which objects may be seen. Rich velvets were popular in the late nineteenth century. In the 1950s pastel colours in flat paint were popular, to be followed by the stronger-coloured hessian and cork finishes of the 1960s. Today the choice is very wide, with fabrics and papers widely used. However, whatever materials are proposed, there is a need to be sure that they will not be harmful to the objects on display. To this end, materials should be tested by conservation staff prior to being used.

Lighting

Since exhibition is essentially a 'visual' experience, light, which is fundamental to it, must be a key factor in any scheme. As such it ranks with shape, colour, form, space and texture as one of the basic design elements. It is also one of the most complex, since it involves an understanding of perception and behavioural psychology as well as of aesthetics. Also, it is highly technical and demands not only an appreciation of the equipment and how it can be used, but also the ability to master the technical calculations involved in achieving the desired effects. Because of the complexities any exhibition designer contemplating a major scheme is well advised to obtain the assistance of a qualified lighting engineer. Considerable help is also available from the manufacturers of lighting equipment, whose technical representatives are generally very pleased to advise on the design of installations.

But lighting, in addition to facilitating vision, can also provide an aesthetic experience which can affect the visitor in a variety of ways, including the creation of different 'moods'. Lighting in an exhibition can be sombre and pensive or it can highlight objects, and bring them out of dark, mysterious voids and enable them to glow and sparkle. Alternatively, it can provide a bright, happy environment reminiscent of being out of doors on a summer's day. To this versatility can be added both colour and movement to provide the full range of effects available in the theatre. However, any scheme is generally subject to considerable constraints. Of these, the principal one as far as the objects are concerned must be the limitations imposed by the object's conservation needs. Others may include the availability of suitable equipment, the availability of sufficient electrical power, the effects on heating and ventilating systems, architectural considerations, and maintenance and the size of the exhibition lighting budget.

In addition to these considerations, a concern for creating a quality of light which is right for the objects must be fundamental to any lighting design scheme. Opinion may well differ as to what this might be. For example, in the context of a painting, is it the light by which it was created, the light in which it was intended to be viewed (and probably was for much of its existence, or until the advent of gas and electricity) or a clinical light by which it may be examined—or none of these? No doubt the exhibition brief, which provides the context in which the objects are to be seen, will indicate the approach to be taken.

The pure quality of natural daylight is something which many artificial lighting systems try to emulate and which provides a standard against which artificial light is measured. At best its quality is superb. However, for conservation reasons it is generally not advisable to use it without filters. These, fortunately, have little effect on the visual quality of the light.

One of daylight's greatest advantages is, paradoxically, also its greatest disadvantage. This is its tendency to uncontrollable and unpredictable change. From a positive viewpoint these changes are probably best appreciated when observing art objects, in particular sculpture and paintings. Three-dimensional objects, especially those incorporating low relief work, can look well in sunlight, when crisp shadows are created. Paintings, however, when they are bathed in bright natural light, can assume a glow and appear to radiate light, depending on their coloration. This exuberant mood can change rapidly, even as a cloud passes in front of the sun. Then the effect can be to create a contrasting, sombre, brooding quality . . . and so on . . . through all the subtleties of visual effect and mood which are often so difficult to accept in terms of exhibition design, for the designer tends to want objects to look at their best at all times. The best effect is probably achieved when, following a dull period, a shaft of sunlight dramatically catches and transforms an object and immediately arrests the eye of the viewer. This cannot be arranged to order, except by artificial means. And, for those few seconds when the sun breaks through, the viewer may have to endure many hours patiently waiting in overcast dullness (particularly as far as the UK is concerned).

The means of admitting and controlling daylight within a gallery are of the utmost importance to the effects which can be created in an exhibition. If it is admitted through carefully positioned roof lights and directed and/or diffused by baffles, it may well be capable, on a clear day, of illuminating a gallery with good-quality light. However, if the roof lights are poorly positioned, or if the exhibition area is reliant upon wall fenestration not designed to illuminate the room as an exhibition space, then, as the rays of the sun move round the room, quite problematic bright spots and areas of excessive darkness may be created.

As the amount of illumination provided by daylight varies, so too does the heat. This, when produced by strong sunlight shining through glass into an enclosed showcase, can be very considerable and very harmful. Therefore, even in situations which might, at first, appear to be without hazard, care must be taken to ensure that disasters do not occur. When the designer is considering the use of daylight to illuminate an exhibition, in addition to the practical consideration as to how this might be success-fully achieved, and what back-up systems might be used for evening viewing, he must think about the context in which the objects are to be presented, for it is this which, subject to conservation needs, should dictate the effects required.

There is now a very wide range of lighting equipment available to the exhibition designer. However, for normal gallery applications the most frequently specified equipment includes *fluorescent tubes*, which provide an evenly distributed, 'flat' quality of light, in a limited range of warm/cool white colours; *tungsten spotlights*, which are used to highlight large objects or create pools of light; and *low-voltage spotlights*, which are ideal to illuminate small objects with a beam of bright light. Within this basic range are numerous refinements. They include focusing and framing devices, bulbs of different colours and strengths (wattage), and an infinite selection of designs of fittings. Of these, many are adjustable and are designed to plug into track systems, whereas others are designed for use in fixed positions. Selecting, matching and combining the various types of lighting to suit the objects, their context and the environment is where the skill of the designer is required. Exactly how light is used in the context of any particular exhibition will depend essentially on the effect the designer is trying to create and the demands of the objects. Control is all-important if a balanced effect is to be achieved. Excessive reflections, especially in the glass of showcases, but also from any polished surface, including the floor, should be avoided and lights should not be positio-ned so that they shine into the eyes of visitors as they move around the exhibition. It is worth remembering here that the angle of incidence is equal to the angle of reflection, so that if it is not possible to reposition lights unwanted reflections may be removed by tilting the glass in showcases, if that is the source of the reflection. Cases placed opposite each other often benefit from this treatment, and adjusting the light level outside cases can be helpful in certain circumstances.

Gallery lighting should consist of three separate systems: house lights, for working and cleaning purposes; display lights, for when the exhibition is open to the public; and emergency lights for use should either of the other systems fail. Approval of this last set should normally be obtained from the relevant fire or safety officer.

There are, of course, as many different approaches to the design of lighting schemes as there are exhibitions, and each will depend on the effect required and what is considered best for the objects. Some objects, like pictures, generally require an even distribution of light over their surface, and in an exhibition consisting only of paintings the aim might be to achieve an evenness of lighting throughout, or simply to concentrate on illuminating the pictures. Others, particularly large, three-dimensional objects, may benefit from a more dramatic approach which can be achieved by variation in the levels of light. The more contrast, the more drama—but the more drama the more difficulty is experienced by the visitors in adjusting to the changes in level and ultimately in seeing the object. A good lighting scheme is one which is safe for the objects and visitors, which enables the objects to be seen, which contributes to the overall design of the exhibition, and which is easily and economically maintained.

Lighting schemes need to be designed with maintenance in mind. In particular, fittings should be positioned in such a way that they are easily accessible for tubes and lamps to be changed without in any way putting objects at risk. This also applies to showcases, where lamps, at least, should be located in an area which is separated from the space in which the objects are positioned for display by a physical barrier such as a rigid transparent or translucent sheet, depending on the light effect required. However, for greater safety, fittings should, if possible, be located remotely, and any likely difficulties with reflections considered and overcome at the design stage.

Colour

It is perhaps invidious to take 'colour' from its associated basic design elements of shape, form, texture and space and give it the status of an individual exhibition element. However, its significance is such that it must form an important consideration in virtually every exhibition, and therefore warrants a special, if brief, mention.

To many people the selection of colours is something which is governed largely by individual taste, and, to a certain extent, this is undoubtedly true. Some people do have a 'good eye for colours' and can select and combine them intuitively to good effect, whereas others need to refer to the many theories of colour for guidance. In fact there has been a great deal written on both the theory and the application of colour, and the interested reader is referred to this wealth of specialized literature.

In the context of exhibitions and associated graphics the task of devising colour schemes is very much an essential part of the designer's function, and should therefore be left to those trained to do it. Colour is not simply concerned with superficial visual effect. Aspects such as psychology and symbolism may also need consideration, and a knowledge of the science of colour and colour theories is necessary if true colour values are to be presented. The use of colour is also subject to the whims of fashion, as any history of interior design will demonstrate. Hence the predisposition of the Victorians to use dark, rich colours and, in the more formal displays, to show pictures against deep red backgrounds, making their gold frames appear especially rich.

It is interesting to note E.T. Hall's comments on the decoration of museums and galleries. Writing in 1912, he commented:

> As to the colour of walls, there is a great difference of opinion. Nearly all are agreed that the background for pictures should be dark. At the National Portrait Gallery in London the latest decoration to the second floor range of galleries has been black. This may be good for the pictures, but the conspicuous black remains on the retina of the eye and is obtrusive. I think it may be safely said that a background is successful in inverse proportion to its obtrusiveness.

Recent years have seen an increase in popularity of the plain white background against which to display modern works of art. Among the reasons for this are that white is not thought to interfere with the colour values in the picture, and that it reflects light around the exhibition space whilst absorbing ultra-violet radiation. It has also enjoyed great popularity in domestic interior design. However, as a background to pictures many galleries now prefer to use sensitive light greys. These reduce the contrast and glare of the hard white, whilst at the same time they maintain colour values. Not so long ago, for general display purposes, the preference was for stronger colours like orange, slate and sludge green, which in their turn had superseded the soft pastel shades of the 1950s.

When he is devising a suitable colour scheme, the designer will be concerned with a number of complex issues. Much will depend on the requirements of the exhibition brief and the nature of the exhibition. Perhaps the two most important considerations will be the objects to be displayed (especially if their colour is a significant factor), and the atmospheric qualities or 'mood' to be achieved in the exhibition environment.

The objects suggest colours in two ways. The first is by their own physical coloration, and the designer may select one or more of the colours and echo them in backgrounds and other related elements to produce a co-ordinated scheme. In doing so, he may make extensive use of shades and tints to provide a tonal range or, alternatively, contrasting colours may be chosen in order to create a more vibrant effect, although this approach needs careful handling if colour values are not to be visually distorted. A turquoise object, for example, can be made to appear very blue when displayed against a green background—or very green if displayed against blue. The second way in which objects will suggest colours is through association and symbolism. Thus nautical objects may be associated in Western cultures with navy blue, agricultural implements with earth colours, and so on. More significantly, where a colour is selected for its religious or nationalist significance, it is important that the association of object and colour is a correct one, and one which will not give offence.

Colour again makes a significant contribution to the atmosphere to be created in an exhibition. If the brief requires an intimate, relaxing and welcoming design solution, then colour psychologists recommend that such a mood can be achieved by the use of dark, warm colours, with the glow of orange, reminiscent of the fireside. Undoubtedly pools of warm light attract visitors, and darkness tends to make spaces appear small and enclosed. Contrasting with this, if a light 'open' atmosphere is required, then pale colours should be used, with an abundance of white or 'off-white'—which can create a cool environment if combined with tints of blue or similar cool colours. Pattern, too, has an effect. Small-scale patterns have a tendency to enlarge a space visually, whereas those which are large have the opposite effect.

Colours can be categorized in various ways. A popular concept is to divide them into the 'warm' or 'cool' families mentioned above. 'Warm' colours are the reds, oranges and yellows, together with those colours which combine them to a detectable degree (for example, brown, and some greens). 'Cool' colours are predominantly the blues, but can include blue-greens, blue–pinks and tints of colours formed by the addition of white. 'Neutral' colours are essentially black, the greys and white. These relate well together and generally show, without visual distortion, any other colour to advantage. 'Earth' colours are the ochres, which form a unified palette, as do 'natural' colours, which tend to be thought of as the 'earth' colours, but with the emphasis on colours associated with the harvest, e.g. straw, grain and 'natural' hessian.

Beyond this stage, definitions become more complex and differ according to theory and system, and whether they relate to coloured light or pigment. It was Sir Isaac Newton who, in 1666, discovered that white light when passed through a prism of glass could be split into seven segments of coloured light—violet, indigo, blue, green, yellow, orange and red. Since Newton's discovery two of the most widely accepted colour systems to have been put forward are those of Ostwald, who like Newton recognized seven primary colours, and Munsell, who decided on five. The three primary system is a popular one, and one which is widely recognised by designers. This relates to mixing pigments, and has red, blue and yellow as the fundamental colours (figure 10.1) from which all other colours may be obtained by mixing. When each primary is mixed with another the secondary colours are obtained. Red and blue make purple, blue and yellow make green, and yellow and red make orange. Tertiary colours are those which are made by mixing two secondaries.

When light is mixed (additive colour mixing), crimson, ultramarine and green light will produce the whole visible spectrum, with red and green, overlapping to give yellow, red and ultramarine producing

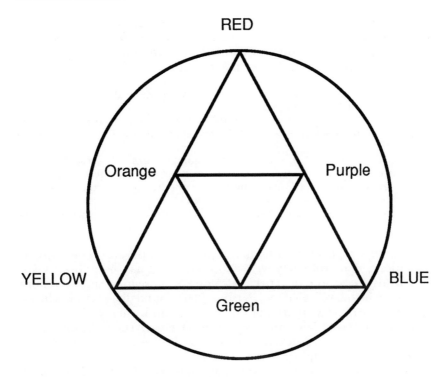

Figure 10.1   Basic colour wheel

magenta, and ultramarine and green giving blue. Where all three 'primaries' overlap, white is produced. In subtractive colour mixing, the printing inks of yellow, cyan and magenta are regarded as the primaries and are used extensively to produce most other colours. However, in psychological terms, primaries are those colours (other than black and white) which are perceived as basic, and usually red, yellow, blue and green are thought of in this way. In the analogous colour system (figure 10.1), harmonious colours are any three which are adjacent (e.g. yellow, orange and red), whereas complementary colours are any two which are opposite each other, e.g. red and green or purple and yellow. These give a clashing, vibrant effect when placed together.

Yet another factor to be considered in relation to colour is tone, that is, the lightness or darkness of any given colour. Tone is important, not only for the overall effect which it can create, but also in specific displays. It is much easier to appreciate the shape (silhouette form) of an object when it is seen against a background of a contrasting tone, either darker or lighter than the object itself. Interestingly, it is Leonardo da Vinci who has been credited with the observation that a dark object when seen against a lighter background will appear smaller than it actually is, whereas a light object will appear greater in size when seen against a background which is tonally darker.

A considerable amount of research has been undertaken on the effects which colour can have on human behaviour. Porter and Mikellides (1976) refer to some of this in *Colour for Architecture*. Among the now familiar experiments which they mention are:

1. A noise sounded louder to a listener in a white room than the same noise when heard in a violet room.
2. People in a blue room would set the thermostat four degrees higher than those in a red one—as if to attempt thermal compensation for apparent visual coolness.
3. In a situation where identical twenty-minute lectures were presented to two audiences, one in a blue theatre and one in a red one, the effect was that the 'blue' group felt rather bored, whereas, for the 'red' group, the lecture was found to be interesting, and time passed quickly.
4. A dark blue packing case seemed to feel heavier than an identical crate coloured yellow.

Clearly, this type of information can have application in museum exhibitions. Unfortunately very little research has been undertaken specifically to explore the effect of colour in museum displays. Among the work which has been done, Parsons (1965) found that although black-and-white displays were thought of as too plain by many visitors, such displays obtained high scores in terms of effectiveness. Borun (1977) thought that there is a negative correlation between popularity and the number of background colours used.

For those concerned with making accurate reference to colours in the UK, two systems are widely used. First, the British Standard system, which relates to colours of paints used in decorating, and second the Pantone system, which is used to specify colours in printing.

Exhibition graphics

In 1893 Sir Jonathan Hutchinson thought that 'The object of an Educational Museum should be to educate rather than collect,' and he outlined six features which, he thought, should characterize an educational museum. The museum in question was the Haslemere Educational Museum, the story of which was told by A.S. Edwards (1949). The features mentioned by Hutchinson, summarized later by E.W. Swanton (1903), were:

The liberal use of pictorial illustrations.
The plentiful introduction of models and busts.
Descriptive labels free from pedantry.
Inexpensive reference-books for the use of visitors.
A museum catalogue.
Free handling of inexpensive specimens.

At that time Hutchinson's thinking was quite radical. He recognized that objects alone were not enough and, that for a more complete educational experience the visitor needs aids to interpretation and devices which facilitate a fuller understanding of the objects.

Some seventy years later, it may be recalled, this issue again came to the fore when Cameron (1968) stressed the importance of the objects themselves as the museum's prime medium of communication. His view was criticized by Knez and Wright (1970), who, whilst not disputing the capacity of objects to communicate information about themselves, thought he had underestimated the contribution which interpretive aids can and do make. They commented:

> In order to bring maximum clarity to the verbal message, an exhibitor also employs such supplementary means as diagrams, maps, photographs, models, all of which are interwoven with carefully selected museum objects to provide a satisfying message. By means of design and art skills, the impact of the message—its intellectual cognition and its emotional force—is significantly enhanced . . .

Today this is an issue which is still very much under debate, for the 'heritage industry', as it has become known, and of which museums form a part, has expanded in ways hardly thought possible several years ago. Now the consideration is not using the media for educational purposes, but as entertainments in their own right; so much so, in fact, that the Disneyland concept of images of reality—the models, animations and theatrical illusions—have become a serious threat to museums, on two counts. First, they woo the visitor away from the museum and its real objects to a marketing concept of our heritage which is packaged for the entertainment industry. And second, this concept of pseudo-history may well be something of an educational disaster.

However, this only serves to underline the enormous popularity of interpretive media and therefore their considerable potential. For museums, it emphasizes the need to utilize interpretive media selectively and ensure that a satisfactory ratio of object-oriented exhibitions to media presentations is achieved.

In museums concerned with the presentation of objects as an aesthetic experience, the role of the interpretive aid has often been regarded as minimal, and the view expressed by John Walker in *Art in America* (1944), has found wide acceptance:

> a work of art is not a specimen, not primarily an historical document, but a source of pleasure, analogous to, say, a musical composition. The major purpose of the National Gallery is to allow each painting, piece of sculpture, or other object of art to communicate to the spectator, with as little interference as possible, the enjoyment it was designed to give.

In all other forms of exhibition which present objects and specimens the role of the interpretive aid is an important one, and in none more than in the didactic exhibition. In this the aids to interpretation convey the bulk of the information to be communicated to the visitor, and they should do this in a form which is attractive and can easily be understood.

There is a wide range of interpretive media but none more visual or cost-effective than exhibition graphics, and to these we must now turn. The important role of interpretive aids in providing the visitor with information about the objects displayed in exhibitions has already been stressed. Exhibition graphics include labels (to be discussed further in Chapter 11) and text panels, but also photographs, illustrations, maps and diagrams. As such they play a central role in the visual communication process.

The conditions for successful visual communication to take place have long been recognized, particularly by the advertising industry but also by educationalists. In essence, a successful communication should be designed in such a way that it:

1. Gains the attention of its intended audience.
2. Employs visual elements which relate to the experience of the receiver.
3. Arouses personality traits in the receiver.
4. Employs words and/or symbols which the audience can understand.

It may be said that these conditions reflect those of the effective exhibition, for attraction, holding power and the capacity to deliver a message or maximize the amount of learning achieved in order to bring about change are also the key factors here.

Exhibition graphics, in the form of visual aids (e.g. illustrations, photographs, maps and diagrams) are ideal media for providing answers to many of the questions which the visitor might pose (see Chapter 11). In particular they can provide contextual information about where an object was found and its natural habitat, or how it was made and how it works. Additionally, graphics can be used to draw attention to features too small to be seen easily in the actual object, and focus the attention of the viewer on a piece of decoration or, for example, an inscription on a coin.

Undoubtedly pictures provide a more direct approach to many types of communication problems, but they can engender very mixed responses in viewers. As a pure attraction factor their potential has long been recognized. As early as 1927 Percival White was writing about the investigations of Strong, who had found that, of four newspapers carrying advertisements to sell watches, those carrying illustrations were 124 per cent more effective in terms of enquiries received and 33 per cent more effective in terms of sales than those which were not illustrated. Early work of Nixon (1926), who compared large and small-sized illustrations for their ability to attract attention, demonstrated that large illustrations, not surprisingly, were more effective in gaining initial attraction (although by a modest 4 per cent). But, when measured over a period of between ten and thirty seconds, it was found that the large illustration was only 88 per cent as effective as the small ones. This may well have been because the smaller pictures demanded more concentrated viewing to appreciate their content.

These early studies led to an enormous quantity of research being undertaken, particularly by the advertising industry, in order to gauge the effectiveness of different design approaches. However, much of the work has been inconclusive, as the considerable range of colours, typefaces and designs used in the advertising and packaging industries demonstrates.

One of the most frequently used and cheapest substitutes for reality is the photograph. If any original object is not available for display, nor a replica, then a photograph is often regarded as the next best thing. There is good reason for this. Photographs have an advantage over illustrations and other graphic representations in that for the majority of visitors they represent truth, and are a faithful reproduction of how something actually appeared. No other medium can claim this, for, in the opinion of most visitors, the camera does not lie.

However, photographs do have certain limitations, and possible drawbacks, depending on the context in which they are used. For example, they can give a very false impression of scale unless a known measure such as a figure is included. Even then the perspective can be distorted to produce bizarre results. Similarly, shapes can be distorted or foreshortened to produce very misleading images. Also, they can contain more information than is needed for the purpose intended and so can prove something of a distraction, even becoming ambiguous in certain situations, for they cannot easily convey abstract information and, like objects, rely on captions to explain their meaning.

That said, the photograph is ideally suited to a number of functions. These include:

1. Providing enlarged visual information on a part of an object not easily seen—for example, the legend on a coin or a detail of ornament on a piece of jewellery, or indeed, enlarging the whole.
2. Providing information on the original context or environment of an object, particularly if it is difficult to recreate. For example, a building, an archaeological site or a wildlife habitat such as an oak wood or the Plains of the Serengeti.
3. Giving objects a human dimension by providing, for example, a photograph of the artist responsible for a painting or of a famous general. Photographic portraits establish the human interest aspect of a display.
4. Provide an opportunity to show objects in use. Examples might include farming implements such as a plough or an early scientific instrument. If the photograph is contemporary with the object, so much the better, but reconstructions to demonstrate how objects were used also have much value.

In addition to their functional qualities as elements within a display, photographs also have some very practical advantages. These include their relative cheapness and, not least, their capacity to operate on both small and very large scales. They also can be very exciting visually, with an infinite number of techniques available to the photographer in both colour and black-and-white.

Although lacking the authentic reality of the photograph, the illustration compensates for this by its flexibility. Indeed, at one extreme it can be almost indistinguishable from a photograph, with full polychromatic realism, whilst at the other it can be a brief, bold visual statement, bordering on the symbolic in its simplicity and minimalism. Nevertheless, in the mind of today's visitor it never quite acquires the credence afforded the photograph, and he is always slightly suspicious and doubting. There are possibly two main reasons for this. First, there is an awareness that the accuracy of an illustration is dependent on the skill and knowledge of the artist; and, second, it is known that the artist is working to instruction and the integrity of that instruction (admittedly not so much in a museum situation) may be doubted. For example, in the context of new architectural developments, everyone has learnt to distrust the attractive 'artist's impression' with its stylized leafy environment and blue sky; but it is accepted, like other blatant distortions of truth, and excused as what is popularly known as 'artistic licence'.

Many types of illustration are, however, taken at face value. This is particularly true of biological illustrations, where it is known that the artist has been concerned with scientific accuracy. In this field the illustration can be particularly important, for certain material cannot easily be photographed, nor may it be displayed in a representational form. For example, some plants come into this category, and in their preserved, dried state bear little resemblance to their live form. Before the advent of the photograph as a widely used method of recording, the illustration was at its height, and works by such people as Audubon, Gould and Ehret are rightly recognized for their considerable artistic as well as technical achievements.

Because it has the flexibility, illustration can do more than record the outer appearance of objects. It can show objects at various stages of development or bring together a range of subjects which might not be seen simultaneously in real life, to demonstrate, for example, concepts like an 'eco-system' in action. In this type of approach illustration can add realism. It can also go further, and combine realism with 'cut-away' views of what might be going on, say, underground. The 'cut-away' has considerable value educationally to demonstrate and explain the hidden structures and workings of things. For example, the workings of a petrol engine or of a nuclear power station can ideally be presented and explained in this way.

Yet another application of illustration is in the field of visual reconstructions, where it can establish how things once appeared. Basing his work on palaeontological, archaeological or historical evidence, and working closely with experts in these fields, the artist provides a visual reconstruction of, say, a dinosaur or a Roman fort. In this field the work of the illustrator is essential if specimens and objects are to be adequately interpreted in this way.

A particular form of illustration, generally figurative, is the cartoon. As a device it can often be used very successfully to attract the attention of visitors (particularly younger ones) and amuse them whilst attempting to communicate a significant point. This approach has been used to take the apparent 'stuffiness' out of museum presentations and demonstrate that they cater for a wide audience. However, cartoons are often associated with light-hearted topics, so it may well be that, although visitors are amused by them, they take little notice of the points they are attempting to communicate. They may smile and forget.

Like illustrations, diagrams can also be very varied in approach and application. Basically their function is to present information in the form of data, or to make explanations as effectively as possible, with an economy of visual elements, in the form of simple visual statements which can be understood easily. The approach is therefore generally schematic, with a tendency towards symbolism and even abstraction. Diagrams can be used effectively to show and explain all kinds of systems, processes and concepts, and, through their clarity of layout, make comprehension for the viewer both quick and easy. Subjects may range from the human digestive system to the schematic representation of ideas behind an exhibition; for the former the shapes used in the diagram may well be simplifications of the shapes of the organs concerned, whereas for the latter any suitable abstract shapes may be used.

Simplified representations are important to diagrams, and especially in systems such as the isotype. In this, the subject matter is represented by standard iconic signs (e.g. the simplified shape of a man or woman, or a car, house or whatever). Each of these also represents a given quantity (e.g. 1,000 men, or 100 cars) and larger quantities are shown by using multiples of the sign, i.e. 200 cars are shown by two car signs: the whole builds up to make a 'visual argument' showing comparisons and so on. Care needs to be taken, however, to explain exactly what each iconic sign means and its unit of quantity in a prominent 'key'. Other useful forms of diagrams are those which show statistics or data schematically in the form of graphs, block diagrams, 'pie charts' and similar devices. These enable the visitor to recognize progressions, percentages, proportions and other concepts instantly which, in pure mathematical forms, are often difficult to understand.

Diagramatic presentations need not, of course, be static. Animated diagrams can be achieved by the use of polarizing filters and back lighting to give the visual illusion of movement. These are ideal to show a progression through a system like, for example, the production of electricity, and can be very effective. Increasingly, however, the computer is being incorporated into exhibitions, with an infinite range of computer graphics at the designer's disposal. These can, of course, be programmed to work independently of the visitor and to provide a continuous presentation, or they can be interactive. This enables the visitor to use a programme in order to obtain information, most of which can be communicated via computer graphics, and even printed out so that the visitor may take it away!

The use of maps and charts is essential if the visitor is to be given adequate information on locations. Generally the visitor's knowledge of geography is poor, and graphic aids which improve the situation must be helpful. Ideally the maps provided should adhere to conventional practice and use recognized symbols and colours, albeit in simplified form. The information which they can convey is considerable, ranging from contours and geological features to political boundaries either now or at any time in history. However, perhaps their most widespread use in the museum is to show the former locations and distribution of the artefacts, and flora and fauna, in the collections.

Outside the displays, the map or plan is an essential orientation device. Morris and Alt (1978) undertook an interesting experiment to help design a map for a large museum. They sought to find out which of two types of map, an axonometric projection or a plan, was the most preferred and effective. The results suggested that although there was a preference for the axonometric, it was not demonstrably easier to read than the plan. They therefore recommended that a design based on a plan but incorporating some pictorial information was probably the best solution.

Models

Since exhibition is a three-dimensional medium, in addition to the display of real objects it is also appropriate for the display of representations of objects, that is, of models. There are many occasions when their use is appropriate and educationally effective. However, there can also be drawbacks, not least the danger of losing the concept of truth which the museum has worked hard to establish. To allow the false, the phony or the imitation to dominate museum exhibitions would be for museums to abrogate their responsibilities. Furthermore, in the minds of many of the public, it might bring into doubt the authenticity of some of the genuine artefacts. Hence the need to use models purposefully, honestly and with restraint. Some of the occasions when there could be good reason to use models are:

1. *The enlargement of objects* otherwise too small or too difficult to see. This need occurs particularly frequently in the showing of biological material such as micro-organisms. It has a long tradition, and during the nineteenth century some very fine models were produced in wax and glass. Popular subjects included single-cell organisms and insects.
2. *The reduction of objects* too large to be seen conveniently. Virtually anything larger than the display space available may come into this category— from human figures to buildings, and from towns to mountain ranges. This approach can also be useful for comparative purposes when the three-dimensional form is particularly important to show certain characteristics of the subject concerned: for example, to show the different species of whales, or different types of vehicles.
3. *To represent objects* otherwise too difficult to show in their natural state. This category applies particularly to natural history material, where many of the preservation techniques used have severe limitations as far as display is concerned, and the use of modelling techniques to represent such material is therefore widespread. For the scientists, preserving an entire organism in alcohol or drying and pressing a botanical specimen may be adequate for their needs, but since the appearance of this type of material is so different from that

which it enjoyed in life, there is a need to show this. The distorted and faded bottled specimens may have an historical justification for inclusion in an exhibition, but if the aim is to create a resemblance of reality a model is the ideal medium.

Taxidermy is a modelling technique which has been developed over many centuries and is particularly successful for birds and mammals, where the original skin is preserved and incorporated in the finished model. At its height it has attained the status of a minor art form, and certainly enjoyed considerable popularity in the late Victorian period, when a glass-domed animal group became a feature of many domestic interiors. For small birds, reptiles and mammals, freeze-drying has superseded taxidermy as a method of preservation, but it is still very dependent upon the skill of the modeller in setting up and positioning the specimen prior to processing. Casting is another long established method which, when combined with modern techniques such as vacuum forming, can produce spectacular results, particularly with material such as fishes. However, there are still occasions when, for the most part, pure modelling and sculpting skills are required to make a representation of reality, even if they are used in conjunction with casting techniques such as the use of flexible moulds. Producing models of human figures is a frequent need, whilst on a larger scale the blue whale in the Natural History Museum, London, represents a spectacular (and very popular) one-off production.

In addition to natural history specimens, there may well be a need to recreate whole environments to provide contexts. The habitats included in diorama presentations are a good example of these, and, on a larger scale, the false 'stone' edifice in the 'Story of the Earth' exhibition in the Geological Museum, London, is a dramatic example. Outside natural history, there are the 'film set'-type environments which may involve the recreation of a room setting, a house, or even a street or village. Unless it is done with care, sensitivity and exactness, as in the exhibitions at the Museum of Mankind, London, where 'The Nomad and the City' was a spectacular success, there can be problems, in which a confusing mix of Hollywood and Disneyland undermines any intention to communicate reality and truth. This lack of authenticity can create a false, often idealized, impression which is over-sentimental, sanitized and dramatic to the point of fantasy.

However, when done well, authentic reconstructions *are* an important educational tool, and do provide the visitor with an insight into the past. Only through this type of work is it possible to appreciate, for example, what megalosaurus or stegosaurus may have looked like (evidence of surface coloration permitting) and fully appreciate their scale in relation to man. Similarly, this technique can be used to show the interior of a Roman villa or any chosen aspect of life in the past. However, the earlier comments regarding the 'film set' approach can also apply here, and fantasy and reality risk being confused. When theatre takes over the result is the type of presentation to be seen at the Jorvik Centre in York. Here, added to the static models, are the sounds and smells of the past. Despite every attempt to ensure accuracy in the individual models, the total experience of exploring the Viking village—knowing it to be false—is fantastic rather realistic.

There are many occasions when in both systematic and thematic exhibitions, it is necessary to make reference to 'key' or celebrated examples of the subject featured. These items may well be in major museums elsewhere in the world, or in their original locations. To include the items in an exhibition a model may be both necessary and justified. Indeed, the Victoria and Albert Museum has in its Casts Gallery an entire exhibition devoted to such celebrated replicas—Michangelo's *David* and the base of the Trajan column among them. Such plaster casts as these, of course, have been widely reproduced and circulated as extension material, and were used in the teaching of drawing and lettering in art colleges throughout the country around the turn of the century.

This need to replicate material has also been experienced by many regional museums as a result of a policy which has meant that much of the important archaeological material found within a region has gone to a national collection.

There may also be occasions, in any museum, when it is felt that objects in its custody are either too rare or too valuable to be safely displayed and are therefore represented by models. In these instances the use of replicas may well be justified, but the public will no doubt be disappointed to know that they are not contemplating the real thing. For many years visitors to the Natural History Museum, London, were shown a cast of the celebrated archaeoptrix, largely unaware that it was not the real specimen. Similarly electrotypes of precious coins and jewels have been displayed without identifying them clearly as such. The modern techniques of casting and electrotyping, and the skill of the model-makers, mean that the quality of much replicated material is extremely high, and visibly indistinguishable from the original, making such confusion possible. This economy of truth is unworthy of museums. Where a replica is used the fact should be stated.

The technique of reconstruction which incorporates extant elements to recreate the form of the whole is important in relation to archaeological material, where, for example, a shard could be used as the basis of a reconstruction of the entire pot. It is also widely used for palaeonto-logical specimens, where, for example, a few fossilized bones may be located within a reconstructed skeleton. This technique is therefore educationally important in providing information on the original location and context of the objects. It can also work on a reduced scale, where, for example, a model building might be used to locate an architectural fragment or show the original location of a piece of sculpture.

The model is an ideal medium for demonstrating important stages in the development of anything from the transition of an egg to a frog, the evolution of the horse or motor car, or the building of a medieval cathedral. It is also a good device for showing before-and-after sequences. For many years a popular exhibition at the Natural History Museum in London showed the various stages involved in the taxidermy process. Other good examples are to be found in the Science Museum and the Victoria and Albert Museum in exhibits which deal with production techniques.

The examples mentioned above have utilized the model as a device to replicate reality, albeit at different scales. Models need not be used solely in this way, for the creative use of the model as a didactic medium has enormous potential. By virtue of the third dimension, it can present and interpret ideas in a way not possible in any other medium. There are many examples of its use in this way, from the schematic representation of the 'zip' characteristics of DNA molecules to the humorous interpretation of a cow as a milk-producing machine which was once featured in a temporary exhibition at the Science Museum, London. Introducing humour to models can be very successful and the use of cartoon characters should not be precluded. Add to this animation and the model immediately becomes an attraction in its own right, as exemplified by the work of Rowland Emmett and his fantastic machines, which owed something perhaps to that earlier exponent, Heath Robinson.

To satisfy the different needs to which models are put, various types of models have evolved. Probably the most frequently used is the reduced or enlarged scale model, which should always have its scale stated. When movement is introduced, the model is described as 'animated' or 'dynamic', and it is this type of model which is so successful in attracting visitor attention. The current popularity of exhibitions of full-size dinosaurs is a good example of this. The traditional favourite, however, is the visitor-operated working model from which the Science Museum in London gained much popularity. Although now regarded as having limited educational value and, sadly, disappearing from exhibitions, such models nevertheless attracted large numbers of eager visitors. Some of them were sectioned or 'cut-away' models, designed to enable the operator to see what was happening inside the outer casing. These were a great help to anyone seeking to understand such things as the workings of a clutch, gears or a crankshaft.

Perhaps the other major model type is the diorama, designed to provide vision 'in the round' and create the illusion of a realistic view, built either full-scale (as in many animal habitat groups) or to a reduced scale, affording a type of 'peep show'. This too has enjoyed considerable popularity over the years and is now experiencing something of a comeback as far as natural history material is concerned, as interest focuses on habitat and ecological issues.

Supplementary exhibition media

The medium of exhibition is one which embraces many other media and uses them to enhance the visitor's experience. Of these, audio-visual techniques are becoming increasingly important in contemporary exhibitions. There are three main reasons. First, audio-visual presentations provide an ideal medium through which the exhibition developers can provide contextual information on the objects and extend their coverage of a subject through visual images and sound effects. Second, many visitors now expect and positively look forward to experiencing some sort of audio-visual presentation. And third, technological advances have created a medium which is more accomplished, more reliable and in many instances more cost-effective than the early mechanical presentations, which often owed more to the amateur world of cine-films and holiday slides than to the sophisticated worlds of television and cinema.

However, in the museum situation one of the biggest problems is always that of balance, and this issue has been much debated. One side expresses apprehension at the growing use of audio-visuals and interpretive aids, whereas the other holds the opposite view, regarding audio-visual as the appropriate medium of the television age. In truth, audio-visual as a medium has many unique qualities, some very positive and attractive, some which are very limiting, depending on the purpose to which the medium is to be put. In a museum the purpose is to support, amplify and interpret the *objects*. In this, audio-visuals fulfil a legitimate and necessary role. However, the position becomes less defensible when, in a museum exhibition context, the medium takes over from the objects and becomes entertainment for its own sake.

The strengths of audio-visual presentations are many. They may be simply listed as:

1. The visual power of large-scale images which may be in colour and which can combine animation and sound to provide an exciting and attractive experience.
2. Technology which now facilitates automatic and programmed presentations.
3. Programmes which can be duplicated easily and cheaply.
4. Programmes which can be repeated easily or run continuously.
5. The opportunity to incorporate existing photogaphs and imagery.
6. The ability to communicate with one or many visitors at one showing and the possibility of interactive presentations.
7. The versatility to combine many different graphic and sound techniques.

Possible disadvantages of the medium include:

1. Relatively high production costs.
2. Comparatively high cost of the hardware.
3. The need for adequate maintenance.
4. The need of space in an exhibition for a 'viewing area'.
5. Its ephemeral nature, which denies the visitor the opportunity to ponder, recapitulate or select from a public presentation.
6. The problem of containing the sound and preventing it from becoming a distraction to other visitors.

Used well, the medium can add enormously to an exhibition. For example, in natural history exhibitions it can show animals living in their natural habitats in a way no conventional museum display can recreate. This ability to show places, scenes and happenings enhances the authentic dimension of an exhibition, and few subjects would not benefit from such treatment, assuming it to be compatible with the aims and objectives of the exhibition. Indeed, for some subjects, like musical instruments or birds, a complete understanding could not be achieved without the use of sound. A particular strength of audio-visual as a medium is its ability to show people doing things and hear them talking about it. This can, in effect, bring people to life, and films of scientists, naturalists or artists at work can greatly assist in the interpretation of otherwise inanimate objects.

Like any other exhibition medium, audio-visual programmes need to be designed and produced in response to a brief which has clearly defined aims and objectives. Then the normal design/problem-solving methodology should be employed in answering the brief. Much will depend on the length of time selected for a presentation. If it is to be made in a 'theatre-like' environment, where the audience is seated (which is ideal), it may run successfully from anything between four and twenty minutes. The length of time necessary to view the programme should be stated. Ten minutes is probably the optimum time. After this there may well be a significant loss of viewers, depending on the subject and the nature of the audience. If, however, seating is not provided, then much shorter programmes are desirable. If the progamme breaks down, the fact needs to be communicated to visitors and back-up material provided to cover the eventuality. This is important, whether it is intended for a comparatively large audience, as a group presentation, or for individuals as a feature within a multi-media display. Where appropriate, times of showing should be given.

Various types of equipment and presentations come under the broad title of audio-visual. The medium had its origins in the single projected slide, but the linked tape-and-slide system was one of the first of the new generation of systems to benefit from sophisticated electronic technology, and is still widely used. Norgate (1973) provided a brief introduction to its use by the museum profession. However, the advances in technology in recent years have been considerable, and this type of presentation may now be controlled by a micro-computer, either as an individual unit or as a whole exhibition system.

Indeed, the micro-computer has taken its place as an exhibition feature, as well as being used extensively 'behind the scenes'. Computer-based exhibits allow for considerable interaction to take place between visitor and 'tutor', and now facilitate a question-and-answer dialogue with ease. The addition of printers means that the information can even be made instantly available for the visitor to take away. Yet another recent development which is expected to have widespread application both in industry and in education is the interactive video disc. However, developing the software is expensive and this may well limit its application in museums unless wider uses can be found for the programmes. For the larger and better resourced museums this may well mean taking advantage of the exciting opportunities offered by the field of distance learning.

Sound alone has, of course, extensive application in museum exhibitions, and specific mention needs to be made of its use in the role of exhibition guide. Technically this may be achieved in various ways, including the use of radio or cassette players to activate personal systems. However, advances in this field are rapid, with increasingly sophisticated equipment being developed at lower cost. Personal audio-guides have now become very popular with visitors, and are ideally suited to the job of supplementing the visual material in the displays (which we know visitors seldom read). They can also be easily programmed to provide commentaries in different languages, making them a useful asset in any major museum.

The standard audio-visual media of slide/tape, film, television, video or sound alone have become well established exhibition communication media. Each has its particular strengths and weaknesses and each has benefited from recent technological developments. Anyone contemplating producing a programme for presentation via one of these media would be well advised to consult some of the many specialist firms who are now active in this field, and seek their advice as to the appropriateness of the proposal, the technical implementation and the costs involved.

Although it is fashionable to think in terms of the new technology in the context of an exhibition, and absolutely right for temporary exhibitions which have an experimental remit, nevertheless many of the long-established supplementary media not only work well but are also very cost-effective. It should also be remembered that, while many are enchanted by the new technology, for many other visitors computers are seen as a gimmick to which they are not attracted, or one of which they can easily tire. These visitors look to the traditional media for the specific functions which they can perform.

Bassett (1984) provides a useful introduction to museum publications, and, of his categories, those which are of particular relevance to an exhibition are 'handlists, handbooks and catalogues for (1) permanent and (2) temporary exhibitions', and 'illustrated guides to museums and galleries'. Catalogues to permanent collections obviously form an essential source of information for scholars and are an important extension of the exhibition (or vice versa), and in concise form are more than adequate to satisfy the needs of the great majority of museum visitors.

In temporary exhibitions the catalogue, as well as meeting the needs of the visitor, is often the only permanent record of the event and, as such, is of immense value to the scholar. Because of their nature and purpose, temporary exhibitions often cover material and explore themes of an esoteric or obscure nature, not possible in permanent collections. This makes the publication of a catalogue all the more important if the research put into the production of the exhibition is not to be lost. In fact in all types of exhibitions the catalogue, or 'book of the exhibition' (to give it a name which seems to attract more sales as a long-term reference work), has an important function. This is to use the convenient format of a book, which may be read in comfort, and which is dependent on words and images to convey information, to extend and develop the substance of the exhibition.

Bassett (1984) rightly draws attention to the fact that museum catalogues, whether of collections or exhibitions, are expected to appeal to a very disparate audience. In this, of course, they are not unlike the exhibitions themselves, and the same briefing procedures should apply to the development of a catalogue as they do to an exhibition, with aims and objectives carefully considered. In some instances, of course, compromises will not be possible, and separate catalogues will be required for the specialist and enthusiast.

The guide to an exhibition or museum can take various forms, from a single sheet giving the briefest introduction and sketch map to an elaborate tome which is scarcely portable and more a catalogue than a guide. Somewhere in between is the practical guide which acts as a source of information on orientation as well as the collections, and is probably presented in such a way so as to make it an attractive keepsake. Visual appearance is obviously an important factor in terms of achieving sales. It is also worth noting that increasingly museums are seeking sponsorship for this sort of production.

Devices which have a specific educational function in relation to exhibitions must also be mentioned in this section. However, discussion of the educational philosophy and practical considerations relating to their use is outside the scope of this work and the reader is referred to Hooper-Greenhill (1990). Such items include worksheets, discovery trails and gallery activites which involve visitors in doing and making things in order to develop and extend their experience of the museum exhibition.

Pacing

An important element in any exhibition is its pacing. This may be defined as 'the rate, intensity and variety of stimuli which the visitor will encounter whilst traversing an exhibition'. It is well known that repetition creates monotony and that the majority of visitors find it both boring and tiring. This exemplifies the need for pacing to provide and regulate a variety of stimuli to which the visitor will be exposed. Good pacing may be likened to a good adventure, with periods of excitement interspersed with opportunities to regain breath and composure before being motivated to explore further.

It is for the designer to ensure that, within an exhibition, good pacing assumes a high priority. Regrettably, however, this is not always done, and, through a desire for standardization or excessive orientation and explanatory material, the excitement and sense of discovery so important to many visitors can be lost. In that case, the visitor, instead of feeling that he is in control on his journey of adventure, can feel that he is simply being processed along an over-refined conveyor belt. 'Over-design' and the presentation of material in all too predictable modules can create a contemporary version of the monotony so much criticized in systematic displays produced in the early part of this century. The 'Aladdin's cave' type of presentation is just the opposite of this. Once the 'method' evolved by many small local history museums, it allowed for a wide range of material, often not unlike that included in the early cabinets of curiosity, to be displayed (and stored) in unrelated profusion. Thus in a single case might be found architectural fragments, birds, coins, ceramics, dolls, furniture, an early ice skate, items of costume, the odd letter and an Egyptian *ushabti*.

Some museums have managed to retain aspects of this type of presentation and provide visitors with the sort of experience which makes them feel that they might 'discover' something. The museums in Wells, Somerset, and Whitby, Yorkshire, have retained something of this charm. It is also to be found in country house-style presentations, where objects are displayed in domestic room settings; some of the best of these are in the Bowes Museum, County Durham. If elements of this 'discovery' quality can be incorporated into the pacing programme the visitor's sense of anticipation and excitement can be retained.

Pacing should be concerned with individual exhibitions and with the museum as a whole. It should also be considered in relation to any itineraries or routes which may be devised for the visitor and communicated in leaflets and guidebooks. Some of the devices which the designer may employ include:

1. *Light*, contrasting areas of darkness and brightness; pools of light; daylight qualities. Animated and static lighting.
2. *Colour*, ranging from light tones to dark and from neutral colours to rich, saturated and bright hues.
3. *Texture*, contrasting smooth and rough; hard and soft.
4. *Scale*, from minute to monumental.
5. *Space*, contrasting open, free spaces with the enclosed and intimate. Transitional and static, busy and relaxing.
6. *Shape*, ranging from angular and hard to curvaceous, soft and flowing.
7. *Intensity*, dense clustering of elements or sparse 'less is more' presentations. Important objects shown in isolation as focal points.
8. *Arrangement*, symmetrical or asymmetrical—formal or informal.
9. *Movement*, dynamic or static; active or passive.
10. *Temperature*, contrasting warm with cool.

It is for the designer to use these devices and apply them whilst designing an exhibition to ensure that it is successful. Too much variety may be as bad as too little. Good pacing is about striking the right balance of stimuli to provide the visitor with a memorable, stimulating experience from which he emerges satisfied rather than exhausted.

11. About objects

Introduction

Objects are what museum exhibitions are about; objects which, for one reason or another, are significant examples of the natural or man-made world. They should be carefully selected for display with a specific purpose in mind, and this is a part of how they are treated in the context of communicating with the visitor. The most likely reasons for selecting an object for exhibition are that, in the opinion of the curator, the object is intrinsically of interest, or information about it is considered of value to the visitor, or the object has a contribution to make to a more general story which the visitor is to be told.

The type of treatment afforded the communication may similarly fall into three categories. At simplest, an object may merely be identified; second, and more normally, information is provided about the object and, third, an object may be interpreted.

While it is sometimes convenient to discuss objects as if they exist in virtual isolation, in practice, of course, they do not, and the context in which an object is seen is of significance to the message which is communicated. The museum is, after all, a very artificial environment where virtually none of the objects which it contains truly belongs; they have been gathered together and placed there for the benefit of the scholar, collector and visitor, and to afford them protection (and/or possibly to exploit them commercially).

Recognizing the incongruity of the situation, many museums try to isolate an object in both visual and contextual terms by placing it in a neutral environment. Here, it may be seen for what it is, but also, perhaps, for what it is not, that is, as an art object. Once the most humble of utilitarian objects is afforded the treatment of being framed within a glazed space and illuminated (as it must be if it is to be protected yet visible), it immediately takes on the preciousness of an art object and the public may find it difficult to see it in any other way.

An alternative to isolating an object is to seek to recreate the environment from which it was taken. This might involve, in the context of a domestic item, the building of a room setting or, in the case of a natural history specimen, recreating a habitat in the form of a diorama. But isolating an object or faithfully restoring its original context are obviously extremes, and there are more subtle ways whereby contexts and environments can be suggested or represented, including the use of graphics. These should ideally enhance the capacity of the objects to

147

communicate and, as stated previously, should not compete with the object or interfere visually.

Contexts and associations are also created by the grouping of objects. These relationships can be used to show developments, make comparisons and so on, depending on the intentions of the selector. Within groups, 'norms' can be and are created through simple majorities, and objects which do not conform will be seen as exceptional (whether or not they really are). Thus, by establishing, for example, a size norm, the exceptional object can be made to appear unusually large or small, and by virtue of its apparent uniqueness, it will be the focus of the visitor's attention. Objects which are to be grouped together need to be selected and positioned with care, for the simple act of placing one object with another, or closer to one rather than another, immediately suggests some form of relationship.

The grouping of objects may occur on a variety of scales. These may range from a small display involving perhaps two or three objects to a whole gallery involving several thousand. The reasons for grouping will also be varied. The objects might be of similar type; similar material; by the same hand; by the same process of manufacture or technique; from the same location, and so on. But they need not always be groups of like. Grouping can also be undertaken to demonstrate contrasts, development and numerous other points. Whatever the reason, the point to be made should be communicated to the viewer without ambiguity, and associations and relationships made explicit, and backed up by written explanations.

Relevant to the object context is the use of 'props'. If they are used in museum exhibitions in the manner which a commercial shop window might present merchandise, the exercise needs to be undertaken with considerable caution and much care. An assessment must be made of the part these extraneous objects are likely to play in the central message to be communicated by the display, and in particular the objects, and what message the props themselves might convey.

A 'prop' may be defined as any item which is introduced to a display for the purposes of aesthetic or contextual enhancement. Confusion can occur between a prop and a display fitting. This latter may be defined as a functional support and should play no part in the communicative aspect of the display. Its purpose is to raise objects and hold them in a position where they may be seen to advantage. Should a support cease to be purely functional and take on a decorative or meaningful role in the display it becomes a prop. If a functional support in the form of a simple white cylinder, for example, is painted to resemble a drum, this applied decoration and new identity moves it from the category of a display fitting to that of a prop. Using props in museum displays for mere decoration, unless undertaken with great care, only serves to distract the attention of the viewer from the objects and create visual interference. Arguably their justifiable uses are to suggest or recreate the original context or environment of the object, or to act as an eye-catching feature which will draw people to look more closely at the display.

In a category on its own is the mannequin or dummy used for the display of costume. When it takes on human form, it comes very close to being a prop, and as such needs to be used with great care. In the display of costume it is important that the characteristics of the mannequin are appropriate to the date, ethnic origin and style of the costumes concerned. Using today's high street mannequins to display, say, eighteenth-century clothing can create an altogether misleading effect.

Related to props, in as much as they are extraneous artefacts introduced to a display to help recreate the original context, are reconstructions and the restoration work done to artefacts. Here the problem is not their incongruity—for this should not occur—it is that by virtue of their relevance they may be mistaken for what they are not, that is, the real objects, or parts of them. Thus such items as replacement axe shafts or the replacement parts of a pot generally need to be seen as such and should not attempt to deceive the visitor into thinking they are original. That said, sensitive and sympathetic restoration is generally more acceptable to look at than examples which make maximum distinction between the original and the replacement, unless undertaken in an exceptional way. The ethics of restoration are a much debated topic, and each artefact and display requires individual assessment.

Object identity

It is frustrating for the visitor if objects are placed on display and are not identified. Arguably all objects exhibited in a museum should be afforded this treatment, even if the prime purpose of the exhibit does not require it. For example, when objects are used simply as decoration or as comparative examples, the aim of the exhibit may not necessitate information to be provided about them. But while, in this situation, information may be a confusing irrelevance, identification of the objects is not. Indeed, this basic provision is arguably obligatory in any situation in an institution which has as one of its main aims the communication of information about its collections. Having invited visitors to take an interest in certain objects by exhibiting them, it should at least reward their curiosity and attention by saying what the objects are.

Quite apart from the use of objects for decoration or for comparative purposes, there is a more significant occasion when it is desirable to provide minimal supporting material about an object. This is when the aim of the exhibition is that the object should 'speak for itself'. This direct communication between object and visitor is intended to enable the visitor's response to be spontaneous and without preconditioning by the museum, even though this may appear contrary to the need for 'intellectual orientation' expressed in a previous chapter: in this particular case, providing information prior to the visitor's contact with the object might well prejudice his/her response. In this situation, information can best be provided after the direct object/visitor inter-action has occurred, for then, irrespective of whether the visitor's experience with the object has resulted in either intellectual or emotional arousal, or both, there is still a need to provide at least a basic identification of what the visitor has been observing. This may serve to confirm or correct any identification which the visitor has formulated for himself, or simply to satisfy curiosity and provide an answer to the basic question 'What is it?'. This much should be readily accessible, and further information, if appropriate, could be provided more remotely.

It will be recalled that Cameron (1968) recognized that as a system of communication the museum depends on real things. Indeed, in any museum the overriding impression should be that the objects themselves have something to communicate. In order to do this, they need to be given some prominence by those arranging the exhibitions. However, the level at which objects can communicate independently of information and other interpretive aids will depend very much on the knowledge and intellect of the visitor. In this respect there is a danger that, through a lack of knowledge, the visitor will not get the most from the experience, or that he or she might make an incorrect assumption or deduction in relation to the object. (This danger is ever present, for even when information is provided, the majority of museum visitors fail to consult it.) However, any lack on the part of the visitor need not prevent an appreciation of those qualities which the object can communicate without a need for the visitor to have specific prior knowledge. These include power, beauty, craftsmanship, and so on. Indeed, any visitor blessed with sight and intelligence has the capacity to respond to an object's colour, shape, line, texture and decoration. The exact nature of the response may well be very complex, and, for the most part will be intellectual and will be based on previous knowledge and experience, however limited it may be. But on certain occasions the response may be emotional, as might be expected when viewing a work of art. Then shock, anger, disgust, sympathy, joy and excitement may well be among the emotions which are aroused in the viewer—like a direct response to a visual phenomenon.

If possible, interference with the capacity of the object to communicate in a direct manner should be minimized. Common instances when, for physical reasons, the full impact of the object is hampered include restrictions on viewing (for example, to the front elevation only, when a side view is also important); obscuring vital details of an object through overcrowding, poor supports or the introduction of badly placed labels; and inadequate or poor lighting schemes, including the distortion of an object's true colour, which occurs when coloured lights are used either deliberately to create an effect or possibly through ignorance.

To sum up, object identity is concerned with satisfying two needs: first, for the object to be as visible as possible and, second, for sufficient information to be provided which will enable the visitor to identify the object, and answer the basic question, 'What is it?'.

Information about an object

As has been stated, the most likely reasons for displaying an object are that it is interesting, that information about it will benefit the visitor or that it forms part of a larger story which is to be told. In all these instances the information which the museum provides about the object may well be crucial to the effectiveness of the display. However, the exact nature and form which the information takes will depend very much on its purpose. In respect of any object there is an enormous amount of information which can be provided, particularly when it extends to background or contextual information. But because not every known piece of information about an object will be relevant to the theme of an exhibition, and because, for practical reasons, it is neither possible nor desirable to attempt to communicate more than a few facts through a maximum of a few hundred words (depending on the medium of communication), selectivity is essential. Deciding on what information is to be communicated in any given situation is a particularly difficult and exacting task. It can be done only with a knowledge of the aims and objectives of the proposed display and its intended audience. Ideally these aims will take into account the visitors' need for information and there will be no necessity to effect a compromise between what the curator wants to say about the object and what the visitor wants to know.

Susan Pearce (1986), in her series of papers 'Thinking about things'; 'Objects, high and low', 'Objects as signs and symbols' and 'Objects in structures' (1987), provides an excellent introduction to the nature and interpretation of artefacts. That there are so many different ways in which an object might be considered makes it essential for those charged with the task of presenting and interpreting objects in the context of an exhibition to have an awareness and understanding of the possibilities. These may range from the traditional art-history approach to one which caters for today's mass-produced material culture.

Pearce provides a useful model for artefact studies on which figure 11.1 is based. This illustrates the areas which may, to a lesser or greater extent, be explored in the context of providing an interpretation of an object.

Irrespective of what orientation material has been made available to the visitor before he or she confronts an object, the full appreciation of it *starts* with an observation of it, and an assessment of its visual appearance. From this the visitor may progress to contexts and thence to more abstract concepts. Below is a list of questions which the interested visitor might reasonably want answered when he/she confronts an unfamiliar object.

   1. What is it?
   2. When was it made?
   3. From what material/s is it made?
   4. Who made it?
   5. How was it made?
   6. Where was it made?

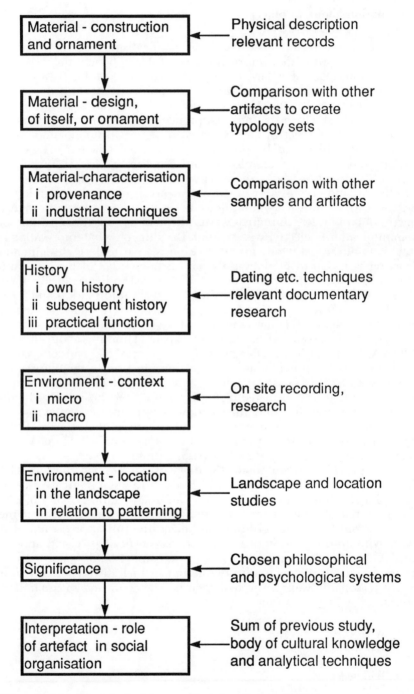

Figure 11.1   Model of object study (after Pearce 1986a)

7. What is its function or purpose?
8. What is its significance?
9. What are its statistics (i.e. size, weight, etc.)?
10. What are its stylistic features?
11. What are its iconographic features?
12. What was the historical, social and economic context of the object?
13. What has been its subsequent history?
14. How does it compare with similar contemporary examples?
15. How does it compare with earlier/later examples?

And, although the museum, as a matter of policy, is unlikely to provide the answer:

16. How much is it worth in monetary terms?

Questions asked about natural history specimens will clearly differ from those asked about man-made objects. In the case of these specimens answers to the following might be sought:

1. What is it? (Common name—and, for the sake of specialists from home and abroad, Latin name.)
2. What is its family, group or type?
3. Where does it live? (Habitat and location.)
4. What does it eat?
5. What are its statistics? (Size, weight, longevity, etc.)
6. What is its life pattern?
7. How does it differ from its opposite sex; older/younger examples; in seasonal appearance, etc.?
8. What is particularly significant about it? (Rarity, etc., or history of specific specimen.)

The lists are not exhaustive, and more specific and relevant questions might be formulated, depending on the exact nature of the object. Whether or not an exhibition seeks to address all or some of these questions will depend on its aims and objectives and, in some instances, on its communication policy. Allowing questions to go unanswered or, indeed, directing specific questions at the public could usefully serve to encourage further investigation, provoke thought or demonstrate that the museum staff do not know all the answers. But over-selectivity and a paucity of information can be a hindrance; a minimum, consistent with the moral obligation of the museum to identify what it displays, is required. In the case of an artefact, this might be to provide answers to questions 1–6 and, for natural history specimens, answers to questions 1–3. Information of this type, which is little more than basic identification, should be placed close to the object, and ideally in a position which makes it possible for it to be seen at the same time as the object, and without any movement on the part of the visitor other than his/her eyes. Normally, however, the information provided in the exhibition would be more extensive and take the form of an extended label, a text panel or an audio commentary. The greater the amount of information given (provided it is consistent with the aims and objectives of the exhibition) the more it should stimulate and satisfy the interest of the audience. However, much will depend on three things: interest value (i.e. the contents); how it is communicated (i.e. style and language) and, lastly, presentation (i.e. design). These aspects are discussed in more detail in the following section, on labels.

Where there is a need to provide more information than this, or it is felt that information which is portable and/or may be retained by the visitor is desirable, use can be made of leaflets and catalogues. These have the advantage of supplementing information given in the exhibition and serving as a permanent source of reference when the visitor gets home. However, some museums and a greater number of art galleries demonstrate a certain reluctance to provide even this minimum information when they have a catalogue for sale. Where nothing more than a reference number is given in respect of a displayed object, the practice is reprehensible. However, for practical, aesthetic and commercial reasons, providing supplementary information in this way is to be encouraged.

Providing information so that it can be understood by non-English-speaking visitors as well as those who speak English is becoming of increasing importance. In museum exhibitions in the UK the English language is used almost exclusively for all museum labels. Exceptionally a few museums have provided information in foreign language where a high immigrant population has justified it. Museums such as Bradford and Leicester are to be commended for this. However, only too rarely have museums provided labels in a foreign language for the benefit of the non-English-speaking visitor. At a time when international travel has become commonplace, when the European free market of 1992 is almost upon us, the Channel tunnel is fast becoming a reality and tourism is a major industry, there is an urgent need for a reassessment of the situation. Certainly those museums which attract substantial numbers of overseas visitors should do more than just provided a brief guide in French, German or Spanish. In the UK the major and specialist museums should prepare translations of the labels and text panels of major exhibitions, case by case. These translations should be available for loan or sale to non-English-speaking visitors. Recommended languages would include Arabic, French, German, Japanese, Russian and Spanish. Another group for whom special labels are required, but are seldom provided, is the blind. In situations where exhibits can be appreciated by the sightless or partially sighted, labels in Braille should be provided.

Interpretation of objects

The word 'interpretation' suggests an unfamiliar language in which meaning needs to be translated and expounded for those who are ignorant of its signs and symbols. So it is with objects, which also need to have their 'secrets' explained. Dana (1927), it will be recalled, spoke of objects being 'silent', and the need for them 'to tell about themselves, their origin, purpose, their relative positions in the development of their kind and countless other details through labels, guides and catalogues'. Interpretation, therefore, needs to go beyond mere identification.

The concept of interpretation in relation to museum objects gained popularity during the late 1950s and early 1960s and owed much to work being undertaken on heritage interpretation in the United States. At the time, Tilden (1957), writing on *Interpreting our Heritage*, gave this definition: 'An educational activity which aims to reveal meanings and relationships through the use of original objects, by firsthand experience, and by illustrative media, rather than simply to communicate factual information.'

Tilden also listed six principles:

1. Any interpretation that does not somehow relate to what is being displayed or described to something within the personality or experience of the visitor will be sterile.
2. Information, as such, is not interpretation. Interpretation is revelation based upon information. But they are entirely different things. However, all interpretation includes information.
3. Interpretation is an art, which combines many arts, whether the materials presented are scientific, historical or architectural. Any art is in some degrees teachable.
4. The chief aim of interpretation is not instruction, but provocation.
5. Interpretation should aim to present a whole rather than a part, and must address itself to the whole man rather than any phase.
6. Interpretation addressed to children (say, up to the age of twelve) should not be a dilution of the presentation to adults, but should follow a fundamentally different approach. To be at its best it will require a separate progamme.

The desirability of establishing, on a personal level, a communication link between the visitor and what he/she is observing is, of course, well known in commercial advertising, and is recognized for its ability to produce successful results. When the viewer relates to things personally, the interest level is higher than if this were not the case. Also, personal experience or involvement provides a baseline of knowledge from which it is possible to progress easily (in the manner of the sound educational principle) from the known to the unknown.

Interpretation is not limited to educational instruction. It may be used to communicate to the viewer ideas and concepts designed to provoke. This is consistent with the fundamental purpose of exhibitions, which is to bring about change, and provocation is a good way to achieve it. Changes in the level of interest of the viewers, changes in attitude, and changes aimed at getting people to stop doing something they shouldn't or to start doing something they should can all come about through interpretation. Indeed, attitudinal change is more likely to be brought about through interpretive displays than through those which merely provide identification of objects or basic factual information. To provoke thought *and* action, consistent with the aims and objectives of an exhibition, must be the ideal to which all interpretive displays aspire.

Since interpretation goes beyond the mere provision of facts and information and *interprets* them in relation to the objects, it can be subjective and express personal views, opinions and assessments, hence its ability to provoke. This is both its strength and its weakness: strength, because it frees the writer to give his/her assessments and evaluations; weakness, because as an opinion it is challengeable. For these reasons, ethics and professionalism are issues which may need to be discussed in relation to the approach adopted in an interpretive scheme, particularly if it is political or controversial. Undoubtedly, for the visitor, having the implications of factual information explained provides a more interesting and stimulating exhibition experience. However, it is incumbent upon the museum to ensure the credibility of the interpretation and uphold the museum's professional standards of scholarship.

Interpretation can be effected through an appropriate labelling system. However, by far the most effective medium of interpretation is the human interpreter. Little can better the ability of a good communicator who is knowledgeable and enthusiastic to make a subject interesting and exciting for his/her audience, particularly as he/she is ideally placed to adjust to the levels of knowledge and specific interests of individual members of the audience. Since it is not possible to have enthusiastic experts on hand to act as interpreters for every group of visitors, an acceptable alternative can be a good audio guide. This has the added advantage of being capable of delivery in many languages, but needs to work in conjunction with a labelling system, rather than as an alternative.

Labels

Traditionally the label has been the main medium used in the museum exhibition to communicate information about an object. It has its origins in the handwritten identification slips of curators and arguably, in the early years, was formulated more to serve their needs than those of the visitor. This practice has been hard to change, despite much having been written about the subject. Among the first to write, and probably the most quoted, was G. Brown Goode (1891), assistant secretary of the Smithsonian Institution and in charge of the United States national museum. He wrote, 'An efficient educational museum may be described as a collection of instructive labels, each illustrated by a well-selected specimen'. Goode went on to qualify this statement, noting that the merit of a label 'depends much more on what you leave out than on what you put in' and could, by virtue of poor presentation, be rendered valueless. He was among the first to acknowledge the problems inherent in writing a label. In 1895 he declared, 'the preparation of labels is one of the most difficult tasks of the museum man'. This view was echoed by Dana (1927) when he advocated their use to overcome his view that objects are silent. 'Labels,' he said, 'can be written to attractive and useful ends only by students of the art of presentation . . . Experts may give facts, but the expert is rarely found who can so present the facts that the reader is moved to an interest and appreciation by them.'

The task of writing the label has traditionally been undertaken by the curator. However, unless he/she is an expert communicator in this medium, it should, as Dana implies, be undertaken by a specialist, a writer or an editor. This has now been recognized by many of the major national museums in the UK, including the British Museum and the Natural History Museum. However, appointments at these museums were made some twenty years or so after the Smithsonian Institution conceived the idea, in 1957, of improving its labels by obtaining the services of a professional writer and appointed George Weiner to the post of Supervisory Exhibits Editor. The use of specialists is also common practice within most design consultancies, and reflects the model of copywriters working with designers in advertising agencies. In those consultancies which undertake museum projects there is a recognition of the need to have an integrated approach to communication, with objects, graphics and text each contributing to the overall message. However, irrespective of whether it is the curator or an editor who actually writes the labels, there are three distinct groups of museum professionals who have an interst in them, as well as the public for whom they are intended: curators, educationalists and designers, all of whom should be present in the exhibition development team.

The curator has responsibility for the academic standards within his/ her department. As the expert in the field he/she has certain professional standards of scholarship to develop and uphold. In the past this has resulted in labels which have been written more as expressions of scholarship, aimed to impress fellow academics, than to communicate information to a largely non-expert public. Still today, to allow a label to contain inaccurate, misleading or inadequate information is seen as a reflection on the professional standards of the curator and the institution as a whole. In this respect, it is interesting to note that George Weiner (1963) on a visit to five large cities of the eastern United States, observed a correlation between the length of labels and the size of the museum. Small museums were seen to have short labels whereas the largest museums he found to be guilty of wordiness. Hopefully, today, there is widespread recognition of the fact that sheer number of words is no indicator of scholarship or status, but meaning, accuracy and appropriateness are, and as the person charged with the responsibility within a museum for scholarship the curator is accountable for the accuracy of the factual content of labels. The overall content, style and presentation of the information, however, may best be formulated by others.

F.J. North of the National Museum of Wales, and author of *Museum Labels* (1957), published in the Handbooks for Curators series, was aware of the difficulties caused by the differences in the language used by curators and that of the public:

It is because the museum has to bridge the gap between expert knowledge and public comprehension that label writing becomes so important and so difficult—important because it is the link between curator and public, and difficult because it means more than translating the results of modern research from the jargon in which it is often recorded into the language of the layman.

More recently B.D. Sorsby and S.D. Horne (1980) undertook a study of the readability of museum labels. They studied a sample of seventy-three labels from seven British museums and through successive applications of the Fry test (Fry 1968; see p. 165) to the labels and to national newspapers which were indicative of the preferred reading of the museum visitors, they came to a somewhat startling and depressing conclusion: 'Our figures indicate therefore that on average about three-quarters of visitors to museums will be unable to pay attention to at least two-thirds of the labels because the vocabulary and sentence structure are too difficult.'

Other research (Robinson, 1931; Borun and Miller 1980) indicates that, irrespective of whether the visitor has a reading age commensurate with that of the labels, there is a general reluctance to pay much attention to them although, by careful design, their performance can be improved. All this needs to be seen from the visitors' point of view. For the curator, making labels attractive to the visitor to encourage his/her attention must be seen as of paramount importance. Most labels which relate to objects (as opposed to text panels) serve both visitor and curator, but all the curator really requires is a reference or code number which will identify the object in relation to more detailed information which may be held in an accession book, index or computerized information retrieval system. The type of information which it was once felt necessary to record adjacent to the object, such as date of accession, donor and details of provenance, previous collection or excavation, should not necessarily be publicly displayed, depending on the aims and objectives of the exhibition.

Educationalists form the second group to have a substantial interest in labels. Their main concern is that the label functions efficiently as an educational tool, and therefore their interest is in content as well as in the educational technology and psychology involved in communicating effectively with the visitor. In this context the label is but one part, albeit a most important part, of the museum as an educational system.

The logical progression from the general to the particular is demonstrated in figure 11.2. If it is to be effective, the visitor needs to be aware of this progression through an orientation process which identifies the various stages clearly. This approach works most easily in systematic exhibitions, but in situations where the refining of the context is not apparent the information needs to be provided or restated in the label at the vital point of contact between object and visitor.

In general terms the task of a label should be made clear by the declared aims and objectives of an exhibit as given in the brief. If the exhibit is a didactic one, and includes specific educational objectives, the role of the label will be particularly important. For the educationalist a label should

1	2	3	4	5	6
Museum Type	Gallery topic	Gallery section topic	Sub - section exhibit	Group	Item

EXAMPLE

Fine and Applied Art	Glass	European	18th Century	Drinking glasses	Air-twist stem glass

Figure 11.2 Logical progression from general to particular (*above*), with an example (*below*)

place more emphasis on explanation than simple identification or facts, and in this context the value of interpretive labels is apparent.

Educationally the label should assist the viewer to discover for him/ herself by making comparisons and giving examples, and by telling the viewer what particular characteristics to look for. Ideally the label should be paced so that it does not become boring, and in this respect the ability to organize information and the art of good writing are important. But possibly the most important function a label can perform is to help and encourage the visitor to understand and respond positively to what he has observed.

Designers are the third group of museum professionals to have an interest in labels. Uppermost in their minds should be the criteria of good design. In this context this should mean: how well do the labels meet the exhibitions aims and objectives, and in particular, how satisfactory are they in terms of function; aethetics; ease of manufacture; initial cost and maintenance; and finally, durability? The content of the label has some relevance to most of these aspects. How the text is written, and how it is subdivided, will, to a certain extent, dictate layout. This, in turn, will affect function and aesthetics, for it is difficult even for good design to overcome the problems of ill conceived text. The quality of written material as well as the layout and use of typefaces will have a direct bearing on the ease of manufacture and cost; the position of the label, together with such considerations as whether it is to be placed inside a showcase or not, will inevitably influence the choice of material and durability.

For the designer there is a great deal of research to draw on with regard to the design of effective labels. Much of it relates to the legibility and readability of print. In *Legibility research, 1972–78* Foster (1980) reviewed no fewer than 400 publications relating to the readability of text. This gives an indication of the quantity of literature available. However, much of it relates to communications graphics and book design and has only general application in the museum situation. A selection of some of the more relevant research findings and observations by museum professionals is given in the next section.

Type style

Spencer and Reynolds (1976) noted: 'There is evidence to suggest that sans serif faces are more legible for children and poor vision readers, and they are widely accepted as being suitable for display purposes.' However, Burt (1959) considered that modern typefaces were the least legible and thought that serifed letters are more legible than sans serif. On this, Spencer and Reynolds (1977) provide the useful comment:

> Many readers claim that they find sans serif faces subjectively less legible than serifed faces, but objective measures of reading performance are often conflicting and it cannot be said that one type style is significantly more or less legible than the other. For relatively short pieces of text such as museum labels it would seem unlikely that legibility would be significantly impaired by the use of a sans serif face.

Undoubtedly there is general agreement that the conventional combination of upper-case (capital) and lower-case type provides the most legible results. Spencer (1968) was aware of this, and his view was confirmed by Fleming (1976) and Allwood (1981). The Royal Ontario Museum study (1976) gives details of the findings of many researchers, including Dandridge (1968), who states that, as far as typewritten material is concerned, 'Tests showed that lowercase type was read almost 12% faster than material set in capitals, and that tested reader opinion was nine to one in favour of lower case lettering.' Neal (1976) confirms this view, suggesting that the use of capitals only may reduce the speed of reading by about 14 per cent. She also makes the useful point that setting in capitals occupies about 40–50 per cent more space than conventional setting.

It emerges that the most legible printed matter is generally that with which the reader is most familiar. Thus for the general newspaper and book-reading public it is a serifed letter printed in black on a white background, set in the usual combination of upper and lower case. However, for the exhibition situation certain adjustments are necessary. These include increasing the type size so that it may be seen over increased viewing distances, adjusting layouts to provide greater clarity and the use of bold, medium, light and italic forms to help 'code' information.

Type size

There may be the odd occasion—for example, when a very small object is displayed and the viewing distance is short—when a type size as small as twelve-point may be used for a label. However, the general consensus of opinion follows that of Carmel (1962) in recommending a minimum type size of twenty-four-point for most museum labels. Weiner (1963 (1)) states that with reference to labelling at the Smithsonian Institution 'We have determined through practice that specimen captions should normally appear in at least 24 point to 30 point type and that main texts and other general texts should be considerably larger—usually 48–60 point.' Neal (1976) also recommends: 'Nothing smaller than 24 points for specimen labels, generally 30 points to 36 points for group labels, with emphasis sometimes being gained by the use of combinations'.

However, rather than provide too many generalized statements, it should be remembered that since so much depends on the typeface used, the location of the label and other environmental factors, it is best that the needs of each situation are assessed by a qualified graphic designer.

Other factors

Although the style of type and its size are the main factors which affect legibility, other factors affect it too. Spencer (1968) makes many helpful observations regarding these. For example, he considers black print on a white ground to be more legible than white on black. Of particular interest to those concerned with labelling pictures in art galleries, where white labels can detract from the pictures, is his discovery that there is no appreciable loss of legibility when type is printed in black on tinted paper, provided the paper is of a minimum of 70 per cent reflectance. He also confirms what many graphic designers have long believed, that unjustified typesetting does not decrease legibility, and provides a useful reminder that reading efficiency is severely reduced by any departure from a horizontal presentation and by departure from a 90° angle of reading. Commenting on the length of lines, Spencer is of the opinion that excessively long lines cause a sharp increase in the number of regressions. Short lines, on the other hand, increase the number of fixation pauses. The use of 'leading' to increase the space between characters, words and lines permits the length of a body of type to be extended without loss of legibility. Spencer and Reynolds (1976) come to the conclusion that an

optimum length of line is one which accommodates between ten and
twelve words, that is, about sixty to seventy characters.

The label in relation to the object

The location of the label in relation to the object should be a logical one,
so that the visitor may easily gain the information he/she seeks, and
relate it to the object without any likelihood of making a mistake.
Generally, labels are best placed below objects, in accordance with
established practice, and may be positioned centrally or to left or right of
the object. In order that the visitor may know where to look for the
information he seeks, it is best that positioning is consistent throughout
an exhibition. Ambiguous situations, where it is unclear whether the
label refers to the object above or below it, are then less likely to be a
problem, but in any case they should be avoided.

Determining the size a label should be in relation to an object can be
difficult, particularly for very small and very large objects. Here scale is
important, and so are the functional requirements of the label. In the case
of small objects such as coins or flies, there is a danger that the size of the
label may visually overpower the object it describes, or the type setting
may necessarily be too small to be legible. In these instances it may be
possible to compromise by providing brief captions and a reference key
where more information can be given. However, introducing a key does
have the disadvantage that many visitors are unwilling to expend the
extra effort required to look up a reference in a key which is remote from
the object.

Labels for large objects, and in particular pictures, can be difficult,
since there is a temptation to make them large enough to be read at the
same distance as it is convenient to view the object. This disregards the
fact that the viewer is mobile, and it can be a mistake anyway, because the
label may then compete, in visual terms, with the object for the attention
of the viewer. In situations like this, where visual interference becomes a
problem, the legibility of the label may reasonably be sacrificed and a size
and colour chosen which will make it unobtrusive yet still readable at a
reduced viewing distance. Where pictures are concerned, encouraging the
viewer to move forward is no bad thing, for by doing so he may be
afforded a new perception of the object, and possibly an appreciation of
the texture and surface of the paint which goes to form the image.

For convenience, most labels are rectangular, with a horizontal
emphasis. This shape emanates from conventional printing, which is in
horizontal bands and which can provide a visually satisfactory border.
The rectilinear form of the label happily echoes that of many display
fittings and showcases. The proportions of labels may vary considerably
and most, depending on their application, can be visually satisfactory.
However, it is the mixing of rectangular shapes of different proportions
which can cause significant visual irritation, and care should be taken to
standardize shapes and sizes wherever possible. Thus a modular system is

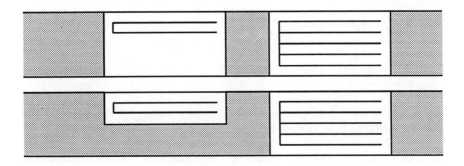

Figure 11.3   Relation between label size and quantity of lettering

to be recommended, where labels are a standard width and depth. Since the overall shape of a label card is normally visually stronger than the lettering which it bears, it is generally better, in design terms, to maintain a constant size even if the amount of lettering varies, as indicated in figure 11.3.

Now that the label as it is perceived by those professional groups within the museum who have a particular interest in its function has been discussed, the viewpoint of those for whom it is primarily intended, the visitors, must be considered. Their attitude is quite straightforward. When their interest is aroused they require information to be readily available. Because the degree of interest varies according to prior knowledge, intellect and purpose, the information required also varies. For the casually interested a word or two will suffice, while for others there is a more substantial need. And whereas a proportion of the casually interested may be wooed into greater involvement, by the completely uninterested they are ignored, not read, and need not exist at all.

These factors suggest that it is unreasonable to expect that, in any survey intended to quantify the numbers of the general public who study museum labels, particularly high scores will be achieved. The public are selective, according to need. Someone who knows an object may not feel . the need to read a label about it, yet someone who is interested, but does not know much about it may be happy to read a relevant label of several hundred words.

Robinson (1930) in his studies at the Buffalo Museum of Science noted that in a given exhibit, about one-tenth of the label was read by one-tenth of the visitors who stopped to look at it. Borun and Miller (1980) in their research at the Franklin Institute had rather better but arguably still very low results. They found that 'whilst visitors read only 18 per cent of the total number of labels available at all displays in the exhibit hall they visited, they did in fact read 68 per cent of the labels on the particular displays at which they stopped'. However, Wolf and Tymitz (1979) in their 'brief exploratory study' of label-reading behaviour as part of their larger study on the visitor perceptions of 'Our Changing Land', the bicentennial exhibit, National Museum of Natural History, Smithsonian Institution, found that most people do read some labels. For those that did, several generalizations were possible: 51 per cent of the visitors sampled read at least one but not more than five labels; 23 per cent of the visitors sampled read between six and fifteen labels; 26 per cent of the visitors sampled read fifteen or more labels.

As people interested in museums we might consider our own behaviour in this respect: how many labels do *we* read on a visit? And is it reasonable to expect the lay public to read more?

Generally speaking, the needs of the visitor might be satisfied by labels which:

1. Identify the object—simply, and in words which can be understood.
2. Put it into context by providing general information.
3. Draw attention to special characteristics/comparisons, etc.
4. Make the experience exciting, interesting and encourage further responses.

However the enthusiast may not be happy with anything less than comprehensive answers to questions 1–16 already discussed on p. 151.

Finding out exactly what visitors want from a label is fairly straightforward: ask them. A number of researchers have, of course, done just that. Among them are Wolf and Tymitz (1978), who, in their study of the 'Ice Age Mammals and Emergence of Man' exhibit at the National Museum of Natural History, Smithsonian Institution, elicited from visitors such comments as 'I like the scientific labels,' 'I'm not big on Latin terms—I want more common terms,' 'The labels are tedious to read,' and 'The labels are easy.' In this instance these contradictory statements may create more problems than they resolve. However, it may be that strengths and weaknesses of labels are identified and the information can be put to good use in development work.

Of course, it is not just by obtaining the views of visitors that the effectiveness of labels can be assessed. Labels, like any other part of the museum's communication system, can be evaluated, and a series of formal tests devised to analyse how efficiently they function in any given situation. Barr (1976) recognized that only when the visitor's interest is maintained at its highest pitch can true communication result. Taking into account the work of various researchers, he suggested that:

They [labels] must first, of course, be truly concise with all extraneous matter pruned out. A journalistic system of headings and sub-headings can be valuable in orientating the reader to the information content. Language should be colloquial, suited to the major target group within the audience, and jargon should either be eliminated entirely or defined in such a way that useful terms are made understandable to the reader. Efforts should be made to include one or two motivational factors in each label and special efforts should be devoted to communicating the scholar's mood of excitement with his objects of study. Remember that the time spent in comprehending an individual label is likely to be 30 seconds or less unless the reader can be motivated to pay unusual attention to it.

Analysis and evaluation of text

The need to know the effectiveness of a given piece of writing has already been demonstrated. Fortunately there are a number of formulas and procedures which have been devised to measure or analyse the character of a piece of prose, and these can be applied to produce useful guidance as to who is likely to be able to read it and how well they may understand it. (See also the full discussion in Klare, 1978, and Harrison, 1979.) Sorsby and Horne (1980) considered the Fry test particularly relevant to the museum label situation, since it has been widely validated by educational technologists and is relatively quick and simple to apply. It provides an assessment of a written passage in terms of an approximate reading age.

THE FRY TEST

1. Select a sample passage of about 100 words.
2. Count the number of sentences in the passage and calculate the number of sentences per 100 words.
3. Count the number of syllables in the passage and calculate the number of syllables per 100 words.
4. Use the graph to determine the reading age for the passage.
5. Test two or more passages and average the results for greater accuracy.

Lakota (1976) advocated the use of two formulae to provide readability indexes, FORCAST and SMOG. Both are easy to apply and generate reading grade levels (American). Since SMOG scores tend to be high, the two methods should be employed. A score of 6 or 7 is considered a reasonable criterion for museums with a general audience.

THE FORCAST METHOD

1. Select a passage of 150 words.
2. Count the number of one-syllable words and divide by 10.
3. Subtract from 20.

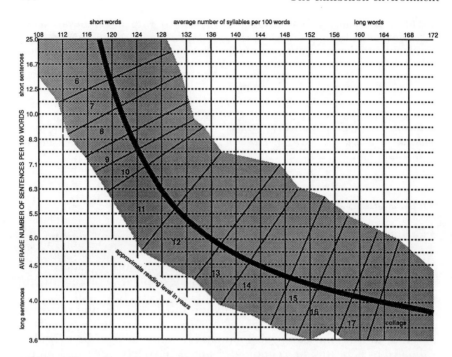

Figure 11.4   The Fry test to calculate reading levels by age. The shaded area indicates the region of maximum readability of the test (after Stansfield's (1981) redrawing of the graph from *Journal of Reading*, April 1988)

THE SMOG METHOD

1. Select a passage of thirty sentences.
2. Count the number of polysyllabic words and calculate the square root.
3. Add 3.

THE CLOZE METHOD

Lakota rightly observes that the above methods produce useful predictive scores but do not measure how the reader actually copes with a particular text. The method he recommends to assess a degree of comprehension and also furnish diagnostic information on which revisions may be made is the CLOZE method.

1. Delete every fifth word in the text and replace it with a blank.
2. Show this to a sample of visitors and ask them to fill in the missing words.
3. Score 1 for each word correctly and exactly restored (irrespective of precise spelling).
4. Calculate the percentage of correctly filled in words.

A score between 57 per cent and 61 per cent roughly equates to full comprehension (i.e. a score of 90 per cent or better on an objective test based on the same material). A score of approximately 55 per cent would indicate a high level of comprehension for materials used with general museum audiences over the age of twelve.

A labelling system

As a major element of a museum's communication scheme labels are best considered as a unified system within a system rather than as individual appendages to exhibits. Having a comprehensive labelling system aids the visitor because, once he/she understands it, it can be used effectively throughout the museum, without the need to learn a new methodology in each gallery. Systemization in this context could mean a standardized order by which information is tabulated, the use of a limited number of typefaces and generally the use of a 'house style' for all graphic text panels. It would also cover the type of information provided and the style of writing. Such a system should not be inflexible but should have the sensitivity to respond to the characteristics of different types of material in varying gallery presentations. However, it does need to be sufficiently consistent to provide the visitor with a constant system of reference with which he/she can become familiar and use efficiently. To devise such a system the views, as previously discussed, of curator, educationalist, designer and indeed visitors should be canvassed, and proposals developed and tested in the exhibitions.

In most museums some form of 'tiered' system of providing inform-ation will probably be appropriate. This enables information to be coded and organized into a hierarchical system, and should be capable of being applied in relation to exhibitions or galleries, sections of exhibitions, sub-sections or individual cases, and ultimately to the object label itself. The characteristic of such a system is that it should consist of a series of headings and sub-headings backed up by more informative bodies of text with the liberal use of paragraphing and the content well organized. If comparative statistics are to be given, simple tabulation of the facts can assist the visitor and increase the speed at which the information may be seen and comprehended. Pictograms, diagrams, symbols, simple maps and other graphics used in conjunction with words can increase their capacity to communicate. However, the use of elaborate graphics and of any keys other than the most simple is best avoided.

A tiered system of labelling which might act as a model for develop-ment in respect of individual museum needs could be, at exhibition level:

1. *Heading* or short title (maximum five words), e.g. 'The garden'.
2. *Sub-heading* or brief explanation (maximum twenty words), e.g. 'An exhibition which traces the history or the garden from Roman times to the present day'.
3. *Detailed elaboration* or conceptual orientation (maximum 100 words). This may state the aims and objectives of the exhibition, the ideas it is intending to

convey and their organization in sections and contents. It may also credit those responsible for the exhibition organization.

4. *Detailed background* or intellectual orientation (maximum 200 words). This should give the background history and serve as an introduction to the subject.

The above approach may be repeated selectively at exhibition section, sub-section and case levels. At object level the tiered system might operate to:

1. Provide a short identification caption (maximum three words), e.g. 'Black-bird'.

2. Expand this with a simple statement or tabulated information (maximum twenty-five words), e.g. Latin name, distribution, sex, plumage, habitat, diet.

3. Elaborate to provide discussion (maximum seventy-five words), e.g. interesting aspects of behaviour, etc., which the viewer could observe.

In many situations, information contained in 2 and 3 above might be omitted from the label, particularly if it is referred to in a caption covering the group as a whole, e.g. 'British garden birds'.

This type of tiered system provides information at exhibition, section, sub-section, case and finally at group and object levels. These levels and the type of information given may be clarified further by the selective and consistent use of different styles and sizes of typeface, the use of standard, bold or italic faces, by the use of capitals and lower-case and by such design elements as colour.

To sum up, the label plays a key role in communicating a range of information to the museum visitor, and in many instances forms the link between object and viewer. As such it needs to be given the most serious consideration and should never be regarded as an afterthought, that is, something which is quickly typed out and added once the exhibition is set up. Indeed, labels, and their content, style and design, should be recognized as a vital part of the museum's communication and orient-ation systems.

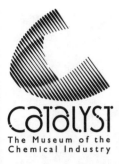

CATALYST
The Museum of the
Chemical Industry

A

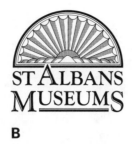

ST ALBANS
MUSEUMS

B

C

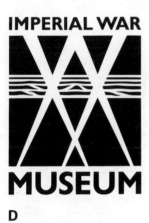

IMPERIAL WAR

MUSEUM

D

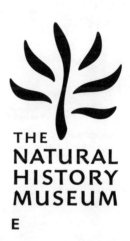

THE
NATURAL
HISTORY
MUSEUM

E

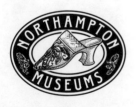

F

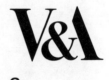

G

Plate 1. Museum logos: (a) CATALYST, The Museum of the Chemical Industry, Widnes (reproduced by courtesy of CATALYST); (b) St Albans Museums, Museum Service logo, designed by Clare Pollak and Clare Cook, 1988 (reproduced by courtesy of St Albans Museums); (c) London Transport Museum, designed by Pocknell and Co., 1990 (reproduced by courtesy of London Transport Museum); (d) The Natural History Museum, London, designed by Wolf Olins in association with NHM staff, 1989 (reproduced by courtesy of the Natural History Museum) ; (e) The Imperial War Museum, London, designed by Minale Tattersfield & Partners, 1989 (reproduced by courtesy of the Imperial War Museum); (f) Northampton Museums, designed by Northampton Borough Council,1988 (reproduced by courtesy of Northampton Museums); (g) Victoria and Albert Museum, London, designed by Alan Fletcher of Pentagram, 1988 (reproduced by courtesy of the trustees of the Victoria and Albert Museum).

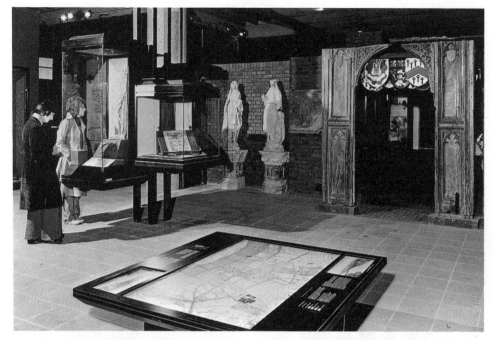

Plate 2. Museum exhibition design. The Saxon and Medieval Gallery, Museum of London. An example of exhibition design with a strong environmental emphasis, demonstrating the need for structural as well as communication design skills. (Reproduced by courtesy of the Museum of London.)

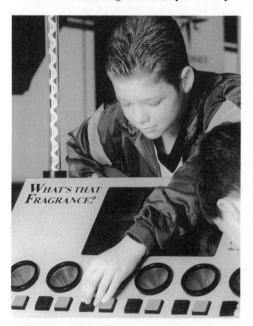

Plate 3. 'What's that Fragrance?' An interactive exhibit about fragrance chemicals in CATALYST's Industry in View gallery, designed to engage the least regarded of the senses. (Reproduced by courtesy of CATALYST.)

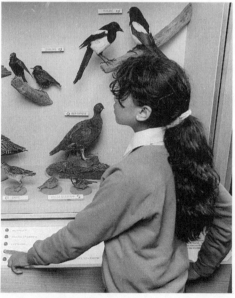

Plate 4. 'Bird Songs'. An interactive unit matching bird songs to specimens. Natural Sciences Galleries, Cliffe Castle Museum, Keighley. Designed and produced by Bradford Art Galleries and Museums, 1990; photo, Norman Taylor, Larkfield Photography.

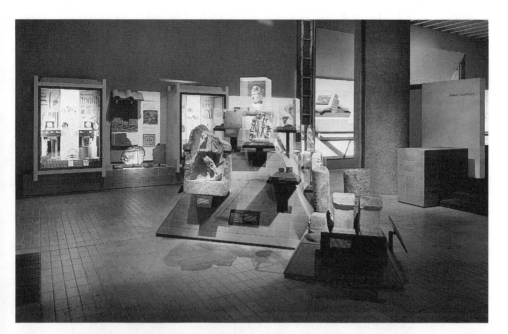

Plate 5. Exhibitions conceived as sculpture. The Roman Gallery, Museum of London. An example of compostion in three dimensions which recognises the importance of solids and voids in an architectural setting. (Reproduced by courtesy of the Museum of London.) This plate, like 6, 7, 8 and 9, shows examples of exhibitions where good design and a sensitive use of materials, colour and texture have contributed to achieving elegant, almost timeless, solutions.

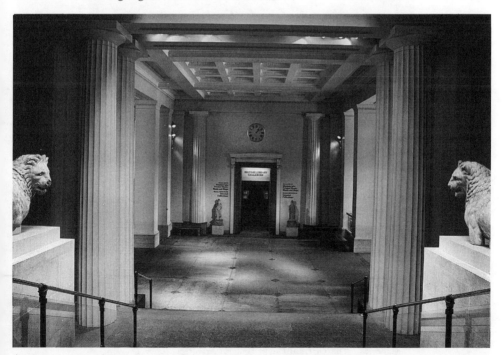

Plate 6. The British Museum, London. The view of the main entrance hall, 1985. Designed by the British Museum Design Office. (Reproduced by courtesy of the Trustees of the British Museum.)

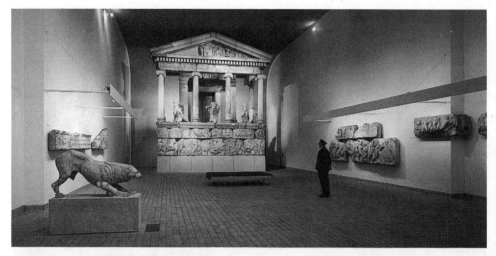

Plate 7. The British Museum, London. The Greek and Roman Galleries, the Neried Monument. Designed by Russell and Godden, 1969. (Reproduced by courtesy of the Trustees of the British Museum.)

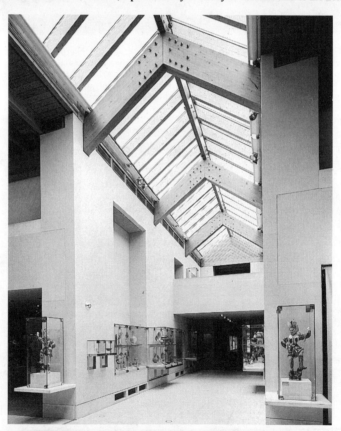

Plate 8. The Burrell Collection, Glasgow Museums and Art Galleries. The Oriental Daylit Gallery. Architect, Barry Gasson, 1983. (Reproduced by courtesy of Glasgow Museums and Art Galleries.)

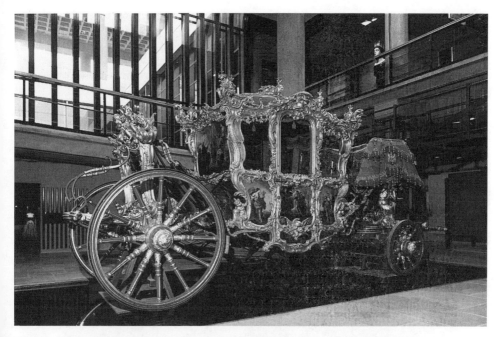

Plate 9. Museum of London. The Lord Mayor's Coach. Designed by Powell and Moya, 1976. (Reproduced by courtesy of the Museum of London.)

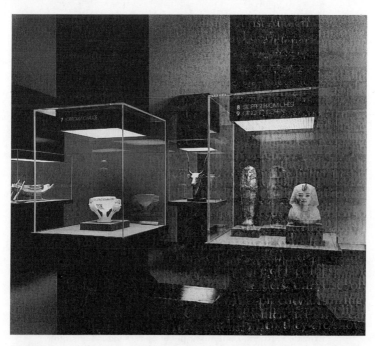

Plate 10. 'Treasures of Tutankhamun', a 'special exhibition'. Second room: small exhibits of alabaster and wood, British Museum, London, 1972. For those who visited, one of the most memorable of all the 'blockbusters'. Designed by British Museum Design Office. (Reproduced by courtesy of the Trustees of the British Museum.)

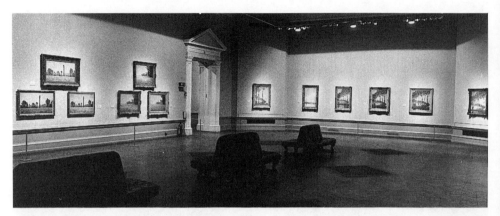

Plate 11. 'Monet in the 90s'. A special exhibition at the RA which broke all previous attendance records. The Royal Academy of Arts, 1990. Designed by Ivor Heal. (Reproduced by courtesy of the Royal Academy of Arts; photo by Steven White.)

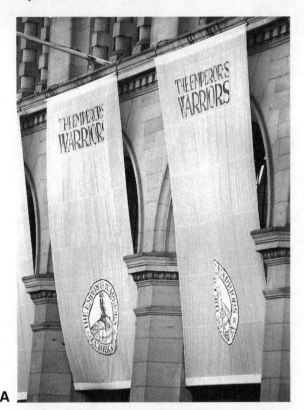

A

Plate 12. 'The Emperor's Warriors'. A 'blockbuster' exhibition at the City of Edinburgh Art Centre in 1985. (a) Banners on the outside of the Centre. (Logo designed by Graphic Partners, Edinburgh; photo by Alexander Topp.); (b) Terracotta warriors and horses from the burial enclosure of Qin Shinhuang, the first Emperor of China (died 210 BC). Exhibition designed by Alexander Topp and staged under the direction of Herbert Coutts, City Curator. (Reproduced by courtesy of Edinburgh City Museums and Art Galleries.)

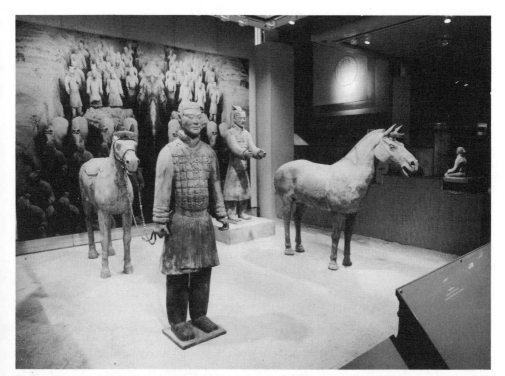

B

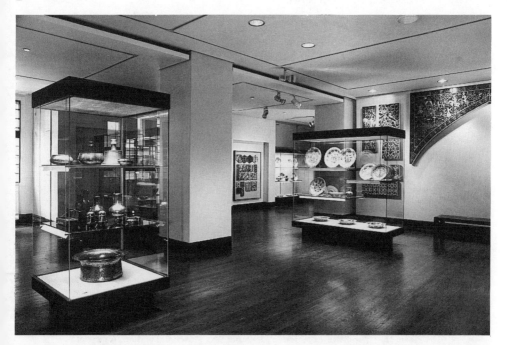

Plate 13. Aesthetic exhibition. The John Addis Islamic Gallery, The British Museum, London, 1990. Designed by the British Museum Design Office; photo by John Donat. (Reproduced by courtesy of the Trustees of the British Museum.)

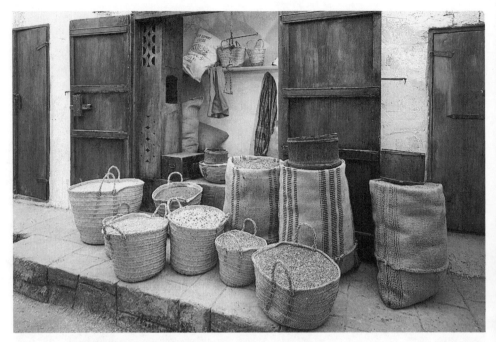

Plate 14. 'The Nomad and the City', Museum of Mankind, London. An evocative exhibition and one of the first to use the complete reconstructed environment technique with great success (1975). Designed by Margaret Hall and Geoff Pickup in association with the British Museum Design Office. (Reproduced by courtesy of the Trustees of the British Museum.)

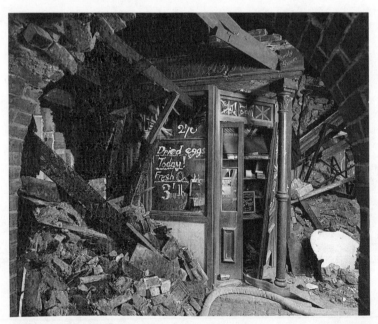

Plate 15. 'The Blitz experience', Imperial War Museum, London. A view of the major, award-winning exhibition. Designed by John Dangerfield of Jasper Jacob Associates in association with Kimpton-Walker plc. (Reproduced by courtesy of the Imperial War Museum.)

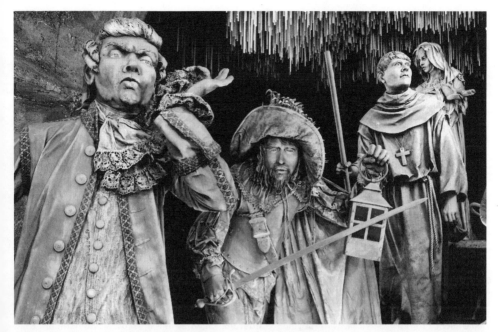

Plate 16. The Jorvik Viking Centre, York, opened 14 April 1984. The 'march past' of a thousand years in time, from the twentieth century back to the tenth in the Centre's Time Tunnel. In view are the eighteenth and seventeenth centuries, with the Middle Ages in the background. Concept by C. I. Skipper, P. Addyman and A. E. Gaynor, designed by John Sunderland, photo by Simon Hill. (Reproduced by courtesy of the York Archaeological Trust.)

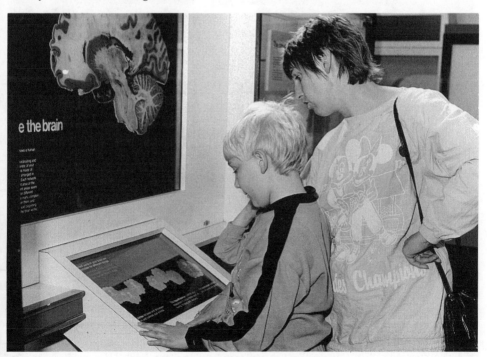

A

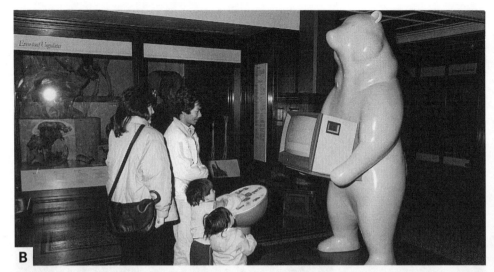

Plate 17. Didactic exhibition: interactive exhibits. The computer has revolutionised interactive exhibits to enable a dialogue to take place between visitor and exhibit. The approach appeals particularly to the younger visitor. (a) An exhibit in the 'Movement' section (revised 1982) of the Hall of Human Biology, the Natural History Museum, London. Designed by David Gosling and Roger Whiteway, Department of Public Services, Natural History Museum; photo by the museum's Photographic Unit. (Reproduced by courtesy of the Natural History Museum); (b) 'Make a Mammal' computer game from the Mammal Gallery of Manchester Museum, 1989. Curator, Michael Hounsome, designed by Andrew Millward, photo by Geoff Thompson. (Reproduced by courtesy of the Manchester Museum.)

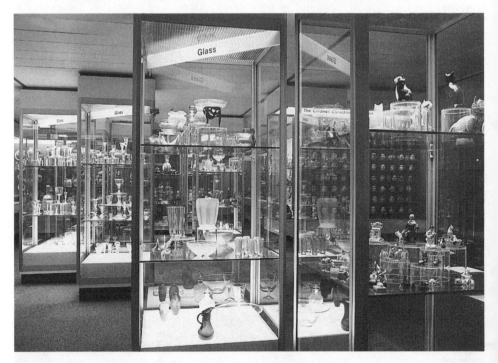

Plate 18. The Ceramic Gallery, Norwich Castle Museum. An object-oriented and systematic permanent exhibition, created in 1978. Curator, Sheenah Smith, designed by Kenneth Heathcote and Nicholas Arber, photo by Peter Honingham. (Reproduced by courtesy of Norfolk Museums Service.)

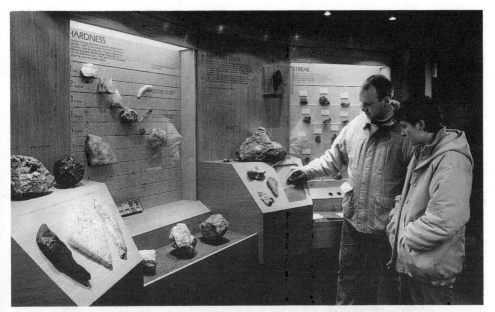

Plate 19. 'Molecules to Minerals'. Natural Sciences Galleries, Cliffe Castle Museum, Keighley. A thematic and participatory permanent display of rocks and minerals. The photograph shows the 'Identification of Minerals' display, with interactive presentation of some methods of identification using specific gravity touch, hardness, magnetism and 'streak'. Design and part production by Bradford Art Galleries and Museums, photo by Norman Taylor, Larkfield Photography.

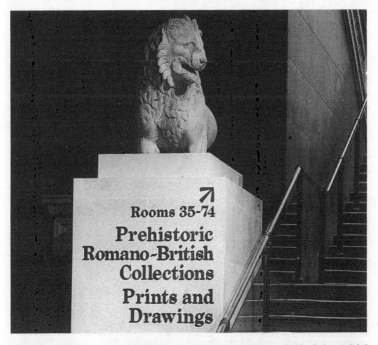

Plate 20. Signs to upper galleries in the main entrance hall of the British Museum, London, forming a part of the museum's internal signing system. Designed by the British Museum Design Office, 1985. (Reproduced by courtesy of the Trustees of the British Museum.)

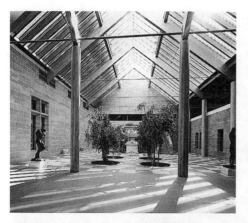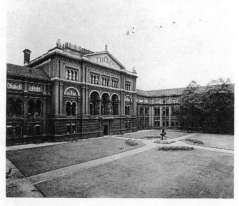

Plate 21. Areas complementing a museum's exhibition galleries. (a) 'The Courtyard' (including the Warwick Vase and Rodin Sculptures), The Burrell Collection, Glasgow Museums and Art Galleries. Architect, Barry Gasson. (Reproduced by courtesy of Glasgow Museums and Art Galleries.) (b) 'The Pirelli Garden', Victoria and Albert Museum, London. (Reproduced by courtesy of the Trustees of the Victoria and Albert Museum.)

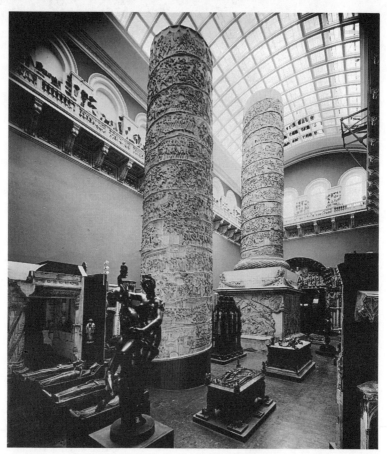

Plate 22. 'The Cast Court', Victoria and Albert Museum, London: general view. (Reproduced by courtesy of the Trustees of the Victoria and Albert Museum.)

Part five.   The museum visitor and exhibition effectiveness

12. *The museum visitor*

Introduction

Visitors are the lifeblood of museum exhibitions. Only as they trickle through and fill the various passageways and spaces to interact with the exhibits do these otherwise passive, dead areas come to life. James Gardner and Caroline Heller (1960) in their book *Exhibition and Display* go further: 'An exhibition does not in fact exist until it is crowded with people, and what really matters is how these people react to what they see.' However, although it is now widely accepted that museums exist to serve the public, this is comparatively new thinking! For centuries entry was restricted to the privileged, and even the British Museum in its early days refused to admit young people under the age of ten. According to one John Britton (Clifford 1987), if what he said is to be believed, the reason for not giving unlimited access to the visitor public was that:

> in England, where ignorance, vulgarity, or something worse, are the character-
> istics of the lower orders, and where frivolity, affectation, and insolence, are the
> leading traits in a class of lounging persons, who haunt most public places, it
> would be the excess of folly for gentlemen, who possess valuable museums, to
> give unlimited admission to the public.

At the time, of course, museums were still something of a novelty; since their contents were generally so far removed from the everyday experience of most visitors, they simply did not know how to respond, and restricting access only exacerbated the problem.

As the nineteenth century progressed, more and more public museums were created. This coincided with improvements in schooling, a greater availability of printed books, including the popular encyclopaedia, and other educational developments. As a result, a wider and more educated public was encouraged to take an interest in museums. So, in the United Kingdom, by the latter part of the nineteenth century, in a climate of philanthropy and educational encouragement, museums thrived on visitors who formed a most appreciative audience.

In the early years of the twentieth century the situation changed. Museum professionals appear to have become increasingly preoccupied with their collections rather than with communicating information about them to the visitor. One reason for this was that museums did not wish to be concerned with education. The Education Act of 1918 had made it possible for local education committees to seek the assistance of museums in the furtherance of local schemes of educational develop-ment, and it was suggested that museums, together with public libraries, should be included in any scheme of education for a local area in

171

England and Wales, and that these institutions should be taken into account in the allocation of state grants to the local authorities. Further, it was suggested that museums and libraries should both be transferred under the powers and duties of the Local Government Board to the Board of Education. This proposal was rejected by the Museums Association, which, in a memorandum, pointed out that in its opinion it would not be in the best interests of museums, since they were not, fundamentally, educational institutions. The functions of museums in order of importance were considered to be (1) collection and preservation; (2) research; (3) education and display. If they were transferred to local education committees, it was thought that the last would be developed at the expense of the first two.

This view was endorsed by a committee of the British Association for the Advancement of Science (1920(1)) which had been formed in 1913 with, as its terms of reference, 'To examine, inquire into, and report on the character, work and maintenance of Museums, with a view to their organisation and development as institutions for Education and Research; and especially to inquire into the requirements of schools.'

A report of the investigation was given at a meeting held in Cardiff in 1920. Among the topics discussed was 'Museums in relation to the General Public', which was approached in respect of the educational work the museum may do for the general public. The report (1920(2)) states:

> The term ['general public'] covers a wide range of needs. It represents the vast majority of visitors to the public museums; we may safely regard them as having little or no special knowledge, and a very large proportion of them enter the museum without any specific purpose. They are just 'looking round'.
>
> For such people the Museum may do a great service . . . By some means or other it should strive to put them *en rapport* with the purpose of the museum. This purpose, for them at least, is to reveal one aspect or other of an ordered universe to people largely uninstructed. These casual visitors are easily overwhelmed by a multiplicity of specimens and of words. The first essential is a definite scheme, carried out with simplicity, boldness and clearness. Elaborate labels, completely logical series, and involved argument do not assist them.

However, in the context of the report the museum's educational function is not made explicit, and is regarded as part of its publications function, which takes its place after collection preservation, study and classification.

Not surprisingly, as museums played down their education and display functions, the large attendances enjoyed in the late nineteenth century fell off, and museums (with some notable exceptions, such as Norwich and Manchester which had progressive educational schemes) became rather neglected in the years between the two world wars and immediately afterwards. Sir Henry Miers (1928) in his *Report on the Public Museums of the British Isles* commented, 'Given definite policy, good buildings, adequate equipment, collections and staff, the duty of a museum to the public has yet to be defined'.

Miers (1929) undertook a very thorough survey of museums, and in an address to the Royal Society of Arts on 23 January 1928 he gave a depressing description of the dismal plight of the less important and less prosperous museums. He painted a picture of deserted rooms with a general air of stagnation, and of visitors who would come and go without much evidence of interest, and who would receive little help towards understanding the exhibits. They would be gazing at rows of things of no interest to them, overcrowded and badly lit; there would be no one to apply to for information.

This confirmed what he had written in his report (1928) regarding the relationship of visitors to museums and vice versa.

> To put it bluntly, most people in this country do not really care for museums or believe in them: they have not hitherto played a sufficiently important part in the life of the community to make ordinary folk realize what they can do . . . This is not surprising when one considers how dull many of them have become and how low the worst of them has sunk.

Nevertheless, even if museums were reluctant to acknowledge and realize their educational potential, Miers was well aware of the possibilities. He likened museums to the broadcaster in that both serve a vast public made up of individuals of all ages, types and classes. He noted that most visitors do not say what they want, and he regarded it as impossible to ascertain what knowledge visitors gained or even how far their curiosity had been satisfied. In raising this issue, Miers was anticipating the interest in visitor surveys and exhibit effectiveness which was to emerge almost fifty years later.

In museums on both sides of the Atlantic during the late 1920s and 1930s it would seem that there was no definite policy on education and the museum visitor. Clearly the educational impetus of the dynamic philanthropists of the late nineteenth and early twentieth centuries had been lost. The report which Miers undertook was at the behest of the Carnegie United Kingdom Trust. This body, realizing the inability of museums to recognize and develop their educational potential, had decided, in 1925, to become actively involved in trying to stimulate interest in, and improve, museums throughout the country. This decision was to bring benefits of inestimable value to museums and their visitors in the years ahead.

Ten years later, S.F. Markham undertook another survey of museums for the trust, and was pleased to report considerable progress with regard to the relationship between museums and their visitors. He commented (1938(1)):

> but undoubtedly the museum function that attracts the greatest public attention, and that which is indeed advanced by a good many people as being the reason why museums and art galleries exist at all, is that field of activity known as visual education.

Also, he reported that there was a general tendancy towards better lighting, more colourful cases, the limitation of reflections and shadows, and spacious exhibition methods. He thought this 'all to the good' and clearly appreciated the relationship between exhibition technique and content and the museum visitor.

Much of the progress which had taken place he attributed to the combined effect of Sir Henry Miers's report and the interest and support of the Carnegie Trust in the educational potential of museums. Markham (1938(2)) felt able to report that . . .

> It may now be said that provincial museums, whilst aware of the importance of proper conservation and of assisting scientists and others in every possible way, recognise more fully than ever that in the future their greatest activity and their greatest claim on public support may be through their education usefulness.

Progress over the next few years was, nevertheless, slow. In part this was due to the intervention of war, but also to a failure to understand that visitors were a vital part of the communication process. In 1954 the Standing Commission reported that:

> There is what we may describe as a rather tepid general recognition of the fact that they [museums] contribute something towards education but there still seems a certain reluctance to accept, in practice, the implications of the fact, so often and so eloquently urged, that they are part and parcel of education itself.

It was largely out of an interest in the effectiveness of the educational function of museums that the visitor, as the measure of effectiveness, became a focus of attention for the researcher. Initially this occurred in America, and gathered momentum in the 1950s and 1960s, when much of the pioneering work of Coleman and Robinson was reassessed and extended by a new breed of researcher. Only gradually was this interest kindled in museum professionals in Britain.

Visitor studies

Museums have been recording visitor numbers almost ever since they first opened their doors to the public. However, in those early days of revolving turnstiles this statistic was, for the most part, the extent of management's interest in the visitor. Numbers were faithfully recorded and possibly included in any museum report as an indicator of the museum's performance. Probably few questioned their validity. The public were thought of as numbers, not as individual visitors, each with a personal identity and specific interest, attitudes and goals. An awareness of this prompted Edward Robinson (1928) to note:

> this casual visitor [to the museum] is in the main a mystery and, if he is to be dealt with effectively, there needs to be added to the talking about him and thinking about him deliberate observation of his behaviour.

Robinson was among the first researchers to become interested in the museum visitor as something more than a statistic. Along with Melton, his contemporary, he contributed much to the study of visitor behaviour in museums.

Writing in 1935, Melton too drew attention to the visitor, and was concerned that exhibition planning should do more than simply cater for the average needs of the public. He cautioned:

> In the first place, the museum visitors vary greatly from one another in their reaction to an exhibit, to a group of exhibits in a single gallery, and to the exhibits in an entire museum. In the second place, as one follows the scale of interest from the level of no interest to the level of maximum interest, there is a continuous variation.

Although it can be said that much of the early work lacked scientific exactness and consisted largely of observational studies, it was, nevertheless, of considerable value. For this was not just research for research's sake. It came about through a genuine desire to identify and understand the problems related to the working of exhibitions, and went beyond mere generalized observation to provide quantified data. As such, it may be regarded as the beginnings of museum market research.

Much of the section on museum marketing in Chapter 3 stressed the importance of satisfying customer needs and market demands. This was demonstrated in the product cycle model in which consumer needs are ascertained through market research and the information thus obtained is applied to the development of new products. In the context of museums, information about the visitor is essential if informed decisions are to be made in respect of all aspects of its services to the public, and especially with regard to its main 'product'—the exhibition.

Museums have been reluctant to think of visitors in terms of being consumers or customers. This has probably been due in part to a certain arrogance emanating from a belief that such commercial terms are more appropriate to 'trade' than a learned profession. It may also be because the provider/customer relationship carries implied obligations on the former to give satisfaction. Such popular phrases as 'the customer is always right' (because he is paying for what he is receiving) have also militated against this concept gaining acceptance. But, in the social and economic climate of today, thinking in these terms can benefit both parties. For they bring a new realism to the analysis of the situation. It was Stephan de Borhegyi who in 1963 put forward the idea of museums using motivational research techniques in order to sell their concepts more effectively and attract more customers. Indeed, de Borhegyi was at the forefront of the resurgence of interest which took place in America in the 1960s, and did much to promote an interest in and an awareness of the importance of the visitors.

By 1975, Pamala Elliott and Ross J. Loomis were able to demonstrate the increased interest in studies of visitor behaviour in museums by producing an annotated bibliography listing 204 entries primarily in the English language.

In the UK Philip Doughty (1968) was one of the first to become interested in the visitor and undertook a statistical survey of the public of the Ulster Museum. His work aroused considerable interest and spurred a whole host of other museums into action, including the Jewry Wall Museum, Leicester (Cruikshank 1972), Norwich Castle Museum (McWilliams and Hopwood 1972), Manchester Museum (Mason 1974) and Portsmouth City Museums (Barton 1973).

All these surveys produced much fascinating information and can usefully serve as 'baselines' against which future developments can be assessed. Some of the findings are given as examples in the sections which follow. However, useful as the information is, some of the methodology in these studies did not (nor was it intended that it should) provide statistically viable data.

In the climate in which museums are operating today it is right that Prince (1985(1)) should again stress the importance of museums maintaining their interest in visitors. He states:

> It thus seems clear, and entirely appropriate, that museums should now seek to apply the same academic rigour to the study of their visitors (and non-visitors) as they do to the study of their collections. Without a deeper understanding of the motivations and aspirations of their actual and potential clients, museums are unlikely to be able to respond effectively to the wider changes in society that are affecting, and will continue to affect, their well-being.

The methods employed to obtain information on the museum visitor are various. The main ones are: formal interviews, informal discussions, written questionnaires, tests (affective and cognitive) and observational studies. Each technique is suited to a particular situation and need, and provides a specific type of information. Since each technique also has its limitations, a combination may be used to provide a more comprehensive range of information. However, ensuring that the visitors studied are a representative cross-section of the general population of visitors is more difficult than it sounds. Not only does it have to be representative of such things as sex, age and so forth, it also has to be related to a visiting time. Many museums experience marked differences in their visitor audience between summer and winter, holiday periods and college term time, weekends and weekdays and even between different times of day, in sunshine and in rain. Thus methods of collecting data must take these variables into account.

The number of subjects to be studied is important if truly representative data are to be obtained. A typical survey of visitors might involve a minimum of 200 subjects. However, if the sample is to be subdivided on analysis, the numbers in the sub-groups may be so low as not to be typical. For example, 200 subjects might yield five subjects who were female and over sixty. These five do not necessarily constitute a large enough sample on which to base data on museum visitors who are over sixty and female. In this situation, depending on the information required, a minimum number in the sub-group of say twenty-five would provide more accurate data. Seeking visitor opinion before and after exposure to an exhibition is a typical approach, the latter being termed an exit survey. Evaluating visitors' response as soon after they have experienced the exhibition as possible is important, as, generally, memories are short and long-term follow-up is very unreliable and difficult to undertake.

In the formal interview the interviewer/s normally obtain information by observation and questions on the subject's profile (sex, age, occupation, etc.), then proceed to ask specific set questions. Some or all of these may be formulated in such a way that they offer multiple-choice answers. This technique ensures consistency between interviews and enables the data processing to be undertaken easily. It is, of course, open to abuse, as questions can be formulated in such a way that they elicit predictable responses.

The informal interview differs from the formal in that, although ideally still structured, the answer opportunities are not prescribed and the subject may answer in any way he/she chooses. Information given in this way is often difficult to record (unless actually taped, or a second interviewer acts as recorder). It can also be difficult to analyse and does not lend itself to statistical data. It is, however, a good technique for getting to know what people are thinking. Because of the openness of the approach, particularly if the interview is unstructured, the technique is dependent for success upon the skill of the interviewer.

Written questionnaires have an advantage in that information is less labour-intensive in its collection and can be undertaken at a distance. However, questionnaires require skill and expertise in compiling if the results are to be valid. Even so, respondents frequently embellish the truth in their answers, and many deliberately lie. This phenomenon is not restricted to questionnaires and occurs in all techniques which require the subject to provide a response.

Tests may be employed for a variety of reasons, to find out what people think or to ascertain specific levels of knowledge or skill. They may be administered in various ways, through interview, questionnaire or by interactive computer technology. Generally, people do not like tests and will not readily submit themselves to assessment. The fear of being found inadequate is too great. However, call it a game and make it fun, or throw out a challenge and give incentives, and people are often only too pleased to be tested and prove how able they are.

Observational studies can take various forms. Tracking and timing selected visitors as they move through an exhibition or a museum is a well tried and tested method of obtaining information. Ideally, of course, it is done without the knowledge of the subject, and notes and timings are recorded as necessary. This can be formalized by the use of set checklists and behavioural rating charts where information on specific activities can be codified for ease of analysis. Other methods can involve the use of video, closed-circuit television and time-lapse photography.

Electronic and mechanical devices can be employed to obtain information on the visitor and his behaviour. Automatic counting devices are now commonplace and, in addition to being used at museum entrances, have an application on interactive displays. Through the use of everything from simple pressure mats to electronic devices visitors can be tracked and their movements monitored.

Although often dismissed because of the high proportion of unconstructive or rude comments received, a 'visitors' comments' facility can nevertheless be a source of useful material. It can take several forms. The exhibition visitors' book, with space for visitors to give their name, address and comments is perhaps the easiest way to obtain visitor feedback. Whereas the bulk of the responses will consist of such comments as 'interesting' and 'enjoyable', some people do take the trouble to write more pertinent comments. Furthermore, the book can provide useful mailing lists. The 'suggestion box' is the other traditional way of encouraging feedback—but can be given more contemporary appeal by inviting visitors to type in their comments on a computer. If, however, personal data relating to visitors are held on a UK museum computer data banks it may well be necessary to register it under the terms of the Data Protection Act 1984. It is a good idea to provide an informal 'visitors' comments' facility of one sort or another in all exhibitions, and to evaluate the response regularly.

Criticism of museums and exhibitions abounds. It comes from within, from the body of museum workers at all levels, from critics and from the public. Much is valid and needs to be considered carefully; and much is ill informed, prejudiced or based on misinformation. Nevertheless, museums need to be alert to any form of criticism, whether coming from a visitor in the form of a private letter, or made public in the letters column of a newspaper. How a museum responds will be a measure of its concern for public relations and its image. As far as comments in respect of exhibitions are concerned, or other relevant public services, it is important that they reach the appropriate staff in the museum who can consider the substance of the comment and take any action considered appropriate.

The museum visitor

Bassett and Prince (1984) state:

> As far as the nature of the museum public is concerned, few generalizations are possible because it differs from country to country, from region to region and even from museum to museum. It is possible to state, however, that almost any museum public is extremely heterogeneous in its make-up, that it is composed of people with a wide range of age-levels and with varying economic, ethnic, social and educational backgrounds.

This is indeed so, and since the make-up of any particular public is likely to be unique—and changing—there is a case for every museum undertaking surveys on a regular basis, to find out who their visitors are. That said, when the various visitor groups are analysed and aspects such as profiles, attitudes, behaviour and reactions are studied, certain facts emerge which are undoubtedly not peculiar to any one situation, but can have wider application to many museums.

Visitor profiles (demographic data)

Information on the individual visitor is essential if the profile of the larger visitor group is to be determined with any accuracy. The type of information required may vary according to specific need, but in general terms the following should provide a useful basis:

1. Sex.
2. Age, possibly in bands which are initially broadly related to educational stages, i.e. up to five, six to ten, eleven to sixteen, seventeen to twenty, twenty-one to thirty-four, thirty-five to sixty-four, sixty-five and over.
3. Educational level: stage of education reached, i.e. GCSE level, to A level; further education; higher education (degree equivalent); postgraduate.
4. Reading level. This might be gauged by obtaining information on reading matter, including newspaper.
5. Main occupation, either broad groups or specific activities can be sought, e.g. 'the arts', education, the forces, housewife, management, office worker, outdoor worker, professional, retired, sales/shop, student, technical, traveller or unemployed.
6. Socio-economic group. This relates to occupation and could be divided into the two main categories, ABC1, or white-collar households, and blue-collar (C2DE). But information may also be sought on such topics as home and car ownership, etc.
7. Spending capacity. This relates to 5 and 6 above, but information could be sought on personal spending in respect of entertainment, books, leisure pursuits, and so on.
8. Place of residence. Distance from the museum could be useful, e.g. within walking distance, local (up to ten miles), within the region (say up to twenty-five miles), outside the region (up to fifty miles), distant (over fifty miles), overseas.
9. Mode of travel to the museum, e.g. walk; public transport—bus/train; private—car/bicycle; organized party/private visit.
10. Nationality and native language.
11. Date and time of visit.

The above may form a basis on which to develop survey material. However, if a questionnaire is contemplated, specific advice from the professional researcher should be sought regarding its composition, particularly if any form of comparative analysis is intended.

Examples of findings

The museum literature is full of fascinating discoveries which museums are making almost daily about their visitors. Given below are some examples of the type of information museums might like to have.

Niehoff (1953, 1968) made a study of the summer and winter visitors attending the Milwaukee Public Museum in Wisconsin. Among the information obtained were such facts as the following. Tourists accounted for 52 per cent of visitors in summer and 22 per cent of visitors in winter. In summer, 35 per cent of visitors were in the ten-to-nineteen age group, whereas in winter the figure was 52 per cent, of which over twice as many were students (53 per cent) as in summer (22 per cent). Contrasting with this, he found that in winter those who were college-trained amounted to 41 per cent, whereas in summer only 21 per cent were in that category. Clearly this information has no application beyond Milwaukee. However, the use to which it could have been put in respect of that museum's exhibition programme may have been considerable.

Another early survey was undertaken by Abbey and Cameron (1960) for the Royal Ontario Museum. Although meticulous in approach, the researchers were surprised by what they considered to be a high number of college-educated visitors (40 per cent). They put this down, in part, to false information being given by a public keen to ingratiate themselves with the young, attractive interviewers.

More recently Alt (1980), who has undertaken extensive studies of visitors at the British Museum (Natural History), provided much interesting information in the 1976–79 survey report. For example, in 1976–84 per cent of visitors had no qualifications in biology. However, by 1979 this figure had fallen to 77 per cent. In that year 2 per cent had a CSE, 9 per cent an O level, 3 per cent an A level, 5 per cent a degree and 4 per cent 'other'.

The distribution of visitors by sex over the period also changed. In 1976 59 per cent were male and 41 per cent female. By 1979 53 per cent were male and 47 per cent were female. The distance of visitors' residence from the museum is also of interest. The 1979 figures were: overseas, 42 per cent; within ten miles, 14 per cent; 10–20 miles, 9 per cent; 21–30 miles, 5 per cent; 31–40 miles, 2 per cent; 41–50 miles, 3 per cent; 51–100 miles, 7 per cent; 101–200 miles, 10 per cent; over 200 miles, 8 per cent.

Prince (1985(2)), in a study on museum visiting and unemployment, thought the evidence he had obtained suggested that museum visiting cannot be explained simply in employment and cost-related terms, and that recent changes in the occupational and demographic structure of the UK have had little impact on museum visiting on a national scale. For, as far as museums were concerned, 'the main trends isolated are that as unemployment has increased museum visiting has decreased, and that this decrease is in line with those for visits to historic and wildlife sites'.

Peter Lewis (1988), from his studies of the spread of visiting at Beamish Museum, discovered the average percentages shown in Table 12.1. It is, perhaps, interesting to compare these figures with Cruikshank's (1972) findings at the Jewry Wall Museum, Leicester, where the visitors' (of whom almost two-thirds were under twenty-five) pattern of attendance was: Monday, 11 per cent; Tuesday, 10 per cent; Wednesday, 16 per cent; Thursday, 17 per cent; Friday, 14 per cent; Saturday 21 per cent and Sunday 11 per cent. Hill (1989), writing in *Design*, reported that the

Table 12.1 The spread of visiting at Beamish Museum

Day	During school term	Outside school term
Monday	12	14
Tuesday	14	17
Wednesday	11	15
Thursday	10	14
Friday	9	10
Saturday	14	6
Sunday	30	24

average visitor to the Science Museum, London, spends 18p during the visit over and above the new admission charge.

The non-visitor to the museum

For a museum, knowing who its visitors are is important if it wishes to retain their interest and support. However, identifying the non-visitor and the reasons for not visiting are of greater importance if the museum wishes to extend or change its visitor profile. But clearly additional numbers, for numbers' sake, are of limited value. Although useful as statistics, they also, of course, indicate a larger number of people who have seen the museum and presumably derived some benefit from the experience. Exactly what needs to be monitored carefully in association with any promotional activity, particularly as simply packing people in can spoil the experience for everyone. Indeed, it has often been said that in museums such as the Natural History Museum in London, where large numbers of children have been known to stampede in uncontrolled packs between galleries, such groups should be excluded at certain times. The introduction of charges has highlighted this for a few who, having paid to gain access to study, do not wish to have their study frustrated as well as lose money in the process. The quality of the visitor experience, and value for money, are important considerations. For large numbers also place visitor amenities such as restaurants and lavatories under considerable strain and may necessitate new capital expenditure on additional facilities. However, more important, they can imperil the safety of the collections unless there are adequate measures for crowd control.

Finding out about the non-visitor can be approached in a variety of ways, the most common being door-to-door surveys in a locality or sampling in shopping areas or similar public places. To adequately answer the question 'Why don't you visit the museum?' questions might be put in the following way:

1. *Museum profile:*
   Did you know you have a local museum?
   Do you know where it is?
   Do you know how to get to it?
   Do you know what it does?
2. *Reasons* ('Why don't you visit it?'), e.g.:
   It's too difficult to get to (no bus route, etc.).
   It's open at inconvenient times.
   There is nothing of interest there.
   It costs too much to get in.
   I have no one to go with.
3. *Motivators* ('What would persuade you to visit it?'), e.g.:
   Exhibitions on ——
   Parking facilities.
   If I knew more about it (regular information).
   More friendly staff.
   Better café.

Answers to questions similar to those proposed above would clearly be useful in enabling a museum to identify and take steps to overcome those negative factors which prevent visitors and, at the same time, develop motivators to increase the museum audience.

Visitor attitudes and interests

An assessment of what the visitor thinks, what motivates him and, above all what interests him is essential to a museum wishing to attract and successfully provide for its public. Visitors coming to the museum with a variety of backgrounds will have an equally wide range of likes, dislikes and attitudes, many of which will have a direct bearing on how they react to the museum experience. Getting to know them will help the museum communicate better with each individual. Some of the areas which are relevant in providing information on the visitor's attitudes and interests include:

1. *Motivation*: the reason for visiting the museum, e.g. research, education, entertainment, curiosity, boredom, to meet people, visit the restaurant, use a free lavatory.
2. *Interests*: general subject areas, e.g. animals, archaeology, art, current affairs, history, natural history, sport, technology.
3. *Preferences*: this could relate to 2 above, where the information obtained might be ranked in order of preference—or could relate to any other aspect on which the museum values visitor opinion. For example, the popularity of exhibits or techniques could be gauged in this way, also future proposals evaluated.
4. *Standards and expectations*: attitudes and prejudices in relation to such topics as war or morality might be sought, as they relate to the presentation of material in the museum. Also the expectations of visitors, whether they are satisfied or not.

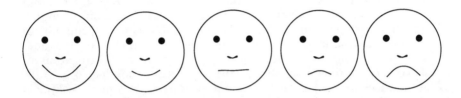

Figure 12.1   A question from a questionnaire at the Franklin Institute, Philadelphia

Minda Borun (1977) in her studies at the Franklin Institute, Philadelphia, devised a novel and extensive questionnaire entitled 'How did you find things in the Franklin Institute? We'd like to know . . .'. In one question using faces similar to those illustrated in figure 12.1, she asked individual visitors, 'How do you feel about your visit?' These figures are also included in a model questionnaire given in her paper 'Exhibit evaluation: an introduction', in *The Visitor and the Museum*, 1977.

Examples of findings

'A Rambling Dissertation on Museums by a Museum Rambler' was the title of a paper by J.A. Manton published in the *Museums Journal*, 1900. Among various observations, he rambled:

So I feel, with regard to art galleries and museums, that your pictures, your treasures, your curios are simply so many odds and ends, so many old stones, so many crocks and pans, unless there is some quickening influence at the back of them . . . I hope some bold adventurer will blow a blast that will wake them to life and usefulness.

Niehoff (1953) in his study of Milwaukee Museum found that some 57 per cent of visitors came to brouse, with no specific exhibit in mind. He also found that life-size dioramas were twice as popular as specimen exhibits. It is interesting to note that the trend continued in the 1980s in Britain, as is evident from the popularity enjoyed by the Jorvik project in York. This exhibition, which consists mainly of life-size tableaux, attracted some 600,000 visitors in its first year (1984) before exceeding its optimum of 890,000 visitors in subsequent years.

Washburne and Wagar (1972) found that above-average interest was shown by visitors in presentations which included motion, changing lights and recorded sound. They also noted above-average interest for violent subject matter, holistic presentations which included cause-and-effect relationships, or a story going beyond mere identification or isolated facts. Shiner and Shafer (1975) in studies conducted at Adirondack Museum, New York, found that the time visitors spent looking at and listening to exhibits ranged from 15 per cent to 64 per cent of that actually required. Ray Pierotti (1973) found that museum visitors are unable directly to verbalize feelings and ideas about their experience.

Alt (1983) provided information on a survey of visitor attitudes to new and old exhibitions at the British Museum (Natural History). In 1981 the museum commissioned research consultants to provide a comparison between four of the museum's galleries in terms of the ways in which they were perceived and evaluated by visitors. The galleries were the Mineral Gallery (opened 1881) and Meteorite Pavilion, the Whale Hall (opened 1937), the Hall of Human Biology (opened 1977) and 'Man's Place in Evolution' (opened in 1979). In a fairly complex evaluation procedure, characteristics associated with the exhibition were formulated and given an importance rating. Four hundred and ten subjects provided data for the exit interviews. In conclusion Alt states, 'Generally, the results . . . have clearly indicated the reasons why visitors evaluate the museum's newer exhibitions more favourably than its more traditional galleries.' Characteristics which obtained high scores for the more recent galleries included 'makes learning easy', 'is thought-provoking', 'gets information across clearly', 'makes the subject seem exciting' and 'designed with the ordinary visitor in mind'.

Cruikshank (1972) undertook a survey of visitor opinion at the Jewry Wall Museum, Leicester, between November 1969 and February 1970. The published results were based on a round figure of 200 completed returns (against 250 distributed and 217 completed). The questions were wide-ranging, and the answers were much quoted by the museum profession in Britain over the ensuing decade. Cruikshank's approach, however, was 'naturalistic', and he did not claim 'statistical significance' for his findings. The following is a brief selection of his findings. Respondents were 53 per cent male and 47 per cent female. Forty per cent were aged eighteen to twenty-five (but, counting school parties, the under-twenty-fives amounted to almost two-thirds of museum visitors). Fifty per cent came chiefly to look around, and 17 per cent to see a particular exhibit. Twenty-nine per cent first got to know of the museum by means of a conversation with a friend, 25 per cent through seeing the Roman site, 23 per cent through a talk at school or college, 12 per cent through a poster and 2 per cent via a newspaper advertisement. Eighty-two per cent did not consider the museum well signposted. Seventy per cent made use of the seating. Seventy-eight per cent wanted an accessible coffee bar. Sixty-eight per cent wanted additional displays of topical interest. Thirty-three per cent were going to buy booklets, 30 per cent postcards, 15 per cent posters and 9 per cent slides. Fifty-seven per cent would have liked to see the introduction of more models they could work; 49 per cent wanted more exhibits they could touch and 36 per cent wanted more open displays.

Brian McWilliams and Joyce Hopwood (1972(1)), in a wide-ranging survey undertaken at Norwich Museum in 1971–72, received the following responses to the question 'What sections interest you most?'. Natural history, 37 per cent; archaeology, 21 per cent; fine art, 18 per cent; the keep, 18 per cent; applied art, 7 per cent; the special exhibition, 6 per cent; the battlements, 5 per cent; geology, 3 per cent, refreshments, 1 per cent; 4 per cent did not know. Interestingly, fine art was more popular in January (25 per cent) than at other times. The peak for natural history was August (42 per cent) and that for archaeology was in July (25 per cent).

Visitor behaviour

Information on how the visitor behaves in the museum has obvious planning implications. Of particular interest are his movements within spaces and how much time is spent on various activities. This information also has relevance to exhibit effectiveness, particularly in relation to the ability of exhibits to capture visitors' attention (attractiveness) and retain their interest (holding power). In order to provide data on visitor behaviour some basic information is useful. This might include:

1. The number of previous occasions a visit has been made to the museum (to establish familiarity).
2. Whether the visitor is alone or accompanied, and if so by whom, and the size of group.
3. Aspects of the visitor's profile, e.g. sex, age, etc.

Observational studies are used to obtain most information on visitor behaviour, and the topics to be studied generally relate to the effectiveness of the museum in satisfying visitors' needs. Numerous studies have been undertaken in this field, and, whereas most relate to specific locations, some generalizations are possible which have wider applications.

Examples of findings

Niehoff (1953) in his study of the Milwaukee Museum in summer 1952 found that visitor attendance was reduced by a quarter for each rise in floor level. Some 33 per cent were first-time visitors and the largest number (46 per cent) spent about an hour in the museum. Melton (1935(1)) noted the significance of the exit. In particular, he found that 'The amount of attention received by an object is a function of its distance from the exits' and 'The exit . . . does more than draw visitors through one section of the gallery and make them neglect other sections. It also . . . competes with the art objects for attention.' Weiss and Boutourline (1963) from their observations at the Seattle World's Fair (1962) state that an important determinant of paths through a pavilion is the location of entrances and exits. Visitors, they noted, were unwilling to go into areas where exits were not apparent. Melton (1935(2)) also discovered that visitors tended to spend a set time in a gallery, almost irrespective of the number of pictures exhibited therein. 'On comparing arrangements of from six to thirty-six paintings in six combinations, increases in the number of paintings did not produce proportional increases in the *total* time spent by visitors in the gallery.'

Borun (1977(1)) in her studies in the Franklin Institute, observed that most visitors came to the museum in family groups, an observation corroborated in many other studies, e.g. Mason (1974), Doughty (1968(1)) and Abbey and Cameron (1960). Robinson (1928(1)) noted that 'The greatest fatigue effect was observed to occur where there was the least walking about on hard floors, but the greatest continuity of observation and the greatests number of pictures observed.' Not surprisingly, he also found that 'An increase in the number of exhibit objects of similar classification tends to decrease the interest of visitors in the pieces present.' This was also noted by Melton (1935(3)), who identified in the visitor two principal types of museum fatigue—muscular fatigue and object saturation.

Wolf and Tymitz (1979) undertook a naturalistic evaluation of the bicentennial exhibit at the National Museum of Natural History, Smithsonian Institution. They obtained a wealth of detailed information based mainly on observation and informal interviews. Typical observations were: 'Female adults are the only visitors we observed stopping at the Indian Culture display. Indeed, they were the only ones to comment on the display during the interview' and 'Adults stay with their children as they visit the exhibit. Parents call out the names of specimens they notice and recognize, e.g. *'Look at the porcupine,' 'Did you see the turkey?'* The smaller and lesser known specimens are not pointed out . . .'

How a visitor behaves in a museum, clearly, is fundamental to an exhibition attaining its aims and objectives, particularly if these are written specifically in behavioural terms. So those responsible for devising exhibitions really do need to know how visitors will behave in any given situation in order that the museum exhibitions may function effectively and the visitor will benefit from the experience.

Visitor reaction

This differs from visitor behaviour in as much as it is more concerned with mental processes than observable physical movements. Nevertheless, it is clearly allied closely to it, and to the studies on exhibit effectiveness with their specific concern with the measurement of visitor reaction and learning. Fundamental to these studies are aspects of educational and behavioural psychology concerning issues like how we learn and the nature of memory and perception.

Learning is a dynamic process which embraces various features, including remembering, perceiving and thinking. It is constructive in relation to developing perceptions, and reconstructive in relation to memories. Growth and change come about through a process of selection, modification and discarding. Cognitive psychologists have developed a theory which identifies the formation of the systems which relate to a person's adaptation to the environment, both physical and social, as a 'schema'. This is modified to a lesser or greater extent as a result of a perception. Once this has happened, the perception is effectively complete and incorporated into a system that will subsequently operate as a living whole, so that the perception cannot reappear as an unrelated item. Distinguishing between the two processes of *remembering*, that is, when a person consults his schemata, and the creative process of *thinking* is clearly difficult. However, when schemata are used in *new* constructions, this is the essence of creative thought.

When a visitor confronts an exhibit, what first occurs is a scanning of the presentation. Usually the eye will first concentrate on a point slightly to left of centre, in the upper quadrant. The visual sensation on the retina of the observer becomes a perception which is coded in the brain to either one or a number of existing schemata. The visitor will want to bring appropriate schemata to bear in order to perceive both the constant features of each item and those which are distinctive. It is this process which gives meaning in the mind to the observed phenomenon. Each time it occurs the structure of the schema is changed to accommodate new experiences and to benefit the understanding of future perceptions.

There is also, of course, an emotional side to learning, known as the 'affective' domain, as opposed to the 'cognitive' (Bloom 1971-2), and here the psychology becomes more complex. However, in this context it is crucial to emphasize the importance of relating the learning process to the emotional state of deriving pleasure. For many, the formal learning situation on which much of the educational work in schools has been based has occurred in circumstances of stress. Learning has become associated with work, and with punishment if the work has not been done well.

However, for others, learning is associated with achievement, which has given satisfaction and pleasure. In the informal learning environment of the museum exhibition it is important to ensure that the visitor is aware of the removal of any stressful coercing factors. This should free him to enjoy the experience. Learning activities become interesting and rewarding if they provide a pleasurable experience. In these circum-stances visitors are certainly more likely to retain more of what they learn, be encouraged to repeat the process, and become increasingly motivated.

To sum up, it can be said that stimuli from the visitor's environment are processed in the central nervous system by the application of schema which are based on past experience, by mood or emotion, and also by genetically determined predispositions. The result is a unique perception which is also accompanied by emotions which are, in part, also deter-mined by it. This may then initiate behavioural activity which can, in turn, act as a modifier to an existing schemata, which in turn may serve to influence subsequent perceptions. Since memory has a long-term capacity, behaviour can be influenced by perceptions which occurred many years previously. The theories which have been developed in relation to the workings of the brain are both numerous and complex. They are, however, important if a full understanding of the visitor's reactions is to be achieved. The interested reader is, therefore referred to the considerable literature which exists on the subject, and in particular to the works of Arnheim, Gagné, Gombrich and Gregory.

Visitors with special needs

A group of visitors deserving a particular mention are those whose needs differ from those of the majority of other visitors—the disabled. The term 'disabled', according to the World Health Organization, may be applied to anyone who has 'any restriction or lack (resulting from an impair-ment) of ability to perform an activity in the manner or within the range considered normal for a human being'. According to some estimates, one person in ten of the population, in some way, is disabled. Although most frequently associated with those confined to wheelchairs, disabilities may be various, causing both mental and physical handicaps.

Nerys Johnson (1984), makes the valid point that the term 'disabled' tends to cause embarrassment both to the person concerned and to other people, and that this, together with the problems of actually being different, can create rather negative situations. She states, 'it could be argued that there is no such thing as a disabled person, only that there is a rich variety of people with differing abilities and needs, requiring different solutions for them all to participate fully in life as a whole'.

A statement by Steve (aged thirty-two and blind since birth) in Eleanor Hartley's *Touch and See* is justification for this view: 'Most people who are born disabled do not consider themselves abnormal—they are ordin-ary people. We have normal ambitions.' However, people's abilities and needs which fall outside the accepted 'norm' are regarded as special and, as such, may be considered, first, in physical terms and, second, in intellectual and emotional terms.

Physical needs

The physical needs start with access. Rosalind Hardiman (1984) considered that ' "Access for all" should be our watchword and active steps
should be taken to achieve this.' Providing good access needs a considered
approach, and is best achieved not through piecemeal improvements to
such things as toilet facilities and ramps at stairways but by an analysis of
the total problem. Routes need to be decided upon and facilitated and
adequate signage provided. Pushing a wheelchair can be very tiring, and
the last thing the person involved may want is to keep trying abortive
routes in an attempt to find the one which allows wheelchair access.

Church (1984) gives some indication of the responsibilities of architects
and designers in this respect, and mentions a number of items which need
particular consideration. These include parking facilities, dipped kerbs,
sliding doors, lifts (but not for use as emergency escapes unless special
provision is made), w.c.s, clear vistas and good signs. He also mentions
an important aspect which is often overlooked, the need for staff to be
briefed and trained to cater for persons with special needs. Also, given
that the purpose of the disabled visitors coming to the museum is
generally to appreciate the exhibitions, these too should be designed with
the physical needs of all visitors in mind.

Intellectual and emotional needs

It was Molly Harrison (1967) who noted that 'irrespective of handicap,
most are curious to discover'. Over the years this statement has been borne
out by admittedly all too few museums who have made some effort to
satisfy the special needs of the disabled, in particular those of the
handicapped. However, it must be said that this group, although
numerous, have not represented a high proportion of museum visitors
and much needs to be done, not only by museums but also by groups
concerned with the disabled, to promote the use of museums in this
respect. Even at the 'Please Touch' exhibition which was specially
designed for the disabled and held at the British Museum in 1983 only 1
per cent of visitors (324) were visually handicapped.

As early as 1913 Deas reported in the *Museums Journal* on an
invitation he gave to blind children to visit Sunderland Museum. It came
about as a result of a chance remark by a teacher of the blind on the
difficulties experienced by the sightless in developing a sense of proportion. Children were given the opportunity to touch and explore animals
(even to sit on a lion's back!). Some five weeks later they were given as a
test making models of the animals they had examined. The results were
reported as 'outstanding'.

More recently Alison Heath (1976) and Anne Pearson (1984, 1989) have
written on various projects for the disabled. Pearson mentions the
qualitative success of the British Museum's 'Please Touch' exhibition
and its value to the general public as well as the disabled. She also reports

on a facility (arranged by the Museum's education service) for deaf visitors, whereby a sign language interpreter accompanies the 11.30 a.m. gallery tour on the first Saturday of every month, thus enabling it to be enjoyed by both the deaf and the hearing.

The British Museum will arrange special tours of its Egyptian and Greek and Roman sculpture galleries for the blind and partially sighted. Similarly, the Tate Gallery (Ellis 1984) will provide special tours for any group of disabled visitors. The Tate's innovative 'Sculpture for the Blind' exhibition was held in 1976, and since then the museum has acquired considerable experience of assisting disabled visitors, including those with mental handicaps. The Natural History Museum, too, responded with facilities within its 'Exploring Woodland and Seashore' exhibition in 1983 and 'Discovering Mammals' in 1985. It would be wrong, however, to suggest that the only recent initiatives have been undertaken in London's national museums. The Horniman Museum and the Gunnersbury Park Museum have both been active in this area, and outside London the National Museum of Wales, Leicester Museum, the Mappin Gallery, Sheffield, and Northampton Museum and Art Gallery are just some which have mounted special exhibitions for the blind.

Eleanor Hartley's booklet *Touch and See* provides a useful introduction to sculpture by and for the visually handicapped, and in particular a discussion of the experimental scheme which was started by the Adult Education Department of the University of Leicester in 1982. This involved a group of visually handicapped people working in the studio on drawings and making sculpture before exhibiting it and appreciating the exhibition. Hartley writes:

> The exhibitions are not just rare occasions for visually handicapped visitors to experience sculpture. The exhibition is itself a learning experience . . . it is designed to lead the visitor through the process of learning-to-see-through-touching, and to illustrate the application of that skill to the creation of the sculptural form.

One of the participants, Jim, aged forty and with tunnel vision, comments, 'One of the important things to me about the 'Touch and See' Exhibition was that my family could come and see the things I made—it showed them that my nuts and bolts are in the right place.'

As a result of the concern felt in museums for the disabled, the Museums and Galleries Disability Association was formed. Early in 1989 the Museums and Galleries Commission appointed a Museums Disability Adviser, whose task is to stimulate and co-ordinate initiatives nationally. The special needs of the disabled extend into all areas of the museum's public services, and beyond. Such is the importance of the issue and its implications that there is a need for most museums to develop a specific policy on their approach to visitors with special needs.

Anthropometric data

Since exhibitions are designed for visitors rather than for objects, a
knowledge of the physical characteristics of the people who will use the
exhibition facilities and spaces is fundamental to the design process.
Everything in these environments, from door handles to showcases, and
from sloping ramps to sign systems, needs to be designed with a
knowledge of the human body and its ability to perform the tasks being
asked of it. If all people were identical in size and shape this would be
relatively simple; but they are not. The skills of the designer must be
employed to devise, fashion and arrange the exhibition components so
that they meet the requirements of the proposed audience. This may
mean that both the short and the tall are catered for, together with
wheelchair users, the very young and the elderly, who, with the handicapped, may need special provision. Almost certainly this will involve
viewing stands, ramps, handrails and similar physical devices to provide
variations on what might be regarded as the norm. If the norm is to be
taken as the average, it should be treated with caution, for it might not
refer to many people, and certainly not necessarily to the majority. For
this reason, percentiles can be better guides to follow. Since a museum
visit is essentially a visual experience for the majority of visitors, enabling
everyone to see an exhibition with ease and without discomfort must be
of paramount importance. To this end, objects must be raised, lowered or
distanced as necessary *in relation to the visitor*. Furthermore, as the
exhibition environment becomes more interactive, with visitors being
encouraged to use computers and other devices, it may be described as a
'workplace' and the ergonomic factors relating to functional ease need
consideration.

A considerable amount of general research has been done on ergonomics and anthropometrics, and the reader is referred to the specialized
studies by the *Architects Journal* (1963), Dreyfuss (1967); Goldsmith
(1977); Murrell (1965); Shackel (1974) and Tutt and Alder (1981) for
detailed information. In the museum field a number of studies have been
undertaken and some of the findings and recommendations are discussed
next.

Vision and viewing

Most people with normal vision can see, without moving the head,
everything within a cone of vision extending outwards from the eyes at an
angle of about 50° (25° each side of straight ahead). (Neal, 1969, suggested
the limit was 60°, whereas Hunter, 1979, has suggested 40°.) This can be
extended by moving the head from side to side, where an angle of about
45° to left and right of straight ahead is normally easily achieved. In the
vertical plane the angle above the horizontal is about 30°, whereas that
below is about 40°. This range may be increased by tilting the head back
or forwards to about 30° either side of its normal position without

Table 12.2 Estimated dimensions of body characteristics of the British population (mm)

| Sex/age group | Standing posture | | Sitting posture | | |
	Height	Eye-level	Height (above seat)	Eye-level (above seat)	Seat width
Men 18–40					
Fifth percentile	1,628	1,524	841	726	328
Fiftieth percentile	1,737	1,633	900	785	366
Ninety-fifth percentile	1,846	1,742	959	844	404
Women 18–40					
Fifth percentile	1,518	1,427	770	681	360
Fiftieth percentile	1,647	1,546	839	735	405
Ninety-fifth percentile	1,742	1,643	882	765	441
Elderly women 60–90					
Fifth percentile	1,454	1,338	739	621	321
Fiftieth percentile	1,558	1,441	798	684	388
Ninety-fifth percentile	1,662	1,544	857	740	455

Note: Data include an allowance for clothing and shoes (28 mm for men, 40 mm for women, 31 mm for elderly women). When reading percentile data it cannot be assumed that whenever the value of the ninety-fifth percentile is observed 95 per cent of the population will be accommodated, for if the critical dimension is in the opposite direction only 5 per cent will be accommodated, and the correct course is to apply the fifth percentile instead. *Source.* Goldsmith (1979), 'Anthropometric data'.

discomfort. Hunter (1979) suggested that, taking into account the vision limit of a cone of 40°, the whole of a picture may be viewed in comfort at a distance of about double its diagonal measurement. At half that distance, or less, details may be appreciated but, depending on its size, the viewer may have to move to encompass it all.

Dandridge (1966) has noted that:

> The eyes tend to move over an observed area in jumps and stops which are termed 'fixations and excursions' . . . the majority of persons tested made the first fixation for all media at a point above and to the left of the centre of the observed field.

These findings confirm those of a number of researchers who have considered the specific topic of how pictures are perceived.

Hamilton (1970) advises that psychologists have estimated that, when the brain is receiving visual and aural impressions simultaneously, about 70 per cent of the intelligence comes through the eyes and 30 per cent through the ears.

An important aspect of vision and viewing is the ability of the visitor to

Table 12.3 Estimated height of children (mm)

Category	Age (years)					
	3	6	9	12	15	18
Boys						
Fifth percentile	879	1,068	1,215	1,345	1,504	1,651
Fiftieth percentile	942	1,143	1,311	1,458	1,633	1,755
Ninety-fifth percentile	1,005	1,218	1,407	1,571	1,762	1,859
Girls						
Fifth percentile	876	1,059	1,204	1,355	1,507	1,534
Fiftieth percentile	930	1,138	1,300	1,468	1,603	1,626
Ninety-fifth percentile	984	1,217	1,396	1,581	1,699	1,718

Note: When reading percentile data it cannot be assumed that whenever the value of the ninety-fifth percentile is observed 95 per cent of the population will be accommodated, for if the critical dimension is in the opposite direction only 5 per cent will be accommodated, and the correct course is to apply the fifth percentile instead.
Source: Goldsmith (1979), 'Anthropometric data'.

read printed material incorporated within an exhibition. This topic is dealt with in the discussion of labels in Chapter 11.

Visual band

There is again general agreement that the most practical 'visual band' (i.e. the strip of wall space that visitors can observe easily as they walk through a gallery) is that which commences about a metre from ground level and extends upwards a further metre. Neal (1976) commented, 'studies have shown . . . that adult museum visitor observes an area only a little over half a metre above his own eye level to a metre below it at an average viewing distance of 60–70 centimetres'.

When considering showcases, Neal (1963, 1969) suggested that in relation to adult viewers they should have an aperture 0.71 m from ground level which extends a further 1.37 m to a height from ground level of 2.08 m, with a depth of 0.61 m and an internal height from ground level of 2.46 m. Hunter (1979), however, has suggested an aperture between 0.75 m and 0.95 m from the ground to between 1.9 m and 2.0 m in height. Obviously the designer has some latitude in these matters, and much will depend on the anticipated audience, the objects and the situation.

In most of these situations it is a matter of applying known data and then of testing proposed dimensions on the intended audience. For example, Snider (1977) has suggested that exhibition developers should themselves visit their projects in a wheelchair in order to appreciate the design implications. For the eye level of adult male and female chair users is about 1.22 m and 1.15 m respectively. This makes the viewing of

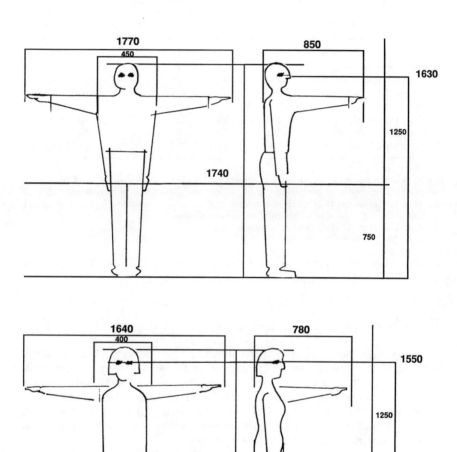

Figure 12.2   Human dimensions: (a) mean average dimensions of adult
British males, (b) mean average dimensions of adult British females (mm)

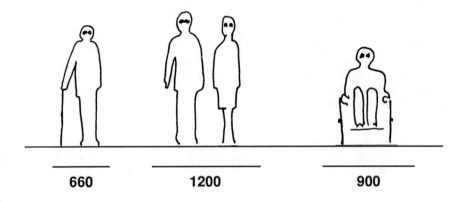

660 1200 900

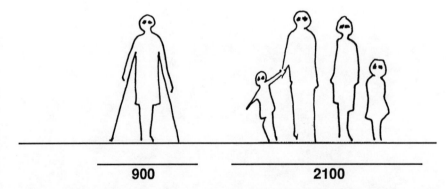

900 2100

Figure 12.3 Minimum human widths to be accommodated (mm)

detailed material above this height very difficult, and particularly so if it exceeds about 1.8 m.

Contrary to popular belief, successful exhibition design is essentially concerned with designing for *people* and not exhibits. A design can be said to 'work' only if it functions effectively and satisfies the needs of its visitors as well as those of the objects it displays. Through compromise it is probably possible to ensure that all visitors gain something, at least, from experiencing an exhibition. However, it will be the design brief which indicates to the designer what his design priorities should be and specifies the visitor group or groups whom he must give priority in his designs. This chapter has emphasized the importance of the visitor in the exhibition context, and has given some indication of his physical and mental make-up and the implications this has for the design of the exhibition environment.

13. Exhibition effectiveness

Introduction

Productivity, efficiency and effectiveness have supposedly been more the concern of industry and commerce than of universities and museums. Indeed, it might be argued that these disciplines have reacted against such impositions, and for good reasons. The advancement of knowledge is an activity which is not easy to assess by either qualitative and quantitative criteria, and the worth of knowledge itself is generally understood only when it is made manifest in some tangible application. However, in recent years two things have happened to change this position as far as museums are concerned. First, since a relatively small group of museum professionals, working mainly in the USA, have concerned themselves with the communication and educational role of the museum, interest in this area has become more widespread and many now seek information about how well the museum performs these functions. Second, as a result of the move towards increased accountability arising from paucity of resources, those responsible for funding museums, many of whom have backgrounds in industry and commerce, have begun to question the extent to which museums are using their funds effectively, and whether they are providing value for money.

Coleman (1939) was among the first to become interested in aspects of exhibition effectiveness and to study how the visitor behaved in the exhibition environment. He commented:

> Attendance is the handiest gauge of relations with the public. When the count goes up the management is pleased, and the annual report gives figures and points to the moral. When the count goes down, the director must have an alibi for the board, and be able to show in print some compensating gain of a higher nature.

Attendance figures still constitute an index of the popularity of museums and exhibitions, and are frequently used comparatively in popularity league tables. The British Tourist Authority publishes annual figures which never fail to attract considerable interest. However, like income received as a result of an admission charge, these particular statistics give little real indication of how well a museum performs as a communicator, and still less about how effective its exhibitions may be.

Writing in *Curator*, Stephan de Borhegyi (1963), who as Director of the

197

Milwaukee Public Museum did much to promote an interest in the visitor's perception of museums and their effectiveness, wrote:

> Only too rarely does the curator consider whether the exhibit will be understood and appealing to the visitor. If he does question its effectiveness he will likely ask another curator if *he* understands and approves it. To make the situation worse, the museum artist tends to design exhibits for the approval of artists in other museums or for designers in the community. The problem, of course, is that museums are not aimed at the understanding and appreciation of curators and artists. No matter how artistic the layout, how scrupulously accurate the scientific label, if the exhibit does not attract the interest or reach the intellect of the average museum visitor, it is simply wasted time, money and effort.

In this statement de Borhegyi summed up the situation not only as it was in America in the 1960s but also how it was in much of Europe as well. Furthermore, many would say that it has a certain relevance even today, although some might take issue with the idea that museum exhibitions appeal only to the 'average visitor', for they would argue that if such a person exists he/she is certainly very hard to define.

The interest of the Milwaukee Museum in visitor reactions to museum exhibitions has been of comparatively long standing. As early as 1952 the museum had been researching into visitor characteristics and had been devising tests for measuring visual communications and the educational and learning impact of its exhibits on the visitor. Some of this research was included in a publication, *The Museum Visitor*, edited by de Borhegyi and Irene Hanson (1968), which did much to promote an awareness of the significance of the topic both in America and Europe. It considered many aspects of the visitor, for, given that the purpose of an exhibition is to bring about some change in its audience, it is only by studying the visitor that this aspect of effectiveness can be assessed. In fact a simple analysis of the museum exhibition communication system suggests that there are three essential elements which are worthy of study: the transmitter – that is, the exhibition structure and the communications media employed; the message – that is, the nature of the communication and its substance; and, finally, the receivers, the visitors and their ability to accept and comprehend the communication. This group was considered in more detail in Chapter 12.

What, then, is exhibition effectiveness? Essentially it is an objective assessment of how well an exhibition (and all its various components) performs its various functions, and, in particular, how well it does so in relation to its declared aims and objectives, for this is the only rational way in which the success or otherwise of an exhibiton can be gauged. There are, of course, other ways of considering an exhibition, but these can become very subjective and, in effect, can be little more than statements of personal preference, such as 'It worked for me' or 'I liked it.' Important as these are—and they *are* important for the individuals concerned—nevertheless, as individual statements they have limited application. It is also worth remembering that, in addition to exhibitions being functional pieces of design whose performance can be assessed, they are works of art and frequently incorporate works of art whose effect on the viewer is difficult to assess. As yet no method of formal evaluation has been devised which will accurately measure the 'oohs' and 'ahs' and gasps of wonder which emanate from the visitor when reacting to this type of emotional experience. However, Hess and Polt (1965) noted that the size of the pupil in the eye reflects the level of interest of a person observing an object, that is, the larger the pupil the greater the level of interest. Also Hess and Krugman (1964) reported the development of a portable camera to determine what the viewer was looking at and his interest level.

In 1968 Harris Shettel and his associates published their paper *Strategies for Determining Exhibit Effectiveness*. Its purpose was to initiate the systematic development of research strategies and testable hypotheses that would make it possibe to evaluate the effectiveness of scientific and technical exhibits better, in particular those designed to attain educational objectives. In his introduction, he stated, 'Exhibit effectiveness is demonstrated on the basis of a measurable change in the behaviour of the intended audience, produced by the exhibit, and consistent with the stated aims or objectives of the exhibit.'

Shettel and his colleagues recognized the enormous number of variables associated with museum exhibition design, and listed the main variables under three headings: 'exhibit viewer variables' (age, sex, socio-economic level, IQ, etc.); 'exhibit design variables' (amount of verbal material, legibility, layout, etc.) and 'exhibit, effectiveness variables', which were concerned with the ability of the exhibition to do its job, that is, to attract the attention of visitors, to hold interest and to bring about a change in the level of such things as interest, attitude and knowledge.

This recognition of the number of variables related to exhibit effectiveness prompted an attempt to rationalize the problem and evolve a system which would eliminate much of the element of chance inherent in a situation with so many variables. Shettel considered that a comprehensive theory of exhibit effectiveness must concern itself with three aspects: (1) initially attracting the visitor; (2) maintaining attraction and (3) maximizing the amount of relevant learning that is achieved on the part of the viewer. In order that this latter might be achieved successfully, he thought that when preparing programmed teaching exhibits a number of principles, if applied, made for particularly effective instructional devices. His strategy began with the need to state exhibit objectives explicitly and carry them out in the conception of the exhibit. The content, he felt, should be presented in small steps, both in intellectual terms, with rational sequence and progression, and in physical terms, with information given in quantities manageable for the viewer. He regarded the type of exhibit employed as of particular significance, and thought exhibits which make the maximum use of relevant, overt responding on the part of the viewer to be better instructional devices than those that do not. Furthermore, he considered exhibits that inform the viewer of the correctness of his responses to be capable of producing a higher level of response than those that do not. Finally, he recognized that exhibits which have been tested on their intended audiences, or 'pre-validated' through a sequence of testing and revising, are more effective than those that are not.

Another prominent researcher active in this field was Screven (1974), who also recognized that 'Museum professionals have strong beliefs that something *is* happening to their visitors, but there is great difficulty in defining what this is, much less measuring it.' In a new department formed in the Smithsonian Institution in 1972 Screven was charged with the task of exploring, on a continuing basis, the museum environment as interactive *milieu*. His aim was to find out how the visitor learns; how the museum affects him and what devices can be used to make the experience more meaningful.

Both Screven and Shettel were interested in developing an exhibit or educational technology relevant to the museum situation which provided a set of criteria against which the effectiveness of exhibits as teaching tools could be gauged. In effect they sought a formula or a design manual which, when applied, would ensure the success of an exhibition as an educational instrument. However, some would argue that seeking to develop an educational technology in museums has, on occasion, over-looked the fact that a large number of visitors come not with the intention of learning but for entertainment. For example, in his paper 'Evaluating didactic exhibits: a critical look at Shettel's work' Alt (1977) concluded that Shettel, in one of his studies, ignored the fact that visitors have different intentions.

Another concern for many is that educational technology based largely on interactive exhibits has been found to have the capacity to function as a teaching tool quite independently of the museum objects, something of which educational establishments are very well aware, and most owners of personal computers too. This presents something of a dilemma for the museum, for with the use of contemporary forms of popular communications media, and the availability of interactive computer-based labelling systems, there is undoubtedly an opportunity to engage the attention of the visitor. However, if it is done at the expense of the object, is the museum betraying its true function?

It is interesting to note that by far the most research that has been undertaken into exhibition effectiveness has been concerned with the communication of information about science, and science is often concerned with abstract concepts. Undoubtedly new technology has a role to play in this, and the 'science centre'/'exploratorium' type of interactive exhibit has a place in the museums of science. However, for other museums, which are more concerned with objects, and in particular in museums concerned with art, the extent to which this type of 'teaching tool' has an application must be limited.

Research and evaluation relating to the effectiveness of a particular solution or element of a solution are necessary activities in a systematic approach to the design of any artefact, including exhibitions (see Chapter

8). The designer needs to have information on what will work, in what circumstances, in order to develop successful solutions. However, what sets exhibitions slightly apart is that no two briefs are ever quite the same, and, more important, besides being functional they are an expressive art form which owes much to their originality. As Gardner and Heller (1960) stressed:

> Successful exhibition design is not, and never can be, a matter of applied formula, and a lot of misunderstanding would be avoided if it were not discussed in such terms. In practice exhibition design is an empirical process with no one infallible answer to any problem.

Effective exhibitions

Carmel (1962) thought that 'The most effective exhibition is not necessarily the one that draws the biggest crowds; it is the exhibition that imparts some measure of stimulation, enjoyment, or knowledge to most of the people who visit it.' There have been numerous definitions of what constitutes an effective or successful exhibition, and probably few would disagree with Carmel in general terms. Similarly, the description that states that 'an exhibition is successful if the visitor can remember its content the next day . . . the next month . . . the next year . . .' also has some credence. But clearly this type of definition can have only limited application. What constitutes an effective exhibition will depend on the viewpoint, be it of the museum or of the visitor, and what it achieves for *them*.

As has already been said, there are three aspects relevant to communicating through museum exhibitions; the exhibition structure and the communications media employed; the message, that is, the nature of the communication and its substance (which includes the objects); and the visitors and their ability to comprehend or indeed react in any other way to the experience. In order to ascertain the effectiveness of an exhibition, each of these three aspects needs to be studied. For the most part, each aspect will be unique to the exhibition in question and have relevance only to that particular exhibition. However, some findings will have application elsewhere and it is on these that the theory of exhibitions as a medium of communications is founded.

Some of the earliest recorded investigations into exhibition effectiveness date from the latter part of the last century. According to Goins and Griffenhagen (1957) as early as 1871 one G.T. Flechner was employing experimental techniques in attempts to develop a scientific method to judge objects aesthetically, and utilizing questionnaires in an art gallery situation. Since then, interest has been spasmodic but it is outside the scope of this work to provide details of all the research that has been undertaken into the effectiveness of exhibitions as a communications media. However, where appropriate, some findings have been included under the relevant topics. For a comprehensive review of the research findings which have application beyond the parameters of the original studies the reader is referred to *Effective Interpretive Exhibitions*, compiled by Geoffrey Stansfield (1981).

Evaluation

Evaluation is a general term which is concerned with the assessment of many aspects of performance and is now frequently applied to museum exhibitions in the context of their effectiveness. Much has been written to try to dispel the impression that evaluation of this type is a judgment of the work produced by a group of individuals or, more seriously, an assessment of the capacities of the people involved. 'Evaluation,' Steven Griggs (1985) tells us, 'Should be considered not as a means of judgement but as a process of *collaboration*; a collaboration between the museum professional and the visitor.' This concept is useful, as neither the curator, the designer, nor indeed any members of the team responsible for the production of an exhibition can, by definition, work in isolation, and none should fail to consider the person for whom the whole exercise is being undertaken, that is, the museum visitor. Evaluation is, therefore, a means to an end—the end being exhibitions which function better and, as a result, give greater visitor satisfaction. Nevertheless an element of measure is fundamental, and needs to be applied to the performance of systems and not to the people involved. Like many other areas of work which were once part-and-parcel of the designer's role, evaluation has now evolved as a separate discipline with its own body of knowledge and its own experts. As such the professional evaluator may be called upon to join the exhibition production team on occasions that warrant it. However, in other circumstances, and in particular for small design elements, the designer may well continue to undertake the necessary research.

Essentially there are three different types of evaluation. The first is concerned with assessing ideas, and occurs early in the exhibition development sequence, at the time the brief is being formulated. It is called *concept research* or *front-end evaluation*. Its purpose is to try to eliminate errors as early in the work programme as possible. In order to achieve this, it will probably involve some form of research and the collection of data which will be used either to validate the proposals or to invalidate them. This may well take the form of surveys (both on a large and a small scale) and involve the use of interview techniques and questionnaires. It may also involve searches of the published literature and, in effect, examine past experience and consider current theory. This pre-planning stage is about testing the proposed audience (or researching new ones), and assessing what the likely response to the development might be. It should therefore provide the basis of informed decisions, and may well feature prominently in any feasibility study.

The second type is *formative evaluation*. This is typically an element within a design activity model and normally follows the initial stage of design development work of which it ultimately becomes a part. Unlike concept research, which is about evaluating the abstract, formative evaluation of exhibitions is concerned with the assessment of tangible elements, but in the early stages of their development when they are in mock-up or prototype form. The mock-up seeks to resemble the finished proposal in the characteristics which might need to be evaluated but is made cheaply and quickly of easily worked, non-durable materials. Whereas the mock-up aims at simulating the final effect, a prototype does not. It is a trial piece or preliminary version, normally intended to be as true as possible to the final proposal, although probably manufactured in a different way. It is particularly important to produce such an item before any mass production is undertaken.

Obviously the purpose of this form of evaluation is to test elements at the developmental stage, to ascertain which function best against the initial criteria, and then attempt to perfect the solution. To achieve this, various techniques might be employed. In terms of how the visitor reacts to a proposed exhibit, questionnaires, interviews and observational studies might be appropriate. In this way information could, for example, be obtained on whether graphics are observed, whether intended sequences are adhered to, or whether labels are understood. Relatively small samples of perhaps twenty or so subjects could provide this information, and the success or failure of some elements may well become apparent after evaluating the response of as few as half this number. This process of testing during the developmental stage is known as pre-validating.

The reaction of the visitor to any given exhibition is not, of course, the only aspect which might need to be tested. Mock-ups and prototypes may also be used by the designer and conservation staff to evaluate the effects of such design variables as proportion, shape, colour, texture, materials and equipment. For example, lighting schemes are often tested in order that the design can be evaluated (in terms of level, shadow effects, etc.) and also so that data can be obtained for conservation purposes (i.e. on levels, heat, etc.). Although technically they might be described as 'formative evaluation', some experiments to test the physical properties of exhibition elements may well be long-term and run over several years. Nevertheless, the results of this type of research may still be applied to new developments.

The final type of evalution is called *summative evaluation*. This, for many, is the most familiar type of evaluation and is undertaken after an exhibition has opened in order to gauge how well it is performing. However, it should not be left until the exhibition has opened before it is thought about. Indeed, many would advocate that as the exhibition's aims and objectives are being set, so the means of evaluating how well they have been achieved should also be considered, for perhaps the main task of summative evaluation is a consideration of how well the exhibition performs against its original aims and objectives. Additionally, new criteria may be devised as new information may be required: for example, the entire exhibition as a system might be considered. This study could make comparisons between types of display and establish how they work together or independently to attract the visitor.

Yet another way in which an exhibition might be assessed, is by critical appraisal. The 'crit' or critique is familiar to all designers who have gone through the design college system of education. Typically, it follows a major project and involves the student group, members of staff and ideally the client for whom the project has been designed. It may also involve an outside expert who contributes to a discussion of the merits or otherwise of the various design proposals. This approach also has applications in the museum situation, and many museums arrange for 'debriefings' or 'post-mortem' sessions on these lines. However, they are generally staff meetings, with the 'client' seen as the curator rather than the visitor to the exhibition. Nevertheless, information on how the visitor is reacting to the exhibition can, and indeed should, be available to the meeting. If this approach is used, arrangements should be made to record the discussion and, ideally, make it available in edited form as a written report. An alternative to group evaluation is to commission an outside expert to undertake a study of the exhibition, as someone who can undertake an unbiased and informed appraisal. After an initial visit when first impressions are recorded, and how the gallery works is observed and also recorded, the assessor may well meet museum staff and be briefed on the aims and objectives of the project. This method, which is surprisingly underused, can and should be very productive, particularly if the consultant is both expert in his/her assessment and sensitive to the museum situation and aware of the issues involved in presenting the report.

A form of critical appraisal is undergone when an exhibition is reviewed by the press, and often the museum sees the person undertaking the review as the consultant in the model above. This is certainly not unreasonable in the case of specialists undertaking reviews for the professional journals, such as those which have appeared in the *Museums Journal* by eminent professionals. However, few other publications aspire to this level of criticism. Certainly reviews in the popular daily press and the popular magazines tend not to review an exhibition, but to discuss the objects on display. This is not surprising as, in part, reviews in the press serve a different function, and reviewers would undoubtedly exclude items from a general publication that they would include in a private report. Nevertheless, press cuttings and letters do, to some extent, provide an indication as to how an exhibition has been received.

Summative evaluation may result in modifications to the exhibition – but, more important, it should provide information on what elements of an exhibition are successful and what are not, and in what circumstances. This information should be available for future projects.

Evaluation methodology. The evaluation process may be divided into four distinct stages:

1. The identification of the characteristics to be studied and the establishing of criteria against which assessment might take place.
2. The devising of suitable evaluation programmes and decisions as to which techniques might be employed.
3. The collection of data.
4. The assessment, evaluation and interpretation of the data.

The first stage is concerned with deciding 'what we want to find out'. Lists of questions in need of answers should be drawn up and categorized. They may be concerned with visitor behaviour, the performance of components, or whatever, and will need to have criteria set against them to enable assessment to take place. Essentially these should be based on the aims and objectives of the exhibition, as that is the normal starting point. However, they could include any facet of the exhibition on which information is required. A priority rating may need to be given, as the programme, if working to a budget, may not be able to undertake all that is desired.

At stage two a programme is devised which will obtain answers to the questions identified above. In doing so, those responsible must take account of the resources available, and any other constraints such as a time scale. Indeed, the methodology involved in the design of such a programme does not differ greatly from that employed in other design disciplines, with the identifiable stages of brief, design development, testing, and implementation and assessment.

Stage three is concerned with the collection of data prior to stage four, assessment and evaluation. This can be undertaken in two ways – informally or formally. 'Informal' is applied to evaluation which is non-rigorous and unstructured. It seeks information in the form of opinions which are based on evidence but may be subject to prejudice and intuition in its interpretation. Often it is not accurately quantifiable, and, unless it is in response to a very specific question the information obtained may be very diverse. This type of evaluation provides a fairly rough-and-ready 'gut reaction' and as such may well be broadly accurate but lacking in detail.

'Naturalistic' evaluation is a term applied to a form of 'informal' evaluation. Wolf and Tymitz (1979), were of the opinion that evaluation strategies are naturalistic if they:

(1) orient more directly to current and spontaneous activities, behaviours and expressions rather than some set of formally stated objectives.
(2) respond to staff and visitor interests in different kinds of information and
(3) account for the different values and perspectives that exist whenever the question of impact is introduced. Naturalistic Evaluation takes a broad, holistic view of the program, exhibit or institution, is more interpretive than judgmental and requires participation from a wide range of people who are to be served by the study effort.
. . . Most important, Naturalistic Evaluation depends upon relating natural behaviours and expressions to the context in which they arise.

In contrast, 'formal' evaluation is both rigorous and structured. It is a systematic approach which seeks to obtain objective information which is both accurate and reliable. It may well be quantified and statistically viable. Both 'informal' and 'formal' evaluation employ a range of different techniques. Broadly these may be divided into three categories – observational, questionnaires and interviews. Observation of how visitors behave in an exhibition is perhaps the oldest-established technique. Whereas it was once undertaken by the researcher tracking and recording what he observed the visitor doing, today, through the use of sophisticated technological aids, including closed-circuit television, video and time-lapse photography the gathering of information has been made easier and more objective. Active in the field of observational studies of visitors in exhibitions have been Robinson and Melton, who undertook some pioneering studies in the 1920s and 1930s, and more recently Wiess and Boutourline (1963), Parsons (1965) and Lakota and Kanter (1975–6).

Questionnaires are probably the most widely used and the most abused of techniques employed in obtaining information. They form the substance of large-scale surveys and can also provide the basic structure of interviews. However, the norm is for them to be distributed in accordance with some method of selection (which may be a random process) and for the recipient to answer a series of questions. Deciding on the questions to be asked, and their structure, order and number, is of particular import-ance, as these factors can have a considerable influence on the answers obtained. For example, preparing a questionnaire in a form that has a series of alternative answers facilitates an easy response but can undoubtedly lead and limit the respondent in his/her answers. The design and preparation of a questionnaire require considerable skill and knowledge if it is to be wholly objective and obtain information which is reliable. Furthermore, in compiling a questionnaire some thought must be given to how the information, once obtained, will be processed, as this will undoubtedly have a bearing on its design, particularly if computers are to be employed.

Similarly, interviewing needs to be undertaken with considerable skill and impartially if it, too, is not to influence the interviewee. It is best undertaken in a structured way, in which the dialogue follows a prescribed sequence in each interview. This ensures that the significant topics are covered, standardizes the procedure and makes the evaluation of the responses easier.

A word of caution: it must be said that whatever techniques are employed there will always be a margin of error. Many people do not like being questioned and certainly do not give honest replies to the ques-tions. With some it is sheer perversity and perhaps a desire to upset the statistics and confuse the issue. With others it is a desire to be helpful and give the answers which they think the interviewers seeks. Others desire to appear more knowledgeable and more interested than perhaps they really are, and/or to impress the interviewer. Whatever the reason, the profes-sional evaluator will be aware of the pitfalls and endeavour to find ways to expose this sort of response and minimize its effect on the validity of the information obtained.

The value of evaluation has to be in the use to which the information obtained is put. Often the data will be essential to support arguments and effect decisions. The uses may range from changes in policy to changes in the design details of exhibition components. On the basis of the research, this should result in the elimination of mistakes and the development of better exhibitions and more satisfied visitors.

Examples of findings

Garvin (n.d.) in an evaluation of visitors of the Cincinnati Science Center, summarized his findings:

> The average fifth grader can name or depict about 15 exhibits three weeks after his visit . . . and there is evidence that this level of recollection is relatively persistent. The exhibits recalled most frequently are those with one or more of the following characteristics:
>
> * It *does* something that is not immediately obvious – and this probably makes a noise
> * The thing it does is completely under the control of the visitor
> * It requires the co-operation of two or more people to discover what it *can* do
> * The thing it *does* lends itself to competition or group play
> * The distinctive legend or symbol is affixed to the apparatus
> * The apparatus itself is familiar to the visitor even if the phenomenon it embodies is not
> * The apparatus or the phenomenon it embodies evokes feelings of mystery, drama, or romance.

Sheppard (1963) undertook some thorough studies of the effectiveness of the MAFF educational exhibits at agriculture shows in the UK. Among some interesting findings he found that 'on the average, farmers learnt something from five[1] exhibits at each stand, whatever the size of the stand, or whatever the number of exhibits seen by them. It follows that stands should display at lease five exhibits.'

T.R. Lee in *Psychology and the Environment* (1976), makes some useful comments on pupil behaviour in relation to environment. He mentions the work of the National Swedish Institute of Building Research, which has evidence to show that in high temperatures people are more easily distracted by noise and less effective at arithmetic tasks. Also the work of Humphreys (1974), who developed elaborate procedures for collecting teachers' assessments of the effects of weather conditions on children's performance. His studies showed that cool days are associated with high industriousness but only moderate energy, hot days with low energy and low industriousness, and windy days with high energy but low industriousness. Wet days, it seemed, produced no consistent expectation.

SUBJECT	SUMMER VISITORS	WINTER VISITORS
Indians	155	97
Mammals	110	72
History	37	45
Guns	34	32
Insects	5	-
Minerals	5	-
Telephone	-	5

Figure 13.1   Exhibition assessment sheet

Jeffrey Taylor (1984) in a study of the relationship between primary schools and local museums in Cumbria came to the conclusion that 'generally, many Cumbrian primary school teachers know very little of the educational facilities provided by their local museum(s)'.

Exemplar exhibition evaluation: a simple method of assessing an exhibition

Questionnaires and assessment sheets employed to evaluate the effectiveness of exhibitions take many forms, depending on their purpose. Anyone contemplating undertaking a survey is advised to consult the specialist literature and talk to those who have completed similar projects.

A selection of topics, in the form of a mark sheet, is given in figure 13.1, which could be useful in assessing a visitor's response to his/her experience of visiting an exhibition. It is suggested that each topic is assessed by giving it a score on a numerical scale of 1–9. Obviously any such evaluation will be highly subjective and the topics suggested are only suggestions and form no definitive list. Indeed, museums should decide on their own topics of interest. Its purpose is more to promote thinking on the sort of topics on which to seek an assessment rather than to act as a model. Nevertheless, should it be used, and ratings be given to the topic lists, a fairly clear picture of many of the strengths and weaknesses of the exhibition in question should emerge. It must be remembered that the information obtained would be of a very general nature, building up to provide an overall assessment. If weaknesses should be identified, or more information required on areas which have apparently been successful, then a more formal method of assessment should be employed. This might best be applied to individual exhibits or components, or even to specific labels.

Note

1 It can be calculated that in 95 per cent of the cases farmers learnt something from between 2.3 and 7.7 exhibits at these stands.

Conclusion

The aim of this book has been to provide the reader with a broad discussion of museum exhibitions. In order to achieve this it has been necessary to consider some of the wider aspects which relate to the subject, and, of these, none is more important than overall museum policy itself for from this all else should follow. The need for policy has been stressed at institution level, and this is no less important at exhibition level. An understanding of those factors which affect policy— namely collections, facilities, visitors, funding body, resources and staff— is essential if the museum's efforts are to be well formulated and responsive to need.

Encouraging museums to prepare policy statements and to address the real issues of what they are about is fundamental. However, to take a balanced, unprejudiced view, and be able to question original premises and evaluate current practice with an open mind is not easy, and this is particularly true in a profession renowned for its inflexibility and conservatism. To be sure, the dangers inherent in a reactionary approach are all too familiar, but so too are those of being over-hasty and of jumping on to the first bandwagon in order to capitalize on a transient market. Fundamentally it is necessary to hold to the basic functions of a museum as being to collect, conserve, research, display and interpret. But what may be questioned is the way in which these functions are performed, the priority given to them, the way in which they relate to each other, and the way in which the whole operation addresses the issue of commercialization. This, in today's political and economic climate has become increasingly necessary. Museums exist for the benefit of the public, and it is for each individual museum to make this apparent through its communications policy and *inter alia* through its functions of display and interpreting.

In this respect, image is of paramount importance, and in a climate which is also becoming increasingly competitive and market-oriented, it matters a great deal. Like the displays in an exhibition, museums themselves are competing with each other for the attention of the visitor. But image, of course, goes beyond this to every facet of a museum's work and covers the entire interface with the outside world, be it with the public, the press, or other members of the profession. Two of the main elements of a museum's image are how it conducts itself and how it presents itself. In the latter, the role of design is clearly of considerable importance, and the increased attention which is being paid to this aspect in recent years is to be welcomed. Good design must be beneficial to the exhibitions, and should be helpful if it is employed to assist in the museum's other operational systems.

The basic concepts of exhibition as a medium of communication have altered little over the years. Its purpose is still to excite, educate and entertain and, ultimately, to stimulate a response on the part of the visitor. Indeed, many of the techniques of presentation have also changed little: the diorama and tableau are two good examples. However, the same cannot be said of exhibition equipment, where showcases, lighting, audio-visuals and interactive computers have all benefited enormously from technological developments. Indeed, as a medium exhibition has always been quick to take advantage of innovations. In the years ahead one can imagine many new technological achievements which will benefit exhibitions. However, it is hard to see a time when the unique experience of an encounter between visitor and *real* object is not sought, even with the advent of the hologram. After all, it was feared by many that photographs would obviate the need to see the subject in original form, but in practice the effect has often been the opposite. Certainly the queues of people, some waiting several hours to see the Monet exhibition at the Royal Academy in London in 1990 bore witness to this. Here many of the works, made familiar through books, were for the first time brought together from all over the world to be presented as a coherent sequence, and attendance at the exhibition broke all records.

This perhaps also emphasizes the important role of the temporary exhibition as a means of bringing together items to illustrate a particular facet or tell a specific story, to the benefit of the lay person and scholar alike. The experimental nature of the temporary exhibition and the excitement it can generate must also be recognized in much the same way as any other contemporary plastic art forms.

Undoubtedly, in the past, one of the factors which inhibited rapid development of museum exhibition design was the mistrust and jealousy which existed between curator and designer. Fortunately today this has been, for the most part, reduced to workable levels and both assume their roles and offer their respective expertise to the common good in a team situation. The more widespread use of outside consultants is having a mixed effect on this, some firms establishing a good rapport with the client while, with others, the apparent intrusion is resented. However, irrespective of the employment status of the designer, what is crucial to the success or otherwise of any project is the way in which exhibition team members work together and their systematic approach to solving the exhibition problem. A prerequisite of this remains a good brief.

Solutions to the brief will inevitably fall into one or more of the three main types of exhibition – emotive (including aesthetic and evocative), didactic, and entertaining. Currently the evocative is enjoying the focus of attention, particularly if it also entertains. Many museums offering this type of presentation are thought by some to be moving their public face away from scholarship towards the leisure industry – where entertainments of this sort have a tendency to come and go.

Another trend is the greater importance being given to orientation.

Preparing visitors for what they are about to experience in an exhibition in geographical, intellectual, conceptual and psychological terms can only benefit all concerned and make for a more efficient use of the exhibition resource. This resource comprises many elements which include showcases, models, graphics, audio-visuals and computer-based displays, and all have important roles to play. However, in a *museum* situation care should be taken lest they usurp the objects as the prime communication medium – for their role is to complement and enhance, not to act as a substitute.

Visitors, of course, are and will always be the lifeblood of exhibitions. They are the people for whom exhibitions are, or should be, designed in the first place, and they should be the subject of the overall aims and objectives. The trend towards purposefully considering what the visitor is intended to gain from the exhibition will make for its more efficient use, but must not preclude the visitor from also using the resource in a non-prescribed way. That museum exhibitions are now appealing to a wider, better informed and more discriminating audience is marvellous. That evaluation techniques are now employed to obtain this information in a systematic way is also all to the good. However, irrespective of what can be demonstrated by the use of statistics and numbers, the real value of any exhibition is the quality of the experience it affords each individual visitor.

A hundred years on, it is hard to improve on the sentiment of the Rev. Henry H. Higgins, when he said in 1890 that:

> The conclusion cannot be far away—that the highest aim of work in Public Museums is not—however ingeniously—to multiply facts in the memories of the visitors, but to kindle in their hearts the wonder and loving sympathy—THE NEW KNOWLEDGE—called for by every page in the remotely-reaching annals of Nature.

If but one visitor leaves an exhibition with a new sense of wonder, understanding or useful purpose, that exhibition can be said to have succeeded.

Bibliography

Introduction

Belcher, M.G. 1982. 'Museum design', M. Phil. thesis, University of Leicester.
Brawne, M. 1964. *The New Museum: Architecture and Display*, Architectural Press, London.
Brawne, M. 1982. *The Museum Interior—Temporary and Permanent Display Techniques.* Thames and Hudson, London.
Hall, M. 1987. *On display—a design grammar for museums*, Lund Humphries, London.

1. Museum policy

Cossons, N., 1988. 'Our museums must blow off the dust', *Sunday Times*, 1 May.
Flower, W., 1893. 'Presidential address', *Proceedings*, Museums Association.
ICOM, 1974. *Statutes*, International Council of Museums, Paris, 1.
Lewis, G., 1984. 'Collections, collectors and museums in Britain to 1920' in J.M.A. Thompson *Manual of Curatorship*, Butterworths, London, 25.
Low, T., 1942. *The Museum as a Social Instrument*, Metropolitan Museum of Art, New York, 7.
Mawson, D., 1988. Letter in *The Times*, 2 December.
Museums Association, 1990. *Museums Yearbook*, Museums Association, London, 7.
Royal Ontario Museum, 1976. *R.O.M. Communicating with the Museum Visitor*, Royal Ontario Museum, Toronto, 229.
Tait, S., 1990. 'Another fine old mess?' *The Times*, 19 March, 19.
Wheatcroft, P., 1990. 'The Fate of the Natural History Museum', unpublished paper submitted to Museums Association Annual Meeting of Members, Glasgow, 10 July.

2. Museum communications policy

Royal Ontario Museum, 1976. *R.O.M. Communicating with the Museum Visitor*, Royal Ontario Museum, Toronto, 240.

3. Museum image, marketing and design

Borun, M., 1977. *Measuring the Immeasurable—a Pilot Study of Museum Effectiveness*, Franklin Institute, Philadelphia, vi.
Casson, H., 1961, 'Annual Conference 1961', *Museums J. 61*, 2: 104-5.

215

Wade, R., 1972. 'Unfamiliarity breeds contempt', in 'Designers in Museums', *Designer*, January, 9-10.

4. Exhibition as a medium of communication

Gardner, J., and Heller, C., 1960. *Exhibition and Display*, Batsford, London, 5.
Read, H., 1931. *The Meaning of Art*, Faber and Faber/Penguin, Harmondsworth.
Swiecimski, J., 1978. 'Form, composition and contents in museum exhibitions', in A. Szemere (ed.), *The Problems of Contents, Didactics and Aesthetics of Modern Museum Exhibitions*, Institute of Conservation and Methodology of Museums, Budapest, 55-70, 67.
Velarde, G., 1988. *Designing Exhibitions*, Design Council, London.

5. Exhibition modes

Clifford, T., 1987. 'Picture hanging in public galleries: a personal view', *Journal of the Royal Society of Arts*, 5374, Vol. CXXXV: 718-34.
Coutts, H., 1986. 'Profile of a blockbuster', *Museums J*, 86, 1: 23-6.
Pope-Hennessy, Sir J., 1975. 'Design in museums', *Journal of the Royal Society of Arts*, October 1975, 5231, Vol. CXXIII: 717-27.

6. Types of museum exhibitions

Allen, D.A., 1949. 'Museums and education' in *Museums in Modern Life*, Royal Society of Arts, 86-106, 86.
Barzun, J., 1969, in K. McLuhan, H. Parker and J. Barzun, *Exploration of the Ways, Means and Values of Museum Communication with the Viewing Public: a seminar*. Museum of the City of New York, New York, 10 October 1967, 65.
Brown Goode, G., 1891. 'The museums of the future', *Annual Report of the Board of Regents of the Smithsonian Institution for the Year ending June 30, 1889*, sect. 3, 427-45.
Cameron, D.F., 1968. 'A viewpoint: the museum as a communications system and implications for museum education', *Curator*, *11*, i: 33-40, 34.
Castillo, A.A., 1989. 'Science Communications through Exhibitions'. M.Phil, thesis, University of Leicester.
Dana, J.C., 1927. *Should Museums be Useful?* Newark Museum, Newark, N.J., 16-22.
Gilman, B.I., 1918. *Museum Ideals of Purpose and Method*, Museum of Fine Arts, Boston, 47.
Hall, M., 1987. *On display, a design grammar for museums*, Lund Humphries, London, 29.
Harden, D.B., 1965. 'In annual conference 1965 Dublin', *Museums J.*, *65*, 2: 143.
Higgins, H.H. 1890. 'Presidential address', *Proceedings*, Museums Association, 37.
Hill, C.R., and Miles, R.S., 1987. 'Development of interactive programmes and maintenance problems', *Bulletin de recherches sur l'information en sciences économiques, humaines et sociales*, 10 September, 127-9, 127.

Knez, E.I., and Wright, A.G., 1970. 'The museum as a communications system: an assessment of Cameron's viewpoint', *Curator, 13*, iii: 204-12, 206-9.
Miles, R.S., and Tout, A.F., 1979. 'Outline of a technology for effective science exhibits', *Special Papers in Palaeontology, 22*: 209-24.
Pott, P.H. 1963. 'The role of museums of history and folklore in a changing world', *Curator, 6*, 2.
Read, H., 1931. *The Meaning of Art*, Faber and Faber/Penguin, Harmondsworth.
Screven, C.G., 1974. *The Measurement and Facilitation of Learning in the Museum Environment: an experimental analysis*. Smithsonian Institution Press, Washington, D.C.
Velarde, G., 1984. 'Exhibition design', in J.M.A. Thompson (ed.), *Manual of Curatorship*, Butterworths, London 394-402, (1) 395, (2) 396.

7. Exhibition policy and planning

Alt, M.B., 1982, in Coles, P. 'Eye Movements and picture perception', *Research in illustration*, 1981 Conference Proceedings, II. Brighton Polytechnic, 140.
Borun, M., 1977. *Measuring the Immeasurable—a Pilot Study of Museum Effectiveness*. Franklin Institute, Philadelphia, vi.
Cameron, D.F., 1968. 'A viewpoint: the museum as a communications system and implications for museum education', *Curator, 11*, i: 33-40.
Coles, P., 1982. 'Eye movements and picture perception', in *Research in illustration*, 1981 Conference Proceedings, II. Brighton Polytechnic, 123-142.
Davies, M., 1989. 'An ace debate with quite a nice museum involved', *Museums J, 89*, 2: 15.
Howell, D.B., 1971. 'A network system for the planning, designing, construction, and installation of exhibits', *Curator, 14*, ii: 100-8.
Miles, R.S., and Tout, A.F., 1978. 'Human biology and the new exhibition scheme in the British Museum (Natural History)', *Curator, 21*, i: 36-50.
Neal, A., 1965. 'Function of display: regional museums', *Curator, 8*, iii: 228-34.
Niehoff, A., 1953. 'Characteristics of the audience reaction in the Milwaukee Public Museum', *Midwest Museum Quarterly, 13*, i: 19-24.
Pearson, N., 1981. *Art Galleries and Exhibition Spaces in Wales*. Welsh Arts Council, Cardiff.
Shettel, H.H., *et al.* 1968. *Strategies for Determining Exhibit Effectiveness*, Project No. V-OII; Contract No. OE-6-10.213. American Institute for Research, Pittsburgh.

8. The exhibition brief

Bruce, Archer, L., 1964. *Systematic Method for Designers*, Royal College of Art, London, 4.
Elliot, M., 1977. Area Museum Service for South Eastern England Design Briefing Procedures, 1.
Hall, M., 1987. *On Display - a design grammar for museums*. Lund Humphries, London, 42.
Hebditch, M., 1970. 'Briefing the designer', *Museums J, 70*, 2: 67-8.
Society of Industrial Artists and Designers, 1974. *The Study of Professional Practice in Graphic and Industrial Design*. SIAD, London.

9. Orientation and environment

Bernado, J.R., 1972. 'Museum Environments for Communications: a study of environmental parameters in the design of museum experiences', PhD dissertation, Columbia University, 107.

Cohen, M.S., 1974. *The State of the Art of Museum Visitor Orientation—a survey of selected institutions.* Office of Museum Programs, Smithsonian Institution, Washington, D.C., 4.

Coleman, L.V., 1950. *Museum Buildings: a planning study,* Vol. I. American Association of Museums, Washington, D.C.

Hall, M., 1987. *On Display - a design grammar for museum exhibitions.* Lund Humphries, London.

Lakota, R.A., 1976. 'Good exhibits on purpose: techniques to improve exhibit effectiveness', in Royal Ontario Museum. *R.O.M. Communicating with the Museum Visitor.* Royal Ontario Museum, Toronto, 245-79.

Lakota, R.A., and Kanter, J.A., 1975/76. *The National Museum of Natural History as a Behavioural Environment,* Parts I and II. Office of Museum Programs, Smithsonian Institution, Washington, D.C.

Lehmbruck, M., 1974. 'Psychology: perception and behaviour', *Museum, 26,* iii-iv: 191-204.

Maclagon, E., 1931. 'Museum planning', *Journal of the Royal Institute of British Architects,* 3rd Series, *38,* 15: 527-48, 543.

Major, D.B., in Klemm G.F., 1837. Geschichte der Sammlungen für Wissenschaft und in Deutschland. Zerbst. Kummer, 153.

Markham, S.F., 1938. *The Museums and Art Galleries of the British Isles,* Carnegie United Kingdom Trust, Constable, Edinburgh, 109-10.

Melton, A.W., 1935. *Problems of Installation in Museums of Art.* Publications of the American Association of Museums, New Series, 14. Washington, D.C.

Royal Ontario Museum, 1976. *R.O.M. Communicating with the Museum Visitor.* Royal Ontario Museum, Toronto.

Winkel, G.H., Olsen, R., Wheeler, F., and Cohen, M., 1975. *The Museum Visitor and Orientational Media: an experimental comparison of different approaches in the Smithsonian Institution.* Smithsonian Institution, Washington, D.C. i.

10. Exhibition elements

Bassett, D.A., 1984. 'Museum publications and museum publishing: a brief introduction with a note on museum libraries', in J.M.A. Thompson (ed.), *Manual of Curatorship,* Butterworths, London, 467-75.

Borun, M., 1977. *Measuring the Immeasurable—a pilot study of museum effectiveness.* Franklin Institute, Philadelphia.

Cameron, D.F., 1968. 'A viewpoint: the museum as a communications system and implications for museum education', *Curator, 11,* i: 33-40.

Edwards, A.S., 1949. 'The story of a local museum', in *Museums in Modern Life.* Royal Society of Arts, London, 41-56.

Hall, E.T., 1912. 'Art museums and picture galleries', *Journal of the Institute of British Architects,* 3rd series, *19,* 11: 405.

Hall, M., 1987. *On Display—a design grammar for museums,* Lund Humphries, London.

Hooper-Greenhill, E., 1990. *Museum Education,* Leicester University Press.

Knez, E.I., and Wright, A.G., 1970. 'The museum as a communications system: an assessment of Cameron's viewpoint', *Curator, 13*, iii: 204–12.
Morris, R.G.M., and Alt, M.B., 1978. 'An experiment to help design a map for a large museum', *Museums J, 77*, 4: 179–80.
Nixon, H.K., 1926. *An Investigation of Attention to Advertisements.* Columbia University Press, New York. 293.
Norgate, M., 1973. 'Linked Tape and Slide Audio-visual Displays', Museums Association Information Sheet 17. Museums Association, London.
Parsons, L.A., 1965. 'Systematic testing of display techniques for an anthropological exhibit', *Curator, 8*, ii: 167–89.
Porter, T., and Mikellides, B., 1976. *Colour for Architecture.* Studio Vista, London.
Swanton, E.W., 1903. 'Notes upon the Haslemere Educational Museum', *Museums J, 2* (1902-3): 118.
Walker, J., 1944. 'The genesis of the National Gallery of Art', *Art in America, 32* 4.
White, P., 1927. *Advertising Research.* Appleton, New York, 538.

11. About objects

Allwood, J., 1981. *Information Signs for the Countryside.* Countryside Commission, Cheltenham.
Barr, D., 1976. 'Interpretative textual material', in Royal Ontario Museum. *R.O.M. Communicating with the Museum Visitor*, Royal Ontario Museum, Toronto, 347-54, 353.
Borun, M., and Miller, M., 1980. 'To label or not to label?'. *Museum News, 58*, iv: 64-7.
Brown Goode, G., 1891. 'The museums of the future', *Annual report of the Board of Regents of the Smithsonian Institution for the year ending June 30, 1889*, sect. 3, 427-45.
Brown Goode, G., 1901. *The Principles of Museum Administration*, rept. U.S. National Museum, pt. 2.
Burt, Sir C., 1959. *A Psychological Study of Typography*, Cambridge University Press, Cambridge, 9.
Cameron, D.F., 1968. 'A viewpoint: the museum as a communications system and implications for museum education', *Curator, 11*, i: 33-40, 34.
Carmel, J.H., 1962. *Exhibition Techniques: Travelling and Temporary.* Reinhold, New York, 105.
Dana, J.C., 1927. *Should Museums be Useful?* Newark Museum, New Jersey, 16-22.
Dandridge, F., 1966. 'The value of design in visual communication', *Curator, 9*, iv: 331-6, 334.
Fleming, A.R., 1976. 'Graphics, colour and visual impact', in *R.O.M. Communicating with the Museum Visitor*, Royal Ontario Museum, Toronto, 289-328, 296.
Foster, J.J., 1980. *Legibility Research 1972-78.* Graphic Research Unit, Royal College of Art, London.
Fry, E.A., 1968. 'A readability formula which saves time', *Journal of Reading, 11*, 7: 513-16, 575-8.
Harrison, C. 1979. 'Assessing the readability of school texts', in E. Lunzer, and K. Gardner, (eds.), *The Effective Use of Reading*, Heinemann, London.

Klare, G.R., 1978. 'Assessing readability', in L.J. Chapman and P. Czerniewska, (eds.), *Reading from Process to Practice*, Routledge, Kegan Paul, London, 248–74.

Lakota, R.A., 1976. 'Techniques to improve exhibit effectiveness', in Royal Ontario Museum, *R.O.M. Communicating with the Museum Visitor*, Royal Ontario Museum, Toronto.

Neal, A., 1976. *Exhibits for the Small Museum*. American Association for State and Local History, Nashville.

North, F.J., 1957. *Museum Labels: Handbook for Museum Curators*, pt. B, sect. 3. Museums Association, London.

Pearce, S.M., 1986a. 'Thinking about things': Approaches to the study of Artefacts, *Museums J, 85*, 4: 198–201.

Pearce, S.M., 1986b. 'Objects, high and low', *Museums J, 86*, 2: 79–82.

Pearce, S.M., 1986c. 'Objects as signs and symbols', *Museums J, 86*, 3: 131–5.

Pearce, S.M., 1987. 'Objects in structures', *Museums J, 86*, 4: 178–81.

Royal Ontario Museum, 1976. *R.O.M. Communicating with the Museum Visitor*. Royal Ontario Museum, Toronto.

Robinson, E.S., 1930. 'Psychological problems of the Science Museum', *Museum News, 18*, 5: 9–11.

Robinson, E.S., 1931. 'Psychological studies of the public museum', *School and Society, 33*, (836), 121–125, 125.

Sorsby, B.D., and Horne, S.D., 1980. 'The readability of museum labels', *Museums J, 80*, 3: 157–9, 157–8.

Spencer, H., 1968. *The Visible Word*. Lund Humphries, London.

Spencer, H., and Reynolds, L., 1976. *The Study of Legibility*. Readability of Print Unit, Royal College of Art, London.

Spencer, J. and Reynolds, L., 1977. *Directional Signing and Labelling in Libraries and Museums: a review of current theory and practice*. Readability of Print Research Unit, Royal College of Art, London 100.

Tilden, F., 1957. *Interpreting our Heritage*. Chapel Hill, University of North Carolina Press.

Weiner, G., 1963. 'Why Johnny can't read labels', *Curator, 6*, 2: 143–56; (1) 149–50.

Wolf, R.L., and Tymitz, B.L., 1978. *Whatever Happened to the Giant Wombat: an investigation of the impact of the Ice Age Mammals and Emergence of Man exhibit, National Museum of Natural History, Smithsonian Institution*. Smithsonian Institute, Washington, D.C.

Wolf, R.L., and Tymitz, B.L., et al., 1979. *'East Side, West Side, Straight Down the Middle': a study of visitor perceptions of 'Our Changing Land', the bicentennial exhibit, National Museum of Natural History, Smithsonian Institution*. Smithsonian Institution, Washington, D.C., 42.

12. The museum visitor

Abbey, D.S., and Cameron, D.F., 1960. *The Museum Visitor, II, Survey Results*. Royal Ontario Museum, Toronto.

Alt, M.B., 1980. 'Four years of visitor surveys at the British Museum (Natural History), 1976–79', *Museums J, 80*, i. 10–19.

Alt, M.B., 1983. 'Visitors' attitudes to two old and two new exhibitions at the British Museum (Natural History), *Museums J, 83*, ii/iii: 145–8.

Architects Journal, 1963. *A.J. Information Sheet 1185, Anthropometric Data and their Application*. A.J. London.

Arnheim, R., 1974. *Art and Visual Perception: a psychology of the creative eye*. University of California Press.

Barton, K., 1973. 'Recording attandances at Portsmouth City Museums: the method and its effect', *Museums J, 73*, iv: 167-8.

Bassett, D.A., and Prince, D.R., 1984. 'Visitor services', in J.M.A. Thompson (ed.), *Manual of Curatorship*, Butterworths, London, 377.

Bloom, B.S. ed. 1971, 1972. *Taxonomy of Educational Objectives; Book 1: Cognitive Domain and Book 2: Affective Domain*. David McKay, New York.

Borhegyi, S.F. de, 1963. 'Museum exhibits: how to plan and evaluate them', *Midwest Museums Quarterly, 23*, 2: 4-8.

Borun, M., 1977. *Measuring the Immeasurable—a pilot study of museum effectiveness*. Franklin Institute, Philadelphia; (1) 9.

British Association for the Advancement of Science, 1920. 'On museums in relation to education', in 'Report of the eighty-eighth meeting of the British Association for the Advancement of Science, Cardiff, 24-28 August 1920, in *Reports on the State of Science, 1920*, 267-80; (1) 267, (2) 270-1.

Church, D.E., 1984. 'The responsibility of the architect and designer', *Museums J, 84*, i: 35-6.

Clifford, T., 1987. 'Picture hanging in public galleries: a personal view', *Journal of the Royal Society of Arts*, 5374, Vol. CXXXV, 718-34, 722.

Cruikshank, G., 1972. 'Jewry Wall Museum, Leicester: trial by questionnaire', *Museums J, 72*, ii: 65-7.

Dandridge, F., 1966. 'The value of design in visual communication', *Curator, 9*, iv: 331-6, 333.

Deas, J.A.C., 1913-14. 'The showing of museums and art galleries to the blind', *Museums J*, XIII, 97.

Doughty, P.S., 1968. 'The public of the Ulster Museum: a statistical survey', *Museums J, 68*, i: 19-26 and ii: 47-53; (1) 47.

Dreyfuss, H., 1967. The Measuring of Man: human factors in design. Whitney.

Elliott, P., and Loomis, R.J., 1975. *Studies of Visitor Behaviour in Museums and Exhibitions: an annotated bibliography*. Smithsonian Institute, Washington, D.C.

Ellis, M., 1984. 'Guided tours: the use of volunteers at the Tate Gallery', *Museums J, 84*, i: 37.

Gagné, R.M., 1970. *The Conditions of Learning*. 2nd ed. Holt, Rinehart and Winston, New York.

Gardner, J., and Heller, C., 1960. *Exhibition and Display*, Batsford, London, 5.

Goldsmith, S., 1977. *Designing for the Disabled*. Royal Institute of British Architects, London.

Goldsmith, S., 1979. 'Anthropometric data', in Tutt, P. and Adler, D. (eds.), *New Metric Handbook*, Architectural Press, London, 23-27.

Gombrich, E.H., 1960. *Art and Illusion: a study of the psychology of pictorial representation*. Phaidon Press, London.

Gombrich, E.H. and Gregory, R.L. (eds.), 1973. *Illusion in Nature and Art*. Duckworth, London.

Gregory, R.L. 1972. *Eye and Brain*, Weidenfeld and Nicholson, London.

Hamilton, E.A., 1970. *'Graphic design for the computer age', Visual Communication for all Media*. Van Nostrand Reinhold, London.

Hardiman, R., 1984. 'Consultation and co-ordination', *Museums J, 84*, i: 36.

Harrison, M., 1967. *Changing Museums*, Longmans, London, 60.

Hartley, E. (n.d.). 'Touch and see', Department of Adult Education, University of Leicester, 26.

Heath, A., 1976. 'The same only more so: museums and the handicapped visitor', *Museums J, 76*, ii: 56-8.

Hill, M., 1989. 'The selling of science', *Design*, 483: 24.

Hunter, G., 1979. 'Museums and art galleries', in P. Tutt and D. Adler, (eds.), *New Metric Handbook*, Architectural Press, London, 286-92.

Johnson, N., 1984. 'Visitors with a physical handicap', *Museums J, 84*, i: 36-7, 37.

Lewis, P., 1988. 'Marketing to the local community', *Museums J, 88*, iii: 147-9, 148.

Manton, J.A., 1900. 'A rambling dissertation on museums by a museums rambler', *Museum J*.

Markham, S.F., 1938. *A Report on the Museums and Art Galleries of the British Isles*; Carnegie United Kingdon Trust, Constable, Edinburgh (1) 83, (2) 84.

Mason, T., 1974. 'The visitors to Manchester Museum: a questionnaire survey', *Museums J, 73*, iv: 153-7.

McWilliams, B., and Hopwood, J., 1972. 'The public of Norwich Castle Museum, 1971-2', *Museums J, 72*, iv: 153-8; (1) 155.

Melton, A.W., 1935. *Problems of Installation in Museums of Art*. Publication New Series No. 14, American Association of Museums, Washington, D.C.; (1) 93, (2) 258, (3) 110.

Miers, Sir H., 1928. *A Report on the Public Museums of the British Isles*, Constable, Edinburgh, 80.

Miers, Sir H., 1929. *Museums and Education*, a paper read before the Royal Society of Arts, London, 23 January 1929, 4-5.

Murrell, K.F.H., 1965. *Ergonomics: Man in his Working Environment*.

Neal, A., 1963. 'Gallery and case exhibit design', *Curator, 6*, i: 77-96.

Neal, A., 1969. *Help! for the Small Museum*. Pruett, Boulder, Colorado.

Neal, A., 1976. *Exhibits for the Small Museum*. American Association for State and Local History, Nashville.

Niehoff, A., 1953. 'Characteristics of the audience reaction in the Milwaukee Public Museum', *Midwest Museum Quarterly, 13*, i: 19-24.

Niehoff, A., 1968. 'Audience reaction in the Milwaukee Public Museum: the winter visitors', in S. de Borhegyi and I.A. Hanson, (eds.), *The Museum Visitor*, Milwaukee Public Museum Publications in Museology, 3, 22-31.

Pearson, A., 1984. 'Visitor services at the British Museum', *Museums J, 84*, i: 37.

Pearson, A., 1989. 'Museum education and disability' in E. Hooper-Greenhill. (ed.), *Initiatives in Museum Education*. Department of Museum Studies, University of Leicester.

Pierotti, R., 1973. 'Be, see, touch, respond', *Museum News, 52*, iv: 43-8.

Prince, D.R., 1985. 'Museum visiting and unemployment', *Museums J, 85*, ii: 85-90; (1) 89; (2) 88.

Robinson, E.S., 1928. *The Behaviour of the Museum Visitor*. Publications New Series No. 5, American Association of Museums, Washington, D.C.; (1) 42.

Shackel, B., (ed.), 1974. *Applied Ergonomics Handbook*.

Shiner, J.W., and Shafer, E.L., 1975. 'How long do people look at and listen to forest-orientated exhibits?' N.E. Forest Experimental Station, Upper Darby, Pennsylvania.

Snider, H.W., 1977. *Museums and Handicapped Students: guidelines for educators*. Smithsonian Institution, Washington, D.C.

Standing Commission on Museums and Galleries, 1954. *Report*, HMSO, London, 32.

Tutt, P., and Adler, D. (eds.) 1981. *New Metric Handbook*. Architectural Press, London.

Washburne, R.F., and Wagar, J.A., 1972. 'Evaluating visitor response to exhibit content', *Curator, 15*, iii: 248-54.

Weiss, R.S., and Boutourline, S., 1963. 'The communication value of exhibits', *Museums News, 42*, iii: 23-7.

Wolf, R.L., and Tymitz, B.L., 1979. *'East side, west side, straight down the middle': a study of visitor perceptions of 'Our Changing Land', the bicentennial exhibit, National Museum of Natural History, Smithsonian Institution*. Smithsonian Institution, Washington, D.C., 32, 15.

13. Exhibition effectiveness

Alt, M.B., 1977. 'Evaluating didactic exhibits: a critical look at Shettel's work', *Curator, 20*, iii: 241-58.

Borhegyi, S.F. de, 1963. 'Visual communication in the Science Museum', *Curator, 6*, i: 45-57.

Borhegyi, S.F. de, and Hanson, I. (eds.). 1968. *The Museum Visitor*. Publications in Museology 3. Milwaukee Public Museum, Milwaukee.

Carmel, J.H., 1962. *Exhibition Techniques: travelling and temporary*. Reinhold, New York, 12.

Coleman, L.V., 1939. *The Museum in America*. American Association of Museums, Washington, D.C., 297.

Gardner, J., and Heller, C., 1960. *Exhibition and Display*, Batsford, London, 17.

Garvin, A.D. (n.d.). *An Evaluation of the Cincinnati Science Center*. University of Cincinnati, 40.

Goins, A., and Griffenhagen, G. 1957. 'Psychological studies, of museum visitors and exhibits at the U.S. National Museum' *Museologist, 64*, 1-6.

Griggs, S., 1985. 'Evaluating Museum Displays', A.M.S.E.E. Information, AMSEE, Milton Keynes, 1.

Hess, H.H., and Krugman, H.E., 1964. 'In the eye of the beholder', *Sponsor*.

Hess, H.H., and Polt, 1965. 'Attitude and pupil size', *Scientific American*, 2-10.

Humphreys, M.A., 1974. Relating wind, rain and temperature to teachers' reports on young children's behaviour', in D.V. Canter and T.R. Lee, (eds.), *Psychology and the Built Environment*, Architectural Press, London, 19-28.

Lakota, R.A., and Kanter, J.A., 1975-6. The National Museum of Natural History as a Behavioural Environment, Parts I and II. Office or Museum Programs, Smithsonian Institution, Washington, D.C.

Lee, T.R., 1976. *Psychology and the Environment*, Methuen, London.

Parsons, L.A., 1965. 'Systematic testing of display techniques for an anthropological exhibit', *Curator, 8*, ii: 167-89.

Screven, C.G., 1974. *The Measurement and Facilitation of Learning in the Museum Environment: an experimental analysis*. Smithsonian Institution, Washington, D.C.

Sheppard, D., 1963. 'The effectiveness of the MAFF educational exhibits at agriculture shows', *Agricultural Progress, 38*, 1: 62-79, 72.

Shettel, H.H., Butcher, M., Cotton, T.S., Northrup, J. and Slough, D.C., 1968. *Strategies for Determining Exhibit Effectiveness*, Project No. V-011, Contract No. OE-6-10-213. American Institutes for Research, Pittsburgh, 2.

Stansfield, G., 1981. *Effective Interpretive Exhibitions*. Countryside Commission, Cheltenham.

Taylor, J., 1984. 'Primary education and local museums in Cumbria', *Museums J*, *84*, 3: 129–34, 131.

Weiss, R.S., and Boutourline, S., 1963. 'The communication value of exhibits, *Museum News*, *42*, iii: 23–7.

Wolf, R.L., and Tymitz, B.L., 1979. *A Preliminary Guide for Conducting Naturalistic Evaluation in Studying Museum Environments*. Smithsonian Institution, Washington, D.C., 2.

Index